Inside
the
Animal
Mind

Inside the Animal Mind

George Page

BROADWAY BOOKS
New York

BROADWAY

A hardcover edition of this book was originally published in 1999 by Doubleday, a division of Random House, Inc.

Broadway Books titles may be purchased for business or promotional use or for special sales. For information, please write to: Special Markets Department, Random House, Inc., 1540 Broadway, New York, NY 10036.

BROADWAY BOOKS and its logo, a letter B bisected on the diagonal, are trademarks of Broadway Books, a division of Random House, Inc.

First Broadway Books trade paperback edition published 2001.

Visit our website at www.broadway.com

Designed by Donna Sinisgalli

The Library of Congress has cataloged the hardcover as:
Page, George (George H.)
Inside the animal mind: a groundbreaking exploration of
animal intelligence / George Page. — 1st ed.
p.   cm.
1. Animal intelligence. I. Title.
QL785.P225   1999
591.5'13—dc21   99-32431   CIP

ISBN 0-7679-0559-8

01 02 03 04 05 10 9 8 7 6 5 4 3 2 1

For Dr. Dennis De Stefano

Contents

∽

Preface

As the executive editor, host, and narrator of the *Nature* series on public television, I have spent many wonderful hours and days observing animals in the wild. A quick count puts me in about twenty countries on exactly five continents over almost two decades. Like many travelers, I found East Africa the most compelling landscape on earth. There is no place like the Masai Mara for getting a real sense of the extremely clever behavior and complex lives of the elephants, lions, leopards, hyenas, wildebeest, monkeys, wild dogs, and many more—the whole rich panoply. Back home in our suburban home north of New York City, I have spent hundreds of equally enjoyable hours in the company of my three dogs and one cat. And like everyone who's ever loved a pet, observed a stalking lioness, watched a bird fly hither and yon in search of just the right nesting material, or held the gaze of a chimpanzee, I've often wondered, "Are these creatures 'thinking' all the while? Without language as we know it, *how* are they thinking"?

For almost 100 years, the behaviorist tradition of psychology in the United States and Europe has argued that these animals have no "minds" at all, in fact. This tradition argues that any belief to the contrary is "folk psychology"—blatant anthropomorphism, whereby we ascribe human characteristics to animals (or even to inanimate objects). Since we cannot get inside the animal's mind as we can get inside our own minds, and since the animal cannot report what's going on—not in a "language" we can readily understand—all we have left are guesses and speculation fatally tainted by anthropomorphism, with no provable facts. But does this reductive hypothesis make any sense outside the laboratory? After all, there is no way to prove conclusively what is going on in another human's mind—no way to prove conclusively that another human is conscious. Can it possibly be true that I am the only conscious creature on this planet? Not likely!

What are animals feeling? Homer said that Ulysses' dog Argos recognized his master after an absence of twenty years. *The Odyssey* is a fable, of course, but we can readily imagine that a dog could have such a keen memory of his master. Indeed, our modern-day pets behave in ways that we feel compelled to interpret in terms of our own emotions. And in the wild, elephants certainly seem to demonstrate sadness, even depression, at appropriate turning points in their lives, as well as behavior that appears to be pure joy. Are the dog and the elephant feeling what we would feel in similar situations? If we could exchange emotional experiences with either animal, would we feel right at home? Again, the behaviorist tradition scoffs at the very notion.

One final question: What difference does it make? Well, what difference does it make how far it is to the end of the universe? Or if there is an "end" to the universe? What difference does it make if quarks are the building blocks of the universe, or if there exist entities even tinier and more fundamental? We humans are curious as cats; we want to know. Just as important, our ideas about animal minds and emotions influence far-reaching questions of ethics and politics.

If we believe or, better yet, determine that animals think consciously and possess the full range of "human" emotions—if their pain is therefore also "suffering"—on what ethical grounds do we support, for just one example, the marine theme parks, whose performing cetaceans are, in the final analysis, enslaved in what are to them puddles? We become hard-pressed to condone animal experimentation, and a growing number of people may decide that they cannot justify eating meat. On the other hand, some ethicists fear that not maintaining a distinction between ourselves and all other animals, including the porpoises and great apes, might set us on a slippery slope that could lead to all manner of abuses of human beings—the same abuses we now put upon these other creatures on the grounds that they are fundamentally different from us. I do not share this fear.

Personally, I very much like the idea that my kinship with the other living creatures of the earth might be much greater than our cultural and scientific heritage has led us to believe. I am comfortable with the fact that, like them, I am an animal and that many of the characteristics that I have so often tossed off as being "just a part of human nature" may, in fact, be aspects of our shared animal natures.

Or as Cynthia Moss, who has studied elephants in East Africa for more than thirty years, put it better: "We are just part of a continuum of species. It isn't just animals and man, I think that is becoming clear. We are just another much more intelligent and masterful animal, but we are all part of this earth."

So questions about animal minds are not merely fascinating. The answers matter.

And I think they matter in terms of the ancient quest for our own identity. How else can we define the human animal without knowing how we are alike and how we are different from other animals? If this is true, does it not follow that we have a profound, even primordial, *need* for our fellow creatures, a need that is as old as our first appearance on the earth?

I first began pondering these issues fifteen years ago when we produced a lengthy series on the human brain for public television. This organ is, as far as we know, the single most complex entity in the universe—a remarkable and perhaps underappreciated fact, but no more remarkable than the fact that the other mammals, all the way "down" to the smallest shrew that lives its entire life underground, have brains of similar structure to our own. Primate brains are practically identical to ours. Only a very few genes may determine the cognitive differences between chimpanzees and ourselves. Common sense and rudimentary logic would seem to suggest that, yes, these animals are thinking and feeling and perceiving the world in some manner that's related to our own. But can we prove it?

As the years rolled by and the crew of the *Nature* series traveled the world, collecting film of an astonishing array of animal behavior, my pile of questions mounted higher and higher. Then, three years ago, we began working on the three-part *Nature* series to which this book is the companion, addressing directly the issues of animal thinking, animal emotions, and animal consciousness. I became somewhat more systematic in my own "studies" and quickly learned that the subject is even more complex than I had imagined, both as it's researched in the laboratory and the field, and theorized about in the ivory tower. In the past decade there has been an explosion of scientific, philosophical, and even quasitheological papers and books exploring various aspects of the problem. In fact, Donald Griffin, the founder of the new specialty of cognitive ethnology, told me in his

office at Harvard as he handed over his personal, ever-growing bibliography, "It's hard for me to keep an up-to-date list of the material,
much less to read it all."

The television series is divided into three one-hour parts: "Thinking,"
"Emotion," and "Consciousness." That division is arbitrary, of
course, but it makes good sense as a way to put some order on this
wide-ranging, complex field. I begin this companion volume with
three short chapters that set the stage for the story, historically and
thematically, and then I roughly follow the tripartite division of the
series. At all times I try to walk the narrow line between making the
complex themes and scientific research clear and accessible, but without oversimplifying. I will succeed if this book can generate just a
fraction of the excitement I feel for what we are learning about the
minds of our fellow creatures on planet earth.

Inside
the
Animal
Mind

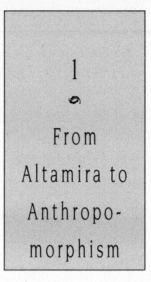

1

From Altamira to Anthropo-morphism

ANCIENT HERITAGE

In the beginning, our lives were totally immersed in the world of animals. In the beginning, in fact, we *were* animals, in the colloquial as well as the technical sense of that word. Our Neanderthal and Cro-Magnon ancestors relied on birds and beasts for food and clothing; they went to the mat one-on-one with tigers and bison and bears, and they took heavy casualties. We were an integral part of a world that was "red in tooth and claw." Surely it is no coincidence that our oldest surviving visual art—the cave paintings at Altamira, Lascaux, and other sites in southern Europe—depict cattle, horses, bison, and deer as objects of hunting and veneration. Animals predominate; there are very few human figures in any of this work. Then there is the idea that our earliest music might have been created in response to the myriad sounds of the natural world. After all, those were the only sounds we heard: There weren't any jets, jackhammers, or jukeboxes around, but there were songbirds in profusion. No wonder Orpheus, the beguiling musician of Greek mythology, could mesmerize a rapt menagerie of wild beasts, who responded to every note of his lyre.

While the very earliest Paleolithic art is dated about thirty thousand years ago, the famous work in southern Europe is dated about 10,000 B.C. Anthropologists believe that those highly artful ancestors were still exclusively hunters and gatherers, but this economic and cultural restriction would soon be overcome. At just about the time the Solutreo-Magdalenian artists were producing their greatest "canvases" at Altamira, the peoples of Mesopotamia and the Middle East were beginning to domesticate mammals. In the long story of our relationship with animals and our still-evolving understanding of the animal mind, domestication marked the beginning of the estrangement that is still with us today. It was a watershed of incalculable importance, as proved by the fact that it was incorporated into all the creation stories of the time.

The first chapter of Genesis says:

And God made the beast of the earth after his kind, and cattle after their kind, and every thing that creepeth upon the earth after his kind: and God saw that it was good. And God said, Let us make man in our image, after our likeness: and let them have dominion over the fish of the sea, and over the fowl of the air, and over the cattle and over all the earth, and over every creeping thing that creepeth upon the earth. So God created man in his own image, in the image of God created he them; male and female created he them. And

God blessed them, and God said unto them, Be fruitful, and multiply, and replenish the earth, and subdue it: and have dominion over the fish of the sea, and over the fowl of the air, and over every living thing that moveth upon the earth.

The subsequent thirtieth verse of that chapter reads: "And to every beast of the earth, and to every fowl of the air, and to every thing that creepeth on the earth, wherein there is life, I have given every green herb for meat: and it was so." Some commentators believe that this verse implies that the Garden of Eden before the Fall was a vegetarian society. I diplomatically take no position on this provocative notion, but there can be no doubt about the disposition of the earth's resources following the Flood:

And God blessed Noah and his sons and said unto them, Be fruitful, and multiply, and replenish the earth. And the fear of you and the dread of you shall be upon every beast of the earth, and upon every fowl of the air, upon all that moveth upon the earth, and upon all the fishes of the sea; into your hands are they delivered. Every moving thing that liveth shall be meat for you; even as the green herb have I given you all things.

In short, God gives mankind dominion over *all* that lives on this earth and He makes it clear that eating meat is condoned. Various passages throughout the Old Testament prescribe respectful treatment for domesticated and wild animals, and the same holds for Judaic Law, but the essential message of the Pentateuch and the legacy of the Old Testament are clear enough: Animals were created, or designated, for our needs. Nowhere in the New Testament is this message challenged. In Matthew 6:26, Jesus says in the Sermon on the Mount, in the verses that precede the beautiful "lilies of the field" image, "Look at the birds of the air, that they do not sow, neither do they reap, nor gather into barns, and yet your heavenly Father feeds them. Are you not worth much more than they?" In his first Letter to the Corinthians, the apostle Paul reiterates this theme when he writes, "For it is written in the law of Moses, 'You shall not muzzle an ox while it treads out the grain." Is it oxen God is concerned about? Or does He say it altogether for our sakes? For our sakes, no doubt. And writing 350 years later, St. Augustine cites Jesus' withering of the apple tree that had failed to bear fruit, and his sending of the devils into the herd of swine, as proof that the natural world is not subject to the concepts of morality that should govern our dealings with other men and women. The natural world is our rightful domain.

Nor could this relationship between man and animal be otherwise in the West, because it flows necessarily from our having been created by God in His image. If humans are kindred to God, aren't we therefore fundamentally different from every animal? As God has dominion over us, so must we have dominion over them. It is logical, and it is written. (And thus, by the way, the adamant prohibition against bestiality in Western culture. Unlike incest, also the subject of strictest censure, bestiality is an act without bad reproductive consequences, so to speak, but it does lower the status of man by moving him away from God and toward the fallen world. It is the gravest insult to the Creator, and thus it is not tolerated.)

I should mention that I was raised a Methodist in Georgia. I recall these biblical passages not in order to challenge the Christian faith in any way but simply to underline the heritage of our culture regarding the nature and status of animals. Besides, our other major cultural influence, the philosophical tradition originating in ancient Greece, was also adamant about the status of animals. Some Greek philosophers did hypothesize something very like a "mind" for wild beasts, but Aristotle was the most important of the philosophers in this field, and for Aristotle man was the only creature possessed of reason, consciousness, and a soul. According to the indispensable *Oxford Companion to Animal Behaviour*, the great thinker discussed, to one degree or another, 540 different species of animals in his writings. He was the first great naturalist, and his ideas about the natural world were the most important from any source for fully fifteen hundred years. As we shall see, Aristotle had some modern-sounding ideas on this subject, but he could also be amazingly uninformed and naïve. He apparently accepted at face value the fable that the mother bear literally licks her progeny into the proper bearlike shape. Certainly the philosopher who rationalized human slavery had no illusions about any concept of "animal rights" as entertained by many of us over two millennia later.

The Romans, too, were fascinated by animals, and the wealth and vast size of their empire allowed them to satisfy this fascination. The emperor Augustus was said to have had a collection of 420 tigers; Nero, 400 bears; Trajan, 11,000 animals of practically every known species. Pliny the Elder was a first-century Roman civil servant and naturalist whose thirty-seven-volume *Historia Naturalis* was packed with almost every imaginable fantasy and falsehood about the natural world—and a few facts as well. We might feel that since he was writing four hundred years after Aristotle he should have made an improvement on the philosopher's idea about the creative power of the mother bear, but Pliny did not. However, his belief in spontaneous generation as the explanation for the sudden appearance of maggots on a carcass was logical enough in that age. What about the report that a distant kingdom in Africa was ruled by a dog-headed race of folks who looked like us from the neck down? Perfectly believable as well, apparently, because there it is in Pliny!

Change came painfully slowly in those days. In fact, Western culture changed very little over a thousand years, so it's not surprising that Christian monks living in the twelfth and thirteenth centuries A.D. were still highly susceptible to such literally fabulous stories, with which they became acquainted in a third-century text that picked up where Pliny had left off. This was the *Physiologus*, or *The Natural Historian*, and the medieval illustrators seized upon these animal stories as a wonderful subject for their new powers of visual illustration. The resulting volumes, now known as "bestiaries," also reflect the residue of the various pagan religions absorbed as Roman Christianity spread north, south, east, and west. Paganism—always, everywhere, and in every form—consecrates animal powers and animal mysteries.

Few medieval men and women thought about hiking up a mountain, which was seen literally as another world, or taking a holiday at the beach, the boundary of yet another demonstrably dangerous world. Just as few ventured forth into the field for the study of natural history firsthand. Thus the stories and images of these bestiaries comprised just about the sum of the knowledge of the animal kingdom for many people for several centuries. Inevitably, I suppose, these bestiaries became more and more fanciful as editors added new stories and the gold-leaf illuminations became more spectacular. Several hundred of these gorgeous books have survived in excellent condition, and they are the best place to find out what a real firebreathing dragon or a lovely mermaid looked like in the flesh.

By and large, pets were not as revered in the Middle Ages as they are today. To keep one could be positively dangerous, in fact, leading to suspicions of witchcraft. Hard as this is for us to believe today, animals were put on criminal trial throughout these centuries. This bizarre cultural artifact is reported by Dorothy Cheney and Robert Seyfarth in their excellent and important book, *How Monkeys See the World*. Cheney and Seyfarth are quoting in turn from *The Criminal Prosecution and Capital Punishment of Animals*, a volume by one E. P. Evans, first published in 1906 and currently out of print, alas. The cited story details the charges against three sows who had been feeding quietly until, "excited and enraged by the squealing of one of the porklings," they trampled the son of the swinekeeper, who died some days later. "After due process of law," the three sows were condemned to death, and so were their peers in the herd, who had "hastened to the scene of the murder and by their cries and aggressive actions showed that they approved of the assault, and were ready and even eager to become *participes criminis*." True story.

Various famous Christians down the ages are remembered for their kindness toward animals—St. Francis of Assisi especially—but, for the most part, the attitude of the mainstream Church toward the animal kingdom had not changed much from biblical days. The message of the Scriptures and the hierarchy of the universe were too plain for all to see. Thomas Aquinas, the great thirteenth-century churchman who reconciled Catholic teachings with the recently rediscovered philosophy of Aristotle, understood that animals can suffer, but he based his opposition to cruelty toward them only upon the supposition that this cruelty might lead in turn to cruelty toward humans or might rebound as an economic loss to the perpetrator. In the great *Summa Theologica*, we are the only creatures who really count. The universe is still 100 percent anthropocentric.

MOVING INTO THE MODERN:
DESCARTES TO DARWIN

But surely ideas about animals changed in the Renaissance? Well, yes and no. Leonardo da Vinci was vegetarian, Montaigne wrote that cruelty to animals was wrong in and of itself, and the tradition of careful observation of the real world gained credence. Even Thomas More, the justly esteemed English statesman and Catholic martyr (and subject of the great movie *A Man for All Seasons*), digressed in his *Utopia* to describe quite accurately the phenomenon of imprinting at birth in barnyard fowl (the newly hatched chick will imprint upon the first creature it sees—man, woman, or beast—and consider that creature "Mom" which, fortunately, it usually is), almost four hundred years before the definitive imprinting work of Konrad Lorenz in the twentieth century. On the other hand, we have René Descartes.

Most of the discussions I've read about Western attitudes toward animals and Western ideas about animal consciousness skip completely over the ancient Greeks and Romans and the first fifteen centuries of Christian thought. Instead they proceed directly to this pivotal French philosopher and mathematician, who lived and wrote in the first half of the seventeenth century. Descartes was adamant in his belief that only human beings are endowed with consciousness. Animals need not apply. Furthermore, Descartes argued that animals were nothing more or less than pieces of soft, fleshy machinery, albeit quite complicated in many cases. He was forced to take this extreme mechanistic position because he had backed himself into a corner in his defense of the immortal human soul, about which he was also adamant, as was everyone else at that time.

As I understand it, Descartes's logic goes something like this:

Human beings have souls, as taught by Christian doctrine and as distinguished by consciousness; animals do not have souls because they cannot have souls, according to Christian doctrine; therefore animals cannot have consciousness either. (One of the early Church's most interesting arguments against animals having souls is that neither heaven nor hell would be big enough to contain the souls of all humans *and* animals that ever lived.) Of course, this is a simplified version of Descartes's thinking, and I'm not a logician, but nevertheless I sense a lot of holes in this remarkable argument. I take comfort from the fact that philosophers have unearthed a lot of problems with it as well. I also think of Benjamin Franklin's famous, irreverent quip that the advantage of our being "reasonable creatures" is that we can always come up with a reason for doing and thinking whatever we want to. Descartes was a brilliant man, sometimes referred to as the father of modern philosophy—*Cogito, ergo sum* and all that— and he made major contributions in optics and mathematics, but as the single most important figure in the story of Western attitudes toward animal consciousness, he makes a contribution that is decidedly, painfully negative and, as I think we have discovered in the twentieth century, dead wrong.

But Descartes was not alone in his rigidly "mechanistic" philosophy. Any number of other brilliant thinkers before and after him subscribed to some version of his view of animal nature. The Englishman Thomas Hobbes was a thoroughgoing materialist with the pessimistic world view that produced his infamous depiction of human life, much less the lives of animals, as "nasty, brutish, and short." Another famous Englishman, Descartes's near-contemporary Francis Bacon, presupposed a mechanistic world suitable for human domination as the basis for scientific empiricism. Surely it is no coincidence that all manner of cruel experimentation on animals became more and more common in the seventeenth century, as these Cartesian ideas were disseminated across Europe:

> They administered beatings to dogs with perfect indifference, and made fun of those who pitied the creatures as if they felt pain. They said the animals were clocks; that the cries they emitted when struck were only the noise of a little spring that had been touched, but that the whole body was without feeling. They nailed poor animals up on boards by their four paws to vivisect them and see the circulation of the blood which was a great subject of conversation.

That appalled and appalling description comes to us from the Enlightenment freethinker Voltaire, writing a hundred years after Descartes. Ironically, however, the results of these grotesque anatomy lessons compelled more and more people to question their morality in the first place, because the experiments demonstrated the essential sameness of physiology among the mammals, including man. Voltaire wrote:

> . . . Judge this dog who has lost his master, who has searched for him with mournful cries in every path, who comes home agitated, restless, who runs up and down the stairs, who goes from room to room, who at last finds his beloved master in his study, and shows him his joy by the tenderness of cries, by his leaps, by his caresses. There are barbarians who seize this dog, who so greatly surpasses man in fidelity and friendship, and nail him down to a table and dissect him alive, to show you the mesenteric veins. You dis-

cover in him all the same organs of feeling as in yourself. Answer me, mechanist, has Nature arranged all the springs of feeling in this animal to the end that he might not feel? Does he have nerves [in order] to be impassive?

David Hume, a contemporary of Voltaire, seconded this pointed sarcasm and added his own: "Next to the ridicule of denying an evident truth, is taking such pains to defend it; and no truth appears to me more evident, than that beasts are endowed with thought and reason as well as man."

Hume and Voltaire and their sympathizers employ what philosophers call the argument from inference. Just as we laypeople infer that other humans feel pain and suffering based on our own experience of pain and suffering, so we must infer the same of the other vertebrates, because the vertebrate nervous system is essentially identical to our own. A hundred years later, Charles Darwin extended this argument from inference about as far as it could go. The scientist who was—and still is, in some circles—reviled as the man who "lowered" mankind to the level of the animal with his theory of evolution and natural selection could just as easily be judged as the man who did everything he could to raise animals as near as possible to the level of humans. Darwin's ideas required that the natural world reveal a continuum of consciousness from the "lowest" invertebrate to the "highest" primate (us). Neither the human mind nor the human emotions could have appeared suddenly and without precedent. They must have evolved from "incipient" predecessors.

THE ANTHROPOMORPHIC INSTINCT

What an intriguing turn of events in Western intellectual history! In the seventeenth century, René Descartes had felt it necessary to deny consciousness to animals as part of a philosophical project to guarantee the existence of the human soul. Now, in the nineteenth century, Charles Darwin had ulterior motives for defending animal consciousness. At the heart of the "conflict" between these two positions was—and still is—the age-old issue of anthropomorphism, which in its simplest terms is the use of human characteristics to describe the nonhuman; or put another way, ascribing human characteristics to nonhumans. To shout at a stalled car for being stubborn is anthropomorphizing, because cars aren't stubborn. Nor is yon lazy cloud really lazy, nor the angry hurricane truly angry as it churns out of the Caribbean and into the Gulf of Mexico.

This is just the way we enjoy thinking and talking. *Why* we tend to relate to the natural world in this way is a fascinating question in its own right, the subject of numerous books and studies, popular and academic. It is also vital to our discussion, because many scientists argue some version of the Cartesian position that to believe that animals are thinking, conscious beings is merely anthropomorphizing. From their perspective, a dog—even one with its four paws planted in concrete, refusing to budge—is no more stubborn than the stalled car. That adjective is an unwarranted assumption on our part in each case.

I strongly disagree, but the naysayers definitely have one valid point. It's true that in the formative years of every human culture, we were obsessed with animals, as I've discussed. One of the earliest writers to appreciate this anthropomorphic tendency was Xenophanes, a Greek thinker of the sixth century B.C. He wrote, "But if oxen and horses . . . could create works of art like those made by men, horses would draw pictures of gods like horses, and oxen of gods like oxen." He's probably right about that. Furthermore, in the formative years of our individual lives, many if not most of us were infatuated with animals. In fact, researchers have found that children dream mainly about animals; as we grow into adulthood, the self emerges as the favorite subject of the incredible dream machine.

I was nine years old when I got my first "very own" dog. She was a cuddly little cur about four months old, part collie and part shepherd with the collie predominant. In a burst of great originality, about which I was not the least bit embarrassed, I named her "Lassie." It was love at first sight for both of us, and we became inseparable. Lassie and I went everywhere together. She would follow me to school and wait for me patiently until school let out. We had to put a stop to this after a few days, however, because it was not safe for her to be running around off-leash even in our small Georgia town.

Lassie slept with me, of course, and would get up at the crack of dawn with my parents so that she could go outside. When it was time for me to get up a little later, Mother would say to Lassie, "Go get George!" Lassie would bound up the stairs at the speed of light and pounce on me with all of her sixty-five pounds. If I did not get up immediately, she would pull the covers off.

Did I consider Lassie a thinking, emotional, and conscious being? To the extent that I thought about such things at all at that age, I most certainly did. Like all children—adults as well—who fall in love with an animal, I was completely anthropomorphic toward Lassie. I would talk to her endlessly, divulging my deepest childhood secrets, and I had no doubt whatsoever that she understood every word I said, even if her reaction was just a little "woof" and a snuggle to get closer to me. I know now, of course, that while Lassie did not understand every word I said to her, she deftly interpreted my body language and the tone of my voice to read my moods. In fact, I have not known a dog since who was so good at making me believe that I was being completely understood. All dogs possess this ability in varying degrees, but Lassie was the champ.

Lassie and I shared a wonderful life together for three years. And then one summer during the war, my parents decided we were going to take a rare four-week vacation, and for the first time ever, we would just close down our big old house for those weeks and let the housekeeper check on it occasionally. I was delighted with the news and said, "Oh, boy, Lassie is going to love this trip!"

"Well," said my father, "your mother and I have given the question of Lassie considerable thought, and we've decided that Lassie would be happier if we boarded her at our vet's very nice kennel. After all, we're going to be driving a lot, and Lassie does have a tendency to get carsick."

I was crestfallen and fought the urge to tell my parents that I just would not go on the trip if I could not take Lassie. Upon reflection, however, I realized that no amount of protesting from me—especially in the form of threats—was going to change my parents' minds, so, reluctantly, I gave in and vowed to myself to make the best of it. That night I dreamed that Lassie and I ran away. But when we got hopelessly lost somewhere in China, the dream of liberation turned into a nightmare. The next day my mom and I took Lassie to the kennel. I tried very hard to "be a man," but as we drove away after leaving Lassie, I could not hold back the tears. I looked over at my mother, and she was crying, too.

We went to Florida and literally toured the state from top to bottom. I had never been to our neighboring state and loved every minute of it. For the first few days I called the kennel every day to check on Lassie. I called on Monday of our last week away, and since we would be home the following Friday, I did not call anymore, knowing that Lassie was fine.

On Thursday of that week, my mother called home from Tampa to check on things while I was cavorting in the hotel's swimming pool. When I came upstairs later, I sensed immediately that something was wrong. My mother's eyes were red, and my father sat in a chair looking completely dejected. Mom gestured for me to come to her, and she put her arms around me. "Son," she said, "I got some bad news when I called home."

I stiffened my body and then heard her say in a cracked voice, almost a whisper, "Lassie died last night." And then all three of us just cried and cried. I had never seen my father cry before.

The vet said his kennel man had checked on Lassie and the other boarders at midnight and Lassie was fine. When he made his rounds at 3 A.M., Lassie was dead. The vet told us he had absolutely no idea why my dog died. He even performed a postmortem and found only that her healthy heart had simply stopped beating. "I've never had anything like this happen before," he said, "and I just feel terrible about it. I know this does not sound very professional of me, but perhaps she missed you so much that she died of a broken heart."

AN IMAGINARY CONTINUITY?

Intimate connection with the natural world may be our most primal and important cultural heritage, but it's also true that today we can only dimly remember it. We have to work hard to stay in touch, through our pets to a degree, but mostly with words. We enshrine the natural world with the popular idioms such as "Mother Earth" and "Mother Nature," although "Stepmother Earth" and "Stepmother Nature" might be more accurate at the end of this millennium. National parks, private gardens, municipal zoos, household pets, and natural-history films such as those on *Nature* are the best most of us can do in an effort to stay in touch. In my opinion, there is not much use in tearing our hair out and wailing over the loss of our sense of intimate belonging in the wide world of flora and fauna. That's just the way it is, and there will be no "going back," not that I can see. This particular horse is definitely out of the barn, and sprinting away about as fast as it can go.

Is our anthropomorphic instinct one way in which we try to stay in touch with the natural world? Many commentators believe so. We see the golden eagle riding the thermals above a beautiful valley and imagine ourselves in that situation and become envious. What sheer fun that must be, what joy, we believe, even though we have absolutely no idea if this is the eagle's own emotion. Or we see a dog cower in the corner after a severe reprimand from his or her owner and we feel sorry for the poor thing—or a little guilty, perhaps, if we are the owner. It seems that we cannot help projecting our attitudes, emotions, and ideas of personality and rationality onto—or into—our household pets and many other animals as well.

Anthropomorphism is also a reflection of our "psychic structure," to quote Paul Shepard in *The Others: How Animals Made Us Human*. Before his death in 1996, Shepard was a professor emeritus of human ecology at Pitzer College. He suggests in this wonderful book that animal stories and anthropomorphizing of every sort set up an "imaginary continuity between animals' lives and our own, [providing] a lifelong shield against alienation. . . . Stories with animals are older than history and better than philosophy."

That is very well said. Stories with animals also make the best cartoons. Many of our most creative cartoonists would be sorely put to the test for subject matter if they couldn't depict talking, thinking, emoting animals. A quick survey of Gary Larson's 1998 "Far Side" desk calendar finds sixteen such jests in the month of August alone. That's sixteen out of thirty-one—and all of them are terrifically clever. The funniest might be the scene on Noah's ark with all the creatures gathered around what we take to be a fresh carcass. (All we see of the deceased are its extended hooves, sticking straight up in the air.) With his hands on his hips and glaring in the direction of the pair of lions, Noah declares sternly, "Well, so much for the unicorn, but from now on, all carnivores will be confined to 'C' deck." The lions look knowingly at each other: classic anthropomorphism with a wicked twist, because we presume that one thing lions do *not* feel is guilt about their carnivorous nature.

Or would Charles Darwin disagree? In his defense of animal consciousness, the great evolutionist was a committed, inveterate anthropomorphizer. *The Descent of Man, and Selection in Relation to Sex*, published in 1871, a dozen years after *Origin of Species*, is full of passages such as this one: "We have seen that the senses and intuitions, the various emotions and faculties, such as love, memory, attention and curiosity, imitation, reason, etc., of which man boasts, may be found in an incipient, or even sometimes in a well-developed condition, in the lower animals." Getting down to details, Darwin wrote, ". . . a dog carrying a basket for his master exhibits in a high degree self-complacency or pride. There can, I think, be no doubt that a dog feels shame . . . and something very like modesty when begging too often for food. A great dog scorns the snarling of a little dog, and this may be called magnanimity."

Perhaps the single most famous such Darwinian passage among biologists is the reference in *Descent* to "ants chasing and pretending to bite each other, like so many puppies." One finds that notorious excerpt in quite a few commentaries! To the scientists who followed in Darwin's footsteps and defended his controversial theory, such passages from *Descent* and others from *The Expression of the Emotions in Man and Animals* were embarrassing. Since these scientists don't like to criticize Darwin, for fear of casting doubt on his main theory, to this day they have tended to focus the onus of blame for this kind of blatant anthropomorphizing on his protégé, G. J. Romanes, who wrote in the same vein in his book published in 1882, *Animal Intelligence*. Romanes's narrative is chock-full of stories about jealous fish and dogs who enjoy a knee-slapping joke.

THE QUANDARY

In her book *Pack of Two*, Caroline Knapp describes her deep love for her dog Lucille and her struggle to balance this love against what she well knows is our tendency to anthropomorphize. Knapp describes how at least once a day Lucille:

> pokes her nose toward my hand. This is the kind of moment that can make me feel in tune with her, that seems to speak to a level of connection between us that I cherish: she is asking me to give her my hand, and when I comply she will sit down and spend several minutes licking it . . . She sometimes places a paw on my wrist to steady my hand, a gesture that feels delicate and tender and full of affection to me. But is it? I'd like to think that this is about love, that Lucille is deliberately seeking me out for a kind of canine kissfest, but it's equally possible that she's indulging one of her other affinities: for the taste of hand lotion. So which interpretation is right? I choose to believe that the hand-licking is about both moisturizer and me (they're my hands, after all), but I am also aware that an element of choice is at

work here, that this is my read, based at least to some extent on my own investment in the idea of loving communion with my dog.

Just so, says Celia Heyes, a comparative psychologist at University College, London, who makes several appearances in the *Nature* series which accompanies this book. Heyes is not a full-blown Cartesian on the question of animal consciousness, but she is an agnostic. We don't know whether animals are conscious, she argues; we don't know whether dogs truly "love" us, but we do know that seeing ourselves in them seems to be the "default" mode to which we humans have been set.

Frans de Waal is a primate researcher whose work is also featured in the *Nature* series. In his book *Bonobo: The Forgotten Ape*, de Waal writes, "When the lively, penetrating eyes lock with ours and challenge us to reveal who we are, we know right away that we are not looking at a 'mere' animal, but at a creature of considerable intellect with a secure sense of its place in the world. We are meeting a member of the same tailless, flat-chested, long-armed primate family to which we ourselves and only a handful of other species belong. We feel the age-old connection before we can stop to think, as people are wont to do, how different we are."

In short, our tendency to anthropomorphize is the "default" mode only because it reflects a deep and vital truth: How else can we view the world, except by listening carefully to our own knowledge and experience and by reacting within the categories our brains allow? When we look into the eyes of a dog, we *do* feel the heart-to-heart connection. To deny this fact is silly and, in the end, fruitless. When we look into the eyes of a bonobo or a chimpanzee, we *do* see "a creature of considerable intellect with a secure sense of its place in the world." René Descartes himself had a pet dog, Monsieur Grat, and I'm willing to bet that he treated him kindly, even while insisting that the animal was merely a machine.

In the early years of our *Nature* television series, we bent over backward not to be anthropomorphic in the narration scripts of our programs. We wanted our films to be scientifically accurate and to be taken seriously. We still do, of course, but the more we have learned about the animal mind, the more we are inclined to give the subjects of our films more credit for some of the intelligent behavior they exhibit right in front of our cameras.

Celia Heyes argues that scientists and others who would know the truth must watch out for the distorting anthropomorphic bias. Fair enough. We should be careful when we're doing science, but when in the name of science we insist on viewing the wild world with no sense whatsoever of "connection," the result is just as unsatisfactory and false as the most far-fetched nineteenth-century tale about the dog who enjoyed the joke.

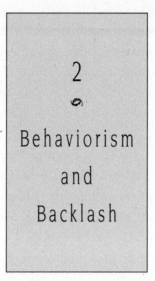

2

Behaviorism
and
Backlash

THE BASIC AGENDA

If I've read about Clever Hans once, I've read about him fifty times. It must be illegal to omit this famous horse from any consideration of our ideas about the animal mind, and I don't want to pay the fine. Hans's owner was Wilhelm von Osten, a Prussian aristocrat who came into a sizable fortune around the turn of the century and immediately set out to prove his prowess as a teacher by instructing a horse in simple arithmetic. And he succeeded in doing so, at least to his own and to many observers' satisfaction. If von Osten wrote down on a card 2 + 4, Hans tapped his forefoot six times; if he wrote 3 × 3, Hans tapped nine times. Even when another individual was in charge of the examination, Hans was usually correct in his computations. He became a sensation, a regular Secretariat in regard to fame.

In 1904, Hans even passed a set of what were designed to be rigorous tests by the director of the Berlin Psychological Institute, one Carl Stumpf. The panel of judges included a circus trainer, a zoologist, a veterinarian, and a politician. Stumped by the horse, Stumpf then turned over the case to his pupil Oskar Pfungst, who ruined all the fun by demonstrating that Hans was not doing arithmetic at all. Instead, he was responding to the very subtle visual cues of his inquisitors.

Now, von Osten was not a con man. Apparently he truly was unaware he had been subtly cueing his horse, just as the other testers had been unaware of their own inadvertent cues. But Pfungst proved that von Osten and the others had indeed been tipping the animal to the answers. Pfungst did so quite simply, by directing the examiner to pose problems written on cards that the examiner could not see. In this case, poor Hans was lost and pawed the ground at random. Pfungst went on to demonstrate that Hans could respond to cues as slight as the raising of an eyebrow or the flaring of a nostril. He was indeed a clever horse, just not in the way his owner wanted to imagine.

The embarrassment of the Clever Hans episode hung over animal studies and comparative psychology for decades, and it still does, to some extent. Indeed, the episode did amply demonstrate the dangers of the anthropomorphic bias and the necessity for rigorous procedure in evaluating animal behavior on a scientific basis. Case closed. In the early twentieth century, it is not much of an exaggeration to state that a diligent program of "de-anthropomorphizing" was undertaken across the board by many researchers, especially those based in America, even if this program took them all the way back to Cartesian ideas about animals as nothing more than complicated pieces of four-legged machinery.

From this perspective, there was no place for "anecdotalism" either—with anecdotalism defined as almost any observation obtained through naturalists' old-fashioned, patient labor in the bush. Like anthropomorphism, this allegation of anecdotalism has been quite important in animal studies throughout this century; I want to present a couple of fieldwork episodes from quite different types of sources to illustrate the problem.

The first comes from *Elephant Memories*, Cynthia Moss's compelling book about her thirteen years living among and studying the elephants in Amboseli National Park in Kenya. In 1980, twins were born to the Amboseli elephant named Estella (even the naming of animals in the field, as opposed to "objective" numbering, is looked on with suspicion by some scientists, but Moss has a strong, complex defense for the practice). One of these twins, Equinox, was male; Eclipse was female. Twins are a rarity among the elephants, and surviving twins even rarer, presumably because the mother can provide only enough milk for one. So, Cynthia Moss thought, this will be quite interesting. Sex differences should come through loud and clear in this "experiment." Indeed, the first time Moss observed Estella nursing the two calves, the male Equinox bullied Eclipse away from the teat on one side, then on the other. Moss writes, "It was always the male, who was slightly bigger, who initiated the aggression, and he was usually successful at disrupting the female's suckling." Within a week, our veteran observer Moss was beginning to doubt that the female would survive, but then one day she watched as the two young elephants ran around and butted and played with each other for ten minutes. Finally the young male got tired and lay down to rest. Immediately Eclipse ran to the teat on the far side of their mother Estella, out of sight of her brother—who was asleep anyway—where she suckled in peace. So this was how the calf had been obtaining her milk ration! Both calves survived and thrived.

Now consider this bizarre episode from Elizabeth Marshall Thomas's bestselling book *The Hidden Life of Dogs*. Thomas also wrote *The Harmless People*, a classic about the !Kung Bushmen of southwest Africa, but this book about her dogs is avowedly, unabashedly, unapologetically anthropomorphic and anecdotal. Yet how could our relationship with dogs be otherwise, Thomas pleads, after thousands of years of codependency (my term, not hers!) between the two species? The story concerns her husband and their dog—one of their dogs. One blistering-hot afternoon in Boulder, Colorado, where the couple lived at the time, Thomas's husband bought an ice-cream cone. When he started licking, he noticed the dog watching with close attention. Sympathetic, he offered the cone to the dog, fully expecting to lose the whole thing with this altruistic gesture. To his surprise, the dog licked daintily and stopped. Man and dog exchanged polite licks a second time, then a third, until they were down to the cone itself (which some of us feel is the best part). Now Thomas's husband took a small bite and offered the stump to the dog, again expecting to lose the rest of it. Instead, the animal astonished everyone again by taking only a small bite, just as his master had. Man and dog then exchanged several more considerate bites.

"Astonishing?" Thomas asks. "Not really. For eight years, my husband and this dog have built a relationship of trust and mutual obligation . . . When two dogs share food, they eat simultaneously while respecting each other's feeding space, which is a little imaginary circle around the other's mouth. But the idea of taking alternate bites is totally human. Even so, the dog fathomed it, and without ever having seen it done. Who ate the tip of the cone? My husband ate it. The dog let him have the last turn."

Do these two stories represent irrelevant "anecdote" from the field or invaluable observation that could be obtained only in the field? The anti-anthropomorphizing camp would dismiss both out of hand as nothing more than whimsical anecdote, wishful thinking, folk psychology—Clever Hans all over again. Their bias became enshrined in the standing joke about "my data, your observations, their anecdotes." And it is true that such evidence must be carefully sifted, but it is also true that the rare behavior serendipitously observed might well be exactly what is most valuable for our understanding of any animal.

Cynthia Moss is a veteran elephant expert. I think her story of Estella and the twins might well demonstrate shrewd thinking by the little female. Here's what Cynthia told me about the practice of culling elephants: "They cull whole families except for the youngest calves and then capture those for sale. And everyone said, 'Oh, that was okay,' because the whole family was killed and no other elephants knew about it. But now we find through our field studies that elephants can hear over long distances—these infrasonic sounds—so they can hear the screams—the death screams of those elephants— maybe from two kilometers away. And then those elephants that remain alive are terrorized, and every time they hear the helicopters go up, they're afraid. They live lives of terror, which is something that we cannot accept."

If we did set aside all such testimony from the field, what could we use for evidence in its stead? At the turn of the century, the answer of the comparative psychologists was . . . laboratory testing. In Russia, Ivan Pavlov conducted his famous experiments demonstrating the conditioned reflexes in salivating dogs. In America, the psychologist and educator Edward Lee Thorndike contrived a classic experiment involving a puzzle box from which famished cats were challenged to escape by finding the correct sequence of release mechanisms. The only way the animal could accomplish this the first time was to happen across the right sequence by pure luck (the same would have been true for a human being). A plate of seafood was the cat's reward. With subsequent trials, the time required for every cat in the experiment to effect its release got progressively shorter, until eventually the animals could escape almost immediately.

Thorndike considered two explanations. This was either a straightforward case of stimulus-response learning, the product of reinforcement, or the cat was rationally thinking its way through the problem, using prior results as a guide. One factor that tipped the scale in Thorndike's eye toward the stimulus-response explanation was the fact that the successfully trained cat would follow the release sequence even if one side of the puzzle cage had been removed and the cat could simply have stepped out and started eating. Given this fact, how could the cat be reasoning? Thorndike decided it couldn't be, and he derived what became known as the "law of effect," which stated that behavior changes because of its direct, immediate consequences and for no other reason. (Later in his career he turned to creating intelligence and learning tests for children.)

In 1913, J. B. Watson codified many of the tenets of Pavlov, Thorndike, and other laboratory researchers and thereby founded the field within psychology that became known as behaviorism. (Watson then had a different kind of "afterlife" from Thorndike. When a sex scandal ruined his career at Johns Hopkins University, he went to work for the J. Walter Thompson advertising agency on Madison

Avenue. In the annals of advertising, he is often credited with inventing the "brand name.")

Although Watson was the official founder of the behaviorist school, these ideas gained public, as opposed to just academic, attention through the notorious pronouncements and investigations of Burrhus Frederic Skinner, who is practically unknown by that name but world-famous simply as B. F. Skinner. Operating from his powerful position at Harvard University, B. F. Skinner succeeded in replacing the overly enthusiastic anthropomorphizing of nineteenth-century naturalists such as Darwin and Romanes with this equally unrewarding, reductive enterprise. Behaviorism held sway in comparative psychology for much of this century, and is still highly influential. Today, the field of cognitive ethology—the study of animal cognition, minds, and consciousness—is, in many respects, a backlash against behaviorism.

Like just about every other school of thought, this one evolved and split into factions with various emphases, which I couldn't begin to parse out, but the behaviorists were united in their belief that as far as scientific investigation of animals goes, all that matters is observable behavior, because only such behavior can be studied with reliability, objectivity, and repeatability—three benchmarks of the scientific enterprise. Everything else is without "cash value." We might believe we can intuit thoughts and feelings in animals, but where's the proof? We don't have any. Furthermore, behaviorists argued, we never will. We can no more scientifically study animal consciousness than we can poetry. The "common sense" of anthropomorphism can be no guide, because common sense has told us in past eras that the sun revolves around the earth and that space and time are constants—how could they be anything else?! But those tenets have been proved incorrect. Thus there is no place in science for "common sense."

I pause to look over at my three dogs and one cat, and I wonder, "What are these creatures thinking?" I ask the same question about all the animals I have observed in the wild. Behaviorists answer, "They're not 'thinking' anything at all, and they're not 'feeling' anything either. They're *behaving*, often in apparently sophisticated and provocative ways, granted, but still just behaving." Or as Skinner wrote in *About Behaviorism*, "Some [mental states] can be 'translated into behavior,' others discarded as unnecessary or meaningless."

Even what we laypeople think of as pure native instinct—breathing is a radical example—was viewed by behaviorists and studied as stimulus-response learning accomplished very quickly, and at a very early age! Behaviorists didn't even try to "understand" their subject. That enterprise, too, was beside the point and loaded with anthropomorphic pitfalls. The best that could be hoped for was accurate, complete description and, perhaps, control. (Skinner frankly acknowledged that his big idea was a philosophy before it was a way of doing science, and as a philosophy it promised profound implications, which were made clear enough by the title of his most inflammatory book: *Beyond Freedom and Dignity*.)

The Interpretation of Dreams, written by Sigmund Freud in 1900, was translated into English in 1913, the year in which J. B. Watson codified behaviorism. Almost needless to say, behaviorists were not impressed by the Freudian agenda, which they considered about as unscientific as a purportedly scientific enterprise could be. When Freudians in turn criticized behaviorism for being unable to deal with the unconscious, Skinner pointed out—with great delight, I imagine—that in fact his approach dealt with almost nothing but the unconscious. After all, we're unconscious twenty-four hours a day of what goes on in our brains. Behaviorists just never used the term in its Freudian sense.

They took great care with language, which was redefined as "verbal behavior" (Skinner wrote a book with that title). Love was "attachment formation." The self was a "repertoire of behavior." They wouldn't use the phrase "the dog threatened the cat" because the term "threaten" anthropomorphically implies some kind of mental state on the part of the animal, some kind of intention or purpose. They might not even have said that the dog "raised its right leg," because this innocuous verb implies the intention to do so. Safer would be to put the phrase in the passive voice: "The right leg is raised," or "The right leg goes up."

As the joke goes, no behaviorist ever changed his or her mind! They became notorious for believing that we do not believe and for thinking that we do not think. Like many, if not most, academic disciplines in this century, behaviorism had contracted a bad case of "physics envy," a widespread malady in twentieth-century science and the academy in general. Many academics—and not just psychologists, by any means—labor in apparent jealousy of the hard-and-fast truths discovered by the physicists and chemists and mathematicians. Forget that these truths can sometimes turn out to be false; at least there is the prospect of solid answers. The incredible discoveries of what we know as the "hard sciences" and the technologies that quickly followed these discoveries have established science as the only purveyor of Truth with a capital T, and comparative psychologists wanted in on the action.

Eventually behaviorism melded with the equally notorious sociobiology as formulated by E. O. Wilson, the famous authority on insects, to yield a more or less unified, ultramaterialist approach to behavior, consciousness, and mind. This viewpoint hypothesizes that all aspects of behavior and culture—human and animal—can be accounted for by a combination of genetic inheritance, handed down through untold generations via natural selection (the focus of sociobiology), and by conditioned behavior "learned" by our brains through reinforcement (the focus of behaviorism). The essence of sociobiology, which was widely derided when it first came to public attention in 1975, is now somewhat back in vogue under the new label "evolutionary biology," without much controversy and with rave reviews for Wilson's latest book, *Consilience*. (It's easy enough to challenge this viewpoint, and I do, but it is much more nuanced than it might appear at first glance. I am simply not ready to admit that my brain is nothing more than the world's best computer; there's too much magic in there. Wilson, who is a charming man, is not ashamed to invoke the language of his upbringing, which was Southern Baptist, so, at least for me, it is very hard not to like this fellow Southerner.)

A BYTE IS NOT A BITE

So we have behaviorism, aided and abetted by physics envy, operating throughout this century as the single most important influence in comparative psychology and the cognitive sciences. A second major influence since the 1960s has been computer science and ideas about "information processing." The most radical cognitive scientists have concluded that "mind" is nothing more than our experience of the brain, in some way. "The mind is what the brain does," according to Steven Pinker. The brain is nothing more than an organ for "information processing"—a fantastically complicated, carbon-based computer. These theories get fantastically complicated, of course but, like behaviorism, they are a profoundly reductive, mechanistic approach to the question of consciousness (including our own).

It is undoubtedly true that a great deal of animal and human behavior is unconscious information processing of some sort. After a complex task is initially learned, it can be accomplished for long periods of time without any sense of conscious awareness. In fact, conscious effort during such tasks just causes problems. The pianist, for example, who laboriously learns a concerto cannot then play that music in a concert with the same "conscious" attention it took to memorize it. If he or she tried to think consciously about every note—disaster! With these difficult skills, the whole point is to transform conscious learning into muscle memory and then to "let it flow."

A more common example of unconscious information processing—the one used by almost every book—is the task of driving a car, which is quite complex when you stop to think about it. The point is that after we have put the key in the ignition, we *don't* stop to think about it. We just drive, and we realize we have been totally inattentive—engaged in conversation with a friend or enjoying a CD, listening to a book on tape or talking on the cell phone—until a sudden event, such as a car pulling out of a driveway into our lane, draws our attention back to the task at hand. Then we become aware that we are, in fact, driving. And when I think carefully about talking with someone when driving a car, I realize that I don't consciously "choose" every word I say. In fact, I don't choose many words in this way. Suddenly I've just said them, and I suspect that is the case with whomever I'm talking with.

Likewise, as I sit at this computer terminal writing these pages, "I" consciously chose the subject, or so it seems, but the specific words in this sentence are suddenly just here. "I" haven't sorted through the confines of my brain to select them, one by one. So there is a good deal of conscious as well as unconscious information processing of some kind going on. Still, it is an incredible leap from these straightforward, less-than-profound insights to the conclusion that human thought is "nothing but" sophisticated information processing. This is the part of the argument that bothers me most.

How would scientists and philosophers who hold this "nothing but" position go about proving it? They might draw an analogy with the idea of the brilliant mathematician Alan Turing, who broke the secret Enigma code of the Axis Powers in World War II and went on to propose a famous test for artificial intelligence, the Holy Grail of his field. Turing proposed that should a computer behind a screen fool an interlocutor in an extended conversation, then that computer must be considered "intelligent" in the same way that we are intelligent, but I wonder whether it's a legitimate challenge in the first place. Let's think about an analogous endeavor in the biological sciences: the creation of a robot that could perfectly mimic the behavior of a laboratory mouse.

Suppose for a moment that a team of computer whizzes does succeed in creating a little robot that perfectly mimics the behavior of the lab mouse in all respects that we can observe. I've seen television footage of the latest robots that roll around on wheels, guided by laser eyes, and successfully avoid all the bigger obstacles. I cannot honestly envision the upgraded, even perfected version that could match the mouse in all respects, but let's suppose it is built. Let's suppose the behavior is identical. This would be a technical feat of a high order, but does anyone care to argue that there would be *no difference at all* between this incredibly sophisticated little machine and this relatively "dumb" little animal?

Recall that the cruel experiments on animals in the seventeenth century backfired, in a way, because they mainly demonstrated the almost identical physiology of the vertebrates. As Voltaire exclaimed,

"Answer me, mechanist, has Nature arranged all the springs of feeling in this animal to the end that he might not feel?" Any twenty-first-century achievement in the field of artificial intelligence will serve only to make a related distinction. Even if the lab mouse is defined as a carbon-based information processor—even if the brain is, as artificial intelligence guru Marvin Minsky famously said, "a computer made of meat"—there remains an undeniable difference between the two test subjects: One is a mobile computer plugged into the wall, one is a mouse with at least minimal sentience. It's that simple. The behavior might be the same, but the means of achieving it are different. No theory can make it otherwise, can it?

THE BACKLASH

The influential MIT linguist Noam Chomsky once said that our human ignorance can be divided into two categories: problems and mysteries. Problems might be solved one day, while mysteries are beyond solution. Until this current era, the cognitive sciences seemed to be stuck investigating what was, fundamentally, the mystery of consciousness. In 1973, the philosopher Thomas Nagel published what became a famous paper in the field, entitled "What is it like to be a bat?" Trying to answer that question, Nagel found himself "restricted to the resources of my own mind, and those resources are inadequate to the task." He answered, in effect, that we'll never know what it's like to be a bat.

Twenty-five years later, some researchers and thinkers in the cognitive sciences argue that we may end up surprised at how much we can learn about what it's like to be a bat or any other creature. No one believes that we'll ever answer every question we might have about animal or human consciousness, but there's not much doubt that scientists working in a variety of fields are moving some of the questions out of the category of mysteries and into the category of problems.

Two thousand years ago, astronomy and medicine, for example, were only marginally scientific; our ancestors didn't have the necessary tools. Three hundred years ago, Sir Isaac Newton discovered the law of gravitation and (along with Gottfried Wilhelm Leibniz) developed calculus—and then he turned his attention to the wonderful world of alchemy because there was no modern science of chemistry. One hundred years ago, we had no way to study the brain and corresponding issues of consciousness. Today we can. Yesterday's EEGs (electroencephlograms) were crude instruments compared with today's CAT (computerized axial tomography) scans and PET (positron emission tomography) scans and ERPs (event related potentials, or patterns of voltage changes in the brain following a stimulus). Tomorrow? There will be something new, we know that. Later we shall consider the fascinating research in this area, but suffice it to say now that we know that certain ERP activity in the human brain is associated with very complex processing of data, and we know that ERP activity in other mammals is almost identical to ours in the same circumstances. This proves nothing, but it certainly raises questions for further research, as does the fact that psychoactive drugs have exactly the same effect on cats and dogs—and other animals, presumably, although our pets are the most extensively treated in this way— as they have on humans.

In philosophy there is a bizarre notion labeled "philosophical solipsism." It has many variants, naturally, but the main one is the idea that I am definitely a conscious human being but you might be a robot, and I can never prove otherwise, because I cannot get inside your head. This notion is taken seriously by few philosophers because of all the inferential evidence to the contrary, but many of the objections to intelligence and consciousness in animals are rooted in an analogous "species solipsism": We humans are conscious, but we will never know about you dogs. Yet this solipsism is no more valid than the other kind. The operative scientific phrase is "inference to the best explanation." I was surprised to learn from Donald Griffin that quarks—the building blocks of all matter, according to the best theories—are actually inferences from the data. Molecules and atoms we can see in electron microscopes, but we cannot see quarks. We infer their existence. Likewise, very little of the evidence supporting the evolution of species has been observed with our own eyes and instruments. Evolution is an inference from the record. Yet many scientists refuse to consider the reality of mental states in animals on the grounds that such states cannot be observed! A glaring inconsistency, as Donald Griffin points out.

No matter how sophisticated the behavior, behaviorists can always simply assert that "it's learned." In fact, that's exactly what radical behaviorism does assert. In order to construct the theoretical framework for such a narrow approach, they are compelled to diminish our sense not only of animals but of ourselves. Furthermore, their reductionism is not even good science. It is true that no one can ever prove that animals have consciousness, no more than I can prove you're not a robot, but to declare today that animals absolutely cannot think or feel is no different from theologians of the Middle Ages testifying that the planet earth cannot possibly orbit the sun. It is just as unscientific as the anecdotal, anthropomorphic assertion that when his owner leaves him alone in the house for ten hours, Fido gets "depressed."

Now the tide is turning. Over the past twenty-five years, an ever-increasing number of ethologists have balked at such arbitrary reductionism. The growing body of evidence we will survey in the following chapters clearly demonstrates that there is more to animal behavior than just instinct and conditioned learning. There is, at the very least, extensive memory and cognition. Even Pavlov's notorious experiments, interpreted correctly, showed more going on with the dogs than knee-jerk salivation, but operating in that early-behaviorist, radically anti-anthropomorphic environment, the Russian could not or did not make the connections. (Nor did he stop to ponder the fact that his experiments drove some of his lab dogs crazy.)

Restricted as they are to artificial settings, many of the laboratory experiments of the comparative psychologists asked narrowly restricted questions and received in return narrowly restricted answers. We need to observe and understand animals in the environment in which they evolved, and where their behavior will make the most sense. Animal intelligence is quite narrowly focused. As we shall see, creatures capable of astonishing mental feats in one area cannot accomplish much at all in another area that does not seem all that more difficult. (If you think this point does not apply to us humans, consider these two skills, language and arithmetic. Language should be extraordinarily difficult—but we pick it up automatically. Arithmetic should be easy by comparison—but months and years of focused labor are required before we master the basics.)

Of course, many biologists and naturalists have always understood the importance of fieldwork, even in the heyday of behaviorism. In Europe especially, there has long been a tradition of field-based naturalism. The validity of field studies is much greater in this century, with much stricter criteria and with much more care taken to account for the biases of the observer. Wolfgang Kohler, whose groundbreaking experiments in the 1920s of the tool-using capabilities of captive chimpanzees, concluded that animals employ insight and purpose in their behavior and lives. (More important, Jane Goodall later proved that chimps living in the wild also used tools.) Konrad Lorenz, the famous researcher whose work with greylag geese nailed down the concept of "imprinting" and who shared the Nobel Prize for Physiology and Medicine in 1973, wrote openly of emotions in animals in his book *Man Meets Dog* and elsewhere. In Japan, studies in ethology have always been fundamentally anthropomorphic, because Japanese culture in general has never accepted the Western cult of rationality.

The concept of the *Umwelt*, used by the nineteenth-century physiologist Jakob von Uexkull to mean the specific sensory world of any given animal, has been deemed of great importance by men and women who actually observe animals in the wild. What is the *Umwelt* of Thomas Nagel's bat? We can't be certain, but we do know that it is much different from our own. A dog's *Umwelt*, heavily reliant as it is on smell as opposed to eyesight, must be drastically different from ours. How can laboratory experiments ever get to the heart of these issues?

Sue Savage-Rumbaugh writes in *Kanzi: The Ape at the Brink of the Human Mind*, "Would the error of sometimes erroneously attributing capacities that did not exist be greater than that of never discovering any emotional or intellectual capacities that were continuous with our own? I think not. At the very least, if one scientist made a mistake and attributed some capacity to an animal that was far beyond its true ability, another scientist would come along and correct this mistake." (The Clever Hans episode is a perfect example.) "As the situation currently stands, we don't even have the right to make the mistake."

Kanzi was published in 1994, and perhaps Savage-Rumbaugh exaggerates. She has a lot of confederates, including the Tufts philosopher Daniel Dennett, whom I will mention often because he's one of the most cogent thinkers about mind and consciousness. Dennett disputes the behaviorist approach. He argues the importance of questions such as "Why does the fiddler crab have this one enlarged claw? What does he intend to accomplish with it?" Behaviorists recoil in horror, but in asking such questions we're not necessarily saying that the crab in fact does know why. We address such questions in order to learn answers from evolution. Even the simplest bacterium has its reasons, Dennett writes with his usual wit. It isn't aware of them, true, but for us to ignore these reasons in our investigations is folly.

This is *pragmatic* anthropomorphism, an important idea that is nicely illustrated for us by one Jerry Garcia—no, not the deceased founder of the Grateful Dead, but the famously inventive experimental psychologist in California. Garcia wrote in *American Psychologist* that he uses anthropomorphism to predict animal behavior "because this works better than most learning theories. I could rationalize this heresy by pointing to our common neurosensory systems or to convergent evolutionary forces. But, in truth, I merely put myself in the animal's place."

A PARTING SHOT

I conclude this brief discussion of the behaviorist philosophy and the backlash against it with a remark by Dr. Nicholas Dodman, professor of behavioral pharmacology and director of the Behavior Clinic at the Tufts University School of Veterinary Medicine. (I think of him as the pet psychiatrist.) "Look," Dodman said to me in a Thai restaurant near Tufts, "if it walks like a duck and talks like a duck, we have to investigate the possibility that it might be a duck."

3

The
Cognitive
Revolution

A FRESH START

The last two decades have witnessed nothing less than a "cognitive revolution." The blasphemous idea that even the lowly duck might have mental states is now in play, and the scientist most responsible for the increasing acceptance of cognitive ethology as a valid field of study is Donald Griffin, professor emeritus of zoology at Rockefeller and Harvard universities. Griffin argues that students of animal behavior have been "haunted" by the specter of Clever Hans errors for long enough. I've mentioned pragmatic anthropomorphism; Griffin's preferred term for the new approach he advocates is "critical anthropomorphism." His books *Animal Thinking* and *Animal Minds* were the groundbreaking texts in this field, and a good deal of my understanding of the background and the issues in cognitive ethology comes from these two volumes, from one long conversation with him in his Harvard office, and from my reading in his forbiddingly enormous, but authoritative, bibliography.

Griffin's first area of study was the mysterious bat. Before his research, our knowledge of bat orientation and navigation was based mainly on the eighteenth-century experiments of Lazzaro Spallanzani, an Italian biologist who was able to establish the important fact that bats primarily use their ears for navigation. The proof was pretty simple, as well as cruel: Subject bats that had had their eyes removed flew around as well as normal bats; other bats with functioning eyes but with their ears plugged ran into problems—*flew* into problems, to be more exact. However, this conclusion was not widely accepted because no human could hear what the bats were hearing. It was Griffin who proved that these remarkable mammals are hearing ultrasound—their own ultrasound. In his research, which began while he was still an undergraduate at Harvard, Griffin got off to a good start by simply pointing a newfangled ultrasound detector at a bat hanging in its cage. The meter went off the charts. So these bats were issuing ultrasound waves. Further work in the lab and outdoors proved that they were issuing the waves from their mouths, because bats trying to navigate with their mouths taped shut had trouble. Griffin proved that the rate of ultrasound emission by the bats increased dramatically when they flew within a meter or so of an object that could be as tiny as a strand of wire. Therefore an insect, even one on the wing, is a huge target, a veritable piece of cake, for a hungry bat. Griffin named the process by which bats navigate "echolocation"; his book *Listening in the Dark* was published in 1958.

Providentially perhaps, Griffin encountered Thomas Nagel just as the philosopher was mulling the ideas that would appear in the seminal paper "What Is It Like to Be a Bat?" Griffin knew more about this subject than anyone on earth, but a long conversation with Nagel first got him interested in the broader questions of consciousness. While Nagel eventually concluded that the *Umwelt* of the bat is so different that we'll never know what its subjective experience is like, Griffin believes that we may be able to learn a lot more than we realize.

At the age of eighty-four, Griffin doesn't give many interviews these days, but he agreed to see me in the small office he keeps in the old Anthropology Museum at Harvard. "It's a creaky old elevator," he had warned over the telephone. "You push the button for the fourth floor, and then for some unknown reason you have to push the unmarked button beside the fourth-floor button. Now, don't forget to push both." This sounded like one of Thorndike's puzzle boxes for testing cats. What would happen if I did forget, which was entirely possible? But I negotiated the terrain, and Griffin greeted me at the doorway to his office. He is tall and distinguished and soft-spoken, hale and hearty and much younger-looking than his age—not exactly how I had visualized such an iconoclastic scholar.

He says almost immediately, "I think everyone would agree that the behaviorist movement started by John Watson and continued by B. F. Skinner here at Harvard was very influential in discouraging, let's say, interest in subjective animal mentality and animal consciousness—up until very recently. Indeed, there are still some strong advocates of the behaviorist point of view."

Because of the explosion of interest and scholarship in the subject of animal minds, it's easy to forget that the cognitive revolution faces serious challenges from within the academy. In fact, Griffin even suspects that his own view may still be a minority view. "There have been a number of people who have been, if not suspicious, at least very cautious," Griffin continues. "One of the leading ones is a Canadian psychologist named Hank Davis. He honored me by likening my book to Salman Rushdie's *Satanic Verses*." Griffin gets a chuckle out of that somewhat hyperbolic denunciation. Another "debunker" I read argued strenuously that the best label for the ideas of the cognitive ethologists isn't "pragmatic" or "critical" anthropomorphism but "anecdotal cognitivism." In the trade, that's a harsh put-down. In a review of Griffin's *Animal Thinking* in *American Scientist*, E. A. Wasserman wrote, "No statement concerning consciousness in animals is open to verification and experimentation. Isn't it time we set aside such tantalizing, but unanswerable, questions and direct our energies to more productive pursuits?" What's ironic here is that Wasserman and colleagues were responsible for some of the first tests demonstrating that "the conceptual abilities of pigeons are more advanced than hitherto suspected." These are famous tests demonstrating the powerful category-creating capacity for the lowly, bird-brained pigeon. In some tests, the birds outperform college students, time and again. We will look at these experiments in detail in the following chapter. Yet the Wasserman paper presenting these findings was titled "Conceptual Behavior in Pigeons."

Behavior. That's the tip-off. As Griffin comments, "Animals may behave as though they utilized simple concepts, but behaviorists are constrained to ignore or deny the possibility that they might consciously think about the categories or concepts. To summarize briefly, the study of animal cognition is now scientifically respectable, but not animal consciousness. In other words, cognition in the sense of information processing in nervous systems, that's okay. But there is a great reluctance to take the further step of saying, well, maybe if there's cognition there is also conscious thinking."

DEFINITIONS

Cognition? Consciousness? The time has come for some definitions. The famous Berkeley psychologist David Krech said, "There is no phenomenon, however complex, which when examined carefully will not turn out to be even more complex." This is definitely true in the cognitive sciences. Almost every philosopher since Plato and Aristotle has wrestled with the problem of consciousness and mind in humans, and many have also pondered the nature of animal minds. In this century, it seems to me, many of the discussions get bogged down in questions of semantics. (For that matter, the same holds for other areas as well. Before the philosophers can discuss "love" or "virtue" or "good" or "God," they have to define these words, and the task turns out to be more difficult than Plato and Aristotle ever imagined. Or so today's deep thinkers have concluded.)

All in all, splitting hairs is child's play compared with drawing meaningful distinctions between "sentience" and "cognition," between "cognition" and "thinking," between "thinking" and "consciousness," between "consciousness" and "self-consciousness." In their fine book *Species of Mind: The Philosophy and Biology of Cognitive Ethology*, Colin Allen and Marc Bekoff refer teasingly (Allen is a professor of philosophy) to "the cold touch of technical philosophy." I know the feeling. Sometimes I found all the academic rigor and necessary skepticism frustrating, but it was also exciting and challenging. For the behaviorists, the confusion is a godsend. They propose something called the "definition objection," which argues that if we can't come up with a strict definition of "consciousness" and other terms, there's nothing to study.

Griffin is ready for this one. He pointed out to me that one of the dirty little secrets of science is that there's no really clear and agreed-upon definition of "gene" either. It is not just a specified sequence of nucleotides on a chromosome, but something much more elusive. Still, thousands of scientists the world over are studying genes, with remarkable results. What's more, he added, "You can't define motivation or learning either, if you want to get increasingly rigorous. All of these are somewhat vague and general concepts. So I am not discouraged by the fact that it's difficult to define consciousness. I think if we knew more about it, it might come easier."

For the definitions that will be "operative" in this book I turn—logically enough, I think—to *Cognitive Ethology*, the volume of essays collected in honor of Donald Griffin in 1991. In those pages "cognition" is defined as "processes by which the sensory input is transformed, reduced, elaborated. . . ." Closely related to cognition is "thinking," defined as "attending to the animal's internal mental images or representations." As laypeople, we might consider cognition and thinking more or less synonymous, but as I read the literature and as Griffin confirms, "cognition" is preferred by those researchers who intend to deny any kind of subjectivity or consciousness for a given animal. They shy away from the word "thinking," which seems to imply just a hint of those verboten qualities.

Griffin explained to me that almost everyone has quietly dropped the first tenet of hard-core behaviorism, the hypothesis that stimulus-response learning accounts for everything. Behaviorists had bet the farm on this mechanism, but too many experiments proved that much more is involved. Furthermore, almost every researcher has drastically modified the second tenet of behaviorism, that scientists should study only observable inputs (environmental factors) and outputs (behavior). Again, there's now too much evidence that learning, memory, representation, and flexible problem solving are all involved. As a fallback position, in effect, scientists who have conceded these two issues employ "cognition" as the catchall phrase. They now view animals as dealing with "representations" that are then "stored" and "processed" and "internally mediated" in one way or another. Here again we see the influence of the computer sciences grafted onto old-style behaviorism.

The following equation from the textbook *Cognitive Ecology* (not *Cognitive Ethology*) strikes me as an appropriate illustration of this general approach to animal behavior. The subject here is the foraging habits of predators in a predator/prey relationship:

$$R = \frac{S\sum_{i=1}^{m}D_i[1-(S/M)^{k_i}]a_i^{1/k_i}\,e_i-(f+bS)}{1+S\sum_{i=1}^{m}D_i[1-(S/M)^{k_i}]a_i^{1/k_i}h_i}$$

This equation may well represent terrific work, nor does working in this vein preclude holding the views of Donald Griffin. I include such higher mathematics at this point only to illustrate in striking fashion the kind of research now directed at understanding animal *cognition*. The key point is that cognition, as the term is used in the cognitive sciences today, does not necessarily entail subjectivity or consciousness. Behaviorist-oriented researchers will grant "cognition" to many animals, while withholding consciousness.

Now we need a definition of consciousness. *Cognitive Ethology*, edited by Carolyn Ristau, says this: "An animal may be considered to experience a simple level of consciousness if it subjectively thinks about objects and events."

Thomas Nagel rephrases this neatly: "An organism has conscious mental states if and only if there is something that it is like to be that organism." English philosopher John Locke had a neat little definition for consciousness: "the perception of what passes in a man's own mind." Only if there is a subjective character to the experience, if it feels like something to be a bug or a bat or a bonobo. Nagel's famous question "What is it like to be a bat?" implies that it's like anything at all. He is assuming that the bat does indeed possess consciousness. Then there is *self*-consciousness, or self-awareness, which adds another level to the progression. We humans have self-consciousness. Some entity I call "I" sometimes leans back in the chair, puts its hands behind its head, and thinks about its own thinking. Do animals have such self-consciousness?

Many of the ethologists and cognitive psychologists who begrudgingly concede the possibility of some kind of mechanical "cognition" still save "consciousness" and "self-consciousness" as higher levels of experience to which only we humans and perhaps the higher primates are privy. Thus the third major tenet of behaviorism, that subjective mental experiences should be ignored, is still alive and well. Some major texts in ethology do not even list "consciousness" in the index. *The Oxford Companion to Animal Behaviour* has no such entry. Griffin and his allies think of this modified behaviorist position as "cognitive behaviorism"—a ploy that still denies animals the essential ingredient, consciousness, by arguing that whatever the animal is experiencing, it must be a far cry from what we experience, by definition. But no one is suggesting that any animal's thoughts are as complex as a human's. As Griffin quips, the distinction may be between my three dogs enjoying a tasty treat and my studying the Battle of Gettysburg. Nor is anyone suggesting we will ever understand animal thoughts in their entirety, any more than we can understand our own. But as Daniel Dennett writes, we can join Donald Griffin in *avowing* the consciousness of the animal without being able to *describe* its nature in full detail.

DRAWING THE LINES

To us humans who enjoy both cognition and consciousness, both seem as one. Can we really get a grip on how another animal might have just cognition without consciousness, or is this distinction just a spurious word game played by the diehard behaviorists? The question is vital for the entire discussion. If cognition were tantamount to consciousness, a lot of the issues discussed in the following pages would be irrelevant. There wouldn't be a debate. But the behaviorists are correct in arguing that cognition does not necessitate consciousness. I have mentioned driving the car: lots of cognition going on, but often more or less unconsciously. However, I don't think driving is the perfect example, because while driving the car we can become conscious at a moment's notice. There is a better way to demonstrate that it is possible to perceive with the senses, and to act on those perceptions, and yet to be completely unconscious of doing so. The phenomenon in question is blind sight, a fascinating subject in its own right. It has been the subject of many, many tests and studies, and it has been interpreted in many different ways.

Blind-sight victims have suffered one of several forms of injury to the part of the brain known as the visual cortex, resulting in a large blind spot in the field of vision. In those cases in which both the left and right visual cortices have been damaged, the individual is completely blind. But some people with this condition can nevertheless perform quite well—much better than chance would dictate—on tests involving the identification of simple shapes and flashes of light. These patients apparently see, and then report what they see, but they have no consciousness of seeing. They have no idea how they score better than chance on the tests. They don't understand any better than the experimenters. Daniel Dennett has his doubts about blind sight and suggests that it could actually be some kind of residual vision. Maybe he's right, but I find the phenomenon useful simply as an aid for picturing cognition without consciousness.

Intuitively, almost all of us "draw the line" somewhere between those creatures we intuitively believe are endowed with consciousness and those who aren't. A survey reported in detail in *Anthropomorphism, Anecdotes, and Animals*, a consistently compelling anthology, reveals that most people draw the line for basic consciousness between the invertebrates and the vertebrates, and then draw another line for some sort of higher consciousness, if not exactly self-consciousness, just beneath the dolphins, primates, cats, and dogs. But we are not necessarily logical in our distinctions. Most of us relegate pigs to the lower category of consciousness, even though pigs are just as intelligent as dogs on any animal-IQ scale. One could conclude from the survey that it pays to be a common household pet rather than a denizen of the barnyard, although such a poll might yield different results since the movie *Babe* came out. That bright piglet lifted the image of his entire species.

Thomas Nagel took into account our propensity to draw lines when he was working on his famous essay. He explained, "I have chosen bats instead of wasps or flounders because if one travels too far down the phylogenetic tree, people gradually shed their faith that there is experience there at all." Daniel Dennett, the other philosopher who has entered our story, wryly observes that it can be tough to draw the line even within our own lives! Was I conscious when I put the newspaper in the refrigerator and threw away the orange juice? Or when I tossed the dirty socks into the toilet instead of the clothes hamper? Hard to say.

Dennett proposes the following clever question to ask in order to determine where you are intuitively tempted to draw the line for a high degree of consciousness: With what creatures would you feel comfortable using the first-person plural "we"? Would you say, regarding your pet dog, "We are going for a walk down the block"? I think you most likely would. Would you say this regarding your horse? Maybe, but to me, this seems like more of a stretch, for some reason. What about you or your child's pet gerbil or parakeet? Now we're losing a lot of folks, I'm pretty sure. Your reticulated python? Very few of us are comfortable with "we" in this case. An oyster? That's where I draw the line!

The foraging dance of the honeybees is more sophisticated in some ways than any such organized means of communication ever observed among any other species on earth, including all the primates except *Homo sapiens*. As Donald Griffin notes, if this complex system employed by the bees were discovered among a troop of monkeys in the jungle, it would be interpreted much differently by scientists and laypersons alike. Why? Most of us do not want to attribute to honeybees the same consciousness we attribute to monkeys. We are suspicious of the role of instinct in such behavior, and we intuitively distinguish among instinct and thinking and consciousness.

Historically, biologists have also drawn a line between instinct and some higher faculty. They have assumed that only learned as opposed to instinctive behavior could possibly manifest consciousness. At least learning *might* require some versatility and adaptability, while it's too easy to envision instinctive behavior, no matter how complex, as 100 percent unconscious. As we shall see, Donald Griffin and the cognitive ethologists challenge this assumption.

However, those of us who believe that many animals do think and do have consciousness have to be careful about assuming that complexity automatically implies one or both. If this were the case, every cell on the planet would be endowed with consciousness, because every single one of them is marvelously complex. (As it turns out, panpsychism does hold that all life forms, and perhaps even all matter, possess mental states, but this is a religious or metaphysical doctrine, not science.) So, finely tuned complexity proves nothing. Learning may not be proof positive either. Primitive invertebrates with very simple neural networks are capable of relatively astonishing results. One particularly well known example within biology is the earthworm, which was studied carefully for decades by none other than Charles Darwin. The earthworm draws a leaf into its tunnel by grasping its narrow tip, rather than the stem end. This is the most mechanically efficient way, without a doubt, but is this the kind of action that instinct could instill? It's not easy to accept this, and Darwin didn't. But if the action is not instinct, does the earthworm *learn* the most efficient way to proceed? This seems to be the only alternative. But do we want to endow the earthworm with consciousness? Most of us draw the line a little higher—but we could be quite wrong.

THE LAW OF PARSIMONY

In all scientific investigation, the law of parsimony gives priority to the simplest possible explanation. Start with the simplest explanation, and if it "works," stop right there. If it doesn't work, consider something a little more complicated. In biology, the corollary known as Morgan's Canon states, "In no case may we interpret an action as the outcome of the exercise of a higher psychical faculty, if it can be interpreted as the outcome of the exercise of one which stands lower in the psychological scale." If a given behavior can be plausibly explained as instinct without need of cognition, draw the line; if information processing—cognition—seems sufficient, then there's no need to invoke conscious thought, so draw the line.

C. Lloyd Morgan was a British psychologist, a colleague of G. J.

Romanes, Darwin's protégé. With his canon, Morgan was essentially reacting against Darwin's and Romanes's excessive anthropomorphism. Promulgated to a less-than-waiting world in 1894, the decree is now viewed as marking the end of the era of systematic anthropomorphism. His canon is sound enough policy, but it was often either misinterpreted or misrepresented as a defense of strict behaviorist explanations. In fact, Morgan accepted some degree of animal consciousness, as he wrote in *The Limits of Animal Intelligence*. He even amended the often misunderstood canon with the following statement: "it may be added—lest the range of the principle be misunderstood—that the canon by no means excludes . . . higher mental processes if we already have independent evidence of their occurrence." Morgan did not doubt that a dog has a juicy bone literally "in mind" when he looks wistfully at his master working over the stove. Or as Stanley Coren writes in *The Intelligence of Dogs*, the canon, if properly invoked, distinguishes between the intelligence required for a dog to find his way home after taking inventory of all the fire hydrants in the extended neighborhood and the intelligence required to read a map of the streets. Dogs have the one talent but not the other.

In the Clever Hans episode, the higher-level explanation—counting—substituted for a more plausible "lower" explanation. This was a violation of Morgan's Canon, and it was found out. But then Clever Hans's failure to do arithmetic was taken as evidence that he was incapable of any thought whatsoever. But couldn't Hans have been thinking about the inadvertent cues of his owner and the other testers? Couldn't he have learned, as Donald Griffin puts it, "I must tap my foot when that man nods his head"? This wouldn't be arithmetic, but it would be some kind of thought.

In the first chapter we met primate researcher Frans de Waal, who convincingly suggested that it is impossible to look into the eyes of a higher primate and not find "the age-old connection." One of the chimps de Waal had in mind was Georgia, a resident at the Yerkes Field Station in the state of Georgia. This mischievous animal has the habit of surprising human visitors to her quarters with a sudden spray of well-aimed water. She does this all the time. If necessary, she'll wait with tight-lipped tension until the victim comes close enough for the prank to have its drenching effect. Other observers have reported similar behavior with other chimps in other facilities, and it could be interpreted as affection or aggression or anything in between; for my current purposes, the specific interpretation doesn't matter. In his forward to *Anthropomorphism, Anecdotes, and Animals*, de Waal describes how he was successful one time in "facing down" Georgia, who he knew was sneaking up on him with a mouthful of water. He writes, "I looked her straight into the eyes and pointed my finger at her, warning, in Dutch, 'I have seen you.' She immediately stepped away and let part of the water drop, swallowing the rest. I certainly do not wish to claim that she understands Dutch, but she must have sensed that I knew what she was up to, and that I was not going to be an easy target."

Any human who acted as Georgia acted with regularity would have been scolded and held accountable, while any animal, even the one closest to us in genetic endowment, the chimpanzee, is still considered by many investigators, in de Waal's phrase, "a mere passive instrument of stimulus-response contingencies." This is absurd, in my opinion—a classic example of what the primatologist Roger Fouts calls the "rubber ruler," with which the explanation depends on which creature is manifesting the behavior. Latter-day behaviorists who withhold consciousness even from chimps—and some do—forget that the second part of Morgan's Canon "by no means excludes . . . higher mental processes if we already have independent evidence of their occurrence." In the case of chimps, we have this evidence in abundance.

ONWARD, THROUGH THE FOG

A professional trainer of the big cats adopted a Rhodesian Ridgeback pup and a lion cub, who then grew up together. The dog, a female, was named Janee, and the lion, a male, Wazoo. They were inseparable, night and day, even sleeping together while rolled up in a ball. Somehow Janee succeeded in convincing the lion that she was the leader of this "pride" of two. She would snarl, bark, and occasionally even nip the lion on the ear in order to bring him to heel. Both animals gave evidence of separation anxiety if they were apart for any period of time. But then, after seven years of this incredibly close relationship, and within the space of a single week, matters changed. The lion suddenly woke up to his role in the larger scheme of things. He realized he was a lion and Janee was a dog. One day, as Janee tried her usual dominant behavior, Wazoo snapped and charged her. Their owner saved the day, but that was the end of a beautiful friendship. This story is from the psychoanalyst Jeffrey Masson's *Dogs Never Lie About Love*. Masson asks in conclusion, "I wonder if either animal is ever nostalgic. Does the dog think back with longing for the day when her closest friend was a lion? Does the lion ever wonder why he spoiled a beautiful relationship?"

It's great to think so, I believe. The story is also a neat exercise in drawing the line. Some might feel that the dog remembers the lion, but not vice versa. But that only underlines the human bias toward dogs. Anyway, even scientists can now entertain such questions without a guilty conscience, because the cognitive revolution has opened wide the door to theories and experiments and fieldwork regarding animal emotions and thought and consciousness. What specific kinds of behavior would plausibly imply mental states and therefore give us something further to investigate? This question has been worried and debated to death, as we should expect. Donald Griffin proposes two overarching categories: adaptive behavior and interspecies communication (his third source of inferential evidence is the physiology of the brain). Here's a list of other candidate behaviors culled from the literature:

Complexity
Learning from the past in a way that can be applied to the future
Plastic memory
Focused attention
Concept formation
Category formation
Tool using
Tool making
"If-then," or "purposive," thinking and behavior
Deceptive behavior
Use of symbolism

Beginning on the next page, we'll look in detail at a wide range of behavior from the laboratory and the field that suggests intelligence. I will be careful to note challenges to these assumptions as well, because every issue in cognitive ethology is open to challenge. In fact, this is not a particularly good subject for those who want sure, easy answers. On the other hand, there's no better subject for fascinating questions, because the world of animals is infinitely rich and infinitely puzzling. Just like our own.

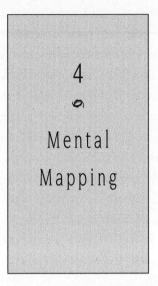

4

Mental
Mapping

FROM BABIES TO BIRDS

Do animals know where they're going or do they roam around aim-
lessly?

Could dogs really accomplish such feats as finding their way
home over hundreds of miles?

Those of us who are dog lovers know that our pets have a very
strong sense of direction. I am sure that my dogs know *their* territories
very well, indeed: Their backyard in New York and a much larger
area of about one square mile around our cabin in the Pennsylvania
mountains. I have no idea, however, whether or not they could find
their way from New York to Pennsylvania, or vice versa, but I would
not be entirely surprised if they could.

How do we begin to learn what is going on in the minds of animals when it comes to getting from one place to the other?

In this case, we start with human babies.

In the middle decades of this century, the famous Swiss psychologist and historian of science Jean Piaget developed his enormously influential model for cognitive development in children. Piaget argued that kids learn in a genetically programmed way that follows clearly marked stages, which arrive on cue at specific ages in most children. Piaget hypothesized and then went a long way toward proving that these stages are mental reflexes, in effect. Learning is just as instinctive as breathing, and we do both, automatically. This depiction of "mental mechanisms" interacting with the environment was very influential among ethologists and comparative psychologists exploring animal behavior. Piaget himself was also interested in these implications; in 1970, he included his own extension of his theories regarding animal cognition in his magnum opus, *Biology and Knowledge*.

An early and essential stage of learning in children is what Piaget labeled "object permanence." To get far in this world, you have to learn that objects can stay put, and then you have to remember where they stay put. The infant has to put together a map—and then many maps, every day. Children acquire their first rudimentary ability in this area between eight and twelve months and finally achieve complete mastery—"stage six"—between eighteen and twenty-four months. It turns out that quite a few birds and mammals, including some of the "lower" primates like squirrel monkeys, achieve one of the intermediate stages of learning object permanence. Some animals achieve total stage-six competence. Cognitive ethologists often refer to this general category of learning in animals by the name "mental maps." (As we saw in the chapter on behaviorism, other researchers won't use the term "mental." They study "cognitive maps," but don't be confused. Mental maps and cognitive maps are different labels for the same ability. The issue is one of interpretation.)

The simplest tests studying the simplest kind of spatial memory date back to at least the 1930s. In these experiments, two cups are placed in front of the animal—a chimpanzee, say. One of the cups is baited with food in clear view of the chimp. Then a screen is lowered. After a delay that varies from test to test, the screen is raised and the subject is free to "search" for the food. About 90 percent of tested chimpanzees accomplished this task easily. They proceeded straight to the baited cup. Macaques scored lower; only about 60 percent went immediately to the food. Since no sensory cues were guiding the animals at the time of the search, researchers concluded that the successful searchers have created the most basic "map" of the most basic kind of scene. Moreover, chimps would still proceed directly to the baited cup even if the setup was rotated slightly to the left or the right.

Such experiments were among the first to challenge the behaviorist bias, according to which learning would take place only as a corollary to immediate stimulus-response conditioning and gratification of immediate needs. Strict behaviorism had a hard time explaining the ability to remember a mental map; it had a hard time dealing with the animal who could "produce his response in the absence of the stimulus," as Jacques Vauclair writes in his invaluable book *Animal Cognition: An Introduction to Modern Comparative Psychology*.

For the *Nature* series on animal minds, we traveled to the Rocky Mountains to observe researcher Sue Healy and her colleagues from the University of Newcastle determine the mental-mapping abilities of the rufous hummingbird. Why does Healy study this particular bird? Mainly because she can. These beautiful little birds migrate north from Mexico all the way to the Canadian Rockies for about six weeks of mating activity in the late spring and early summer before returning home. Male rufous hummingbirds, easily identified by their ruby-red throats, are very territorial and aggressive defenders of that territory. They feed in a flower for only a few seconds before returning to a perch in a tree to check for potential competitors in the mating game. It is therefore fairly easy for Healy to attract just one bird to her experimental setup and then be certain that it is this same bird who has returned a second time, as required for the test. This kind of experimental control is difficult to achieve with most birds, for obvious reasons.

Does the rufous hummingbird have the same or even a superior mapping ability in its springtime mountain habitat as the animal in the lab working with the cups hidden behind the screen? Does the bird remember which flowers it has already visited and depleted of nectar? Healy thought it might, because such feeding efficiency would be a tremendous advantage, saving both time and energy on the arduous migratory trip. She explains, "A typical territory has about two hundred flowers. When the bird empties a flower of nectar, the estimated time before the flower refills is four hours. Rather than coming back to a flower and finding it empty, it would be useful for the bird to be able to remember it and avoid it."

Healy's experimental setup is straightforward. First she sets up a semicircle of eight artificial flowers, which she calls a radial maze. The male rufous who finds this maze to his liking becomes the unofficial master of this domain. Healy watches to make sure, of course, but she knows that this one bird will be the subject of her experiment, because he'll drive away any potential transgressor. Anyone who has watched the action around a hummingbird feeder in those mountains can testify to this. The male rufous is a domineering sort, no doubt about it.

The flowers are baited with very little sucrose, so that a given flower will be depleted *before* the hummingbird abruptly leaves it for another. Since the idea is to determine if the bird remembers that the flower is empty and therefore doesn't waste time and energy finding out on a second visit, this depletion is the vital aspect of this stage of the experiment. The subject bird is allowed to feed at only four of the eight flowers. Then he is shooed away and Healy sits quietly, waiting for him to return, which he almost always does, usually within ten minutes. On the return visit, more than 75 percent of the hummingbirds Healy has studied fly directly to the four flowers they had *not* visited the first time. They did indeed remember the flowers previously visited and depleted, and avoided them.

Only 75 percent of the birds "passed" Healy's test? Maybe that doesn't sound like a high figure, but one of her colleagues back in Newcastle demonstrated that about the same percentage of college students are successful on an equivalent test using overturned cups and pieces of candy. And the bird's brain is seven thousand times smaller than the brain of an undergraduate! Healy always laughs when she tells this story.

But how do the hummingbirds remember the depleted flowers? Do they remember a particular route flown among the eight flowers, or do they remember the specific locations of the four? Locations, not routes, as more tests prove. But is it really location, or is it some identifying characteristic of the particular flower? There is a huge difference. Remembering location indicates the presence of a mental map; remembering color and shape is also a significant feat, but it is not a mental map. To address this possibility that the birds are remembering specific flowers, not specific locations, Healy moves on to the next stage of her investigation, in which she sets up an array of distinctively and individually designed flowers, only one of which has sucrose. The others have just water, which hummingbirds don't like at all. (The birds get all the water they need from nectar. Drinking plain water is a waste of time, and they don't do it.) When the rufous has found the one flower in Healy's radial maze that has been filled with sucrose, she shoos him away *before* the flower is empty. This is key. Unlike the previous test, this one is set up to entice the bird back to the same flower.

After the bird has been banished for the time being, Healy switches the array before his return visit. About 80 percent of the time, the returning bird flies directly to the flower in the same location as the originally baited one, not to that flower itself, which is now in a new position. If Healy does not place any flower in the target location, the bird flies there anyway and circles around, searching for the flower where he knows it should be. The test confirms that the bird remembers location, not specific flowers.

Scientists have confirmed that hummingbirds discriminate colors very well. Why don't they use this talent for feeding purposes? The answer seems to be simple. Most of the flowers in any given territory will be the same kind, and almost identical in color. Therefore color can be a dicey basis for discrimination, but, as Healy puts it, "flowers in real life don't move." (Important point: In the 20 percent of cases in which the bird did not return to the correct location, he selected the original target flower in its new location. This seems to indicate that color remains a secondary consideration that occasionally takes precedence, for whatever reason.)

The Clark's nutcracker may be the world's most studied bird in terms of mental-mapping ability. There is no question that this bird, who inhabits the mountain pine forests of the American Southwest, employs a detailed map of its terrain while harvesting pine seeds in a period of just a few weeks in the late summer and early fall, and storing them in up to two thousand locations. The usual nutcracker cache holds two to five seeds, but a single bird may store a total of up to thirty-three thousand seeds when the cone crop is heavy. Students of this nutcracker estimate that a bird must be able to retrieve three thousand seeds in order to make it through the difficult alpine winter.

In laboratory tests by Vanderwall, Balda, and Turek, the nutcrackers were presented with eighteen cache sites, which they proceeded to use for storing seeds. Then the birds were removed from this experimental environment for eleven days. In further laboratory research with the same birds almost one year later, they were as accurate at finding their caches after 285 days as they were after 11 days. Spectacular feats of memory! As Dr. Russell P. Balda of Northern Arizona University told me, "Not even humans can perform at the accuracy levels that we see in these birds." (This comes as no surprise to me, because I can never find where I put my keys!) The result supported a conclusion that the birds were using a mental map, as did the results when landmarks within the lab were shifted around after the initial caching operation. Then the nutcrackers' scores plummeted.

The landmark thesis was beautifully proved in another set of experiments with chickadees. These birds were trained to feed at one of four boxes attached to a wall of their aviary. Then the array of boxes was shifted laterally on the wall. The shape of the array stayed the same, but now a different box was in the position of the original feeding box, relative to the landmarks in the room. When the birds were returned to the aviary with this new setup on the wall, their first response was to try the box in the same position on the wall as the original feeding box; second choice was the box in the same position relative to the array as the original box; third choice was the box with the same identifying marks as the original box. The only conclusion to draw from this experiment is that landmarks in the overall environment—maps, in a word—are the most important information used by the birds.

Long ago, researchers understood that birds have a talent for simple mapping, but it was only quite recently that they learned—to their great surprise—that certain birds also remember *when* they stored food, not just where. The experiments with scrub jays leading to this conclusion are not directly to my point in this chapter, but I'd be remiss to omit a brief rendition of this important research. The subject jays were given both wax worm larvae and peanuts to store. The key point to understand is that these larvae, usually the preferred food, rapidly lose their desirability over time. When the jays were then given the choice of which food to retrieve, they chose the larvae only if they had stored the worms quite recently. If they had stored them several days earlier, they chose the peanuts instead. Conclusion: The scrub jay remembers when it stores food and then takes this memory into account when considering the menu. This is a remarkable experimental result. Until this research was first published in late 1998, this kind of "episodic memory" was considered beyond the capability of most, if not all, animals. It was a talent that separated us humans from the hoi polloi, as the *New York Times* phrased it. But if the scrub jay remembers when it buries food, why shouldn't other birds and animals?

Of course, no avian mapping or feat of memory can equal the navigational skills of the migratory birds. They are unmatched by any creature. The basic map-and-compass system is not the half of it. Star reading is necessary for these fliers, and magnetic fields may play an important role. The long-haul migratory birds such as the arctic tern, which commutes annually between the two polar icecaps, a round-trip distance of more than twenty-five thousand miles, easily solves navigational problems that bedeviled human navigators right up until this era of the Global Positioning System. It is no exaggeration to state that the migratory birds do not need GPS. They have their own—but how it works exactly, no one knows.

THE CASE OF THE KIDNAPPED BEE

Many insects are successful in the earliest stages of learning "object permanence" and creating mental maps. Once we get past the fact that they are insects, whom we tend to think of as essentially instinctive creatures, we really shouldn't be surprised by this mapping ability, especially in those species that feed on flowers. If mapping would be advantageous for foraging birds, why wouldn't the same hold for flower-foraging insects? Perhaps mapping is just too advantageous not to have evolved among species, be they birds or bees.

Bumblebees are a case in point. G. H. Pyke has studied the food-gathering means of *Bombus appositus* while foraging for monkshood flowers in Colorado. Pyke tags his bees, then films them as they invade a succulent new "garden." In general, the bees start with the flower at the bottom of a given plant and work their way up the shaft until they reach the top, when they shift to a neighboring plant. Pyke learned that these bees, like the rufous hummingbird, almost never waste time and energy returning to the same flower twice. They remember, for a short time, at least, which flowers they have visited, or they leave a scent that serves as a reminder, or both. In any event, as Donald Griffin summarizes in *Animal Minds*, this is not the "simple, stereotyped sort of reactions we are accustomed to expect from insects."

Extremely sophisticated computer analyses of the minutely observed movements of ants support the case for some kind of mapping
ability with these creatures. (As ground dwellers, ants are more amenable to round-the-clock observation than are wasps and bees. Reports of this research are full of equations and phrases like
"trigonometric vector summation.") The latest thinking holds that all
the ants and bees employ some combination of a sun-based compass
and a magnetic compass, as well as the more mundane expedient of
landmarks and mental maps. This landmark hypothesis was first conclusively proved by Niko Tinbergen's classic experiment on the homing instincts of the digger wasp, *Philanthus triangulum*. Tinbergen's
idea couldn't have been simpler. First he arranged a set of pinecones
around a wasp nest that was a busy center of activity. When most of
the wasps were away from the hive, he then moved the cones into the
same relative position around a fake nest. The wasps all returned to
the fake nest.

This was an incontrovertible experiment, replicated many times
and with many modifications. But it was not the last word, by any
means. Consider the modern-day study first reported by James L.
Gould in 1986. Gould is a professor of ecology and evolutionary
biology at Princeton University. I read about this work, which might
be called "The Case of the Kidnapped Bee," in quite a few different
sources, including *The Animal Mind*, published in 1994, which he co-
authored with Carol Grant Gould, a science writer. The protocol
involved a number of different experiments. I'll focus on the one in
which the bees are first trained to follow a route from their hive to a
food source due west, say, about 150 yards away. Then one bee is
kidnapped while en route to this food and carried in an opaque box
to a new site due south of the hive. The two sites—one to the west of
the hive, one to the south—are not visible from each other, but in

some of the trials there is a landmark tree in the vicinity. In the trials with the landmark, most of the bees fly directly from the new release point south of the hive to the old site west of the hive without proceeding to the hive itself for orientation purposes. This route is one the bee has never flown before. Kidnapped bees that are released only thirty-three yards farther from the landmark tree than the first bees have more problems picking out the correct route to the old site. Some become disoriented, while others who do fly off toward the goal do not pick quite as straight a line as the bees released closer to the landmark tree.

A lot of experimental energy has been spent trying to replicate and then explain these "mental mapping" results, which are somewhat more complicated than I have summarized. The consensus is that landmarks are definitely important, if not the whole story, and that the bees use the landmarks to construct some kind of mental map. As Gould writes:

> The complications inherent in testing the cognitive abilities of unrestrained animals in the wild, particularly when they have more than one way to solve a problem, is well illustrated by the bee-map saga. . . . Despite a widespread unwillingness to take indications of insect intellect at face value, there is good evidence that even a few milligrams of highly specialized neural wiring can accomplish a limited set of individually impressive cognitive tasks essential to the natural history of the animal in question.

Gould notes that in comparison with flies and moths, the social insects (ants, wasps, and bees) have excess brainpower relative to body weight, and he adds, "The excess brain power of social insects may well have evolved to solve problems based on goal-oriented strategies—strategies that require a level of cognitive finesse far beyond anything imagined in invertebrates by most researchers as recently as two decades ago."

THE MAZE

The maze has been standard equipment in the laboratory of comparative psychologists since the nineteenth century. In fact, the very first experiments that challenged behaviorist principles were those in which lab rats were turned loose in a maze while they were neither hungry nor thirsty. According to theory, they therefore had no reason to learn anything. But they did. In fact, Piaget was right: Learning is automatic. It is what we animals do at whatever level of which we're capable. The maze is also perfect terrain for testing mental maps under rigidly controlled conditions. Therefore, it's not surprising that a great deal of work has been done in this area with laboratory animals.

In 1993, Chapuis and Scardili showed that hamsters could build a mental map of a maze, even if they had only been in half of it! And for the *Nature* series, the production team re-created this classic experiment with the favored laboratory rat. The setup is similar to Sue Healy's radial maze of flowers, but in this case the maze is shaped like a cartwheel—with rim and spokes. In the learning part of the test, the rat is allowed into only half of the perimeter; the rest of the maze is out of bounds and blocked off. Food is placed at the end of one of the arms, and the rat quickly learns where to find it. It runs straight to the food, *by the shortest route*, every time it is placed in the maze. How does the rat know which route to take?

The obvious answer would be smell. The rat might have simply smelled its way to the food. To test this possibility, food is placed at the ends of *all* the arms. If the rat were working on smell alone, he should have gone to the nearest food source. But the rat isn't using smell. It is using its memory. As far as the rat knows, there is food only at the end of one arm. Using its mental map of the maze, it works out the best route to reach it. Thus, rats can work out alternative routes, just as a London cabbie would if he finds a street unexpectedly blocked. Our television series used a London cabbie's astonishing memory as an extraordinary example of mental mapping. But perhaps the rats in the sewers beneath London's streets are doing the same thing.

As we should expect by now, complicated and behaviorist-oriented explanations have been propounded to explain all of these results. I've read about "habit family hierarchies" and "fractional antedating goal responses." This last incomprehensible theory prompted one commentator to write, "[this] system seems to require more cognitive effort by both the human theorist and the rats." Meanwhile, the law of parsimony that we introduced in the previous chapter proposes that the simplest, most straightforward explanation stands a good chance of being the best one. E. C. Tolman, one of the important researchers in this field, has written, "We believe that in the course of learning, something like a field map of the environment gets established in the rat's brain and the incoming impulses are usually worked over and elaborated into a tentative, cognitive-like map of the environment." (Tolman knew early in this century that any number of maze tests had already confirmed the failure of the strictest behaviorist model, but he was intimidated by the behaviorist influence, as was almost everyone else. Therefore he coined the term "purposive behaviorism"—a classic hedge if there ever was one. Later in his career, he was more candid.)

Psychologist John Pearce of Cardiff University agrees with Tolman. Pearce thinks of a mental map as something like an aerial photograph based on landmarks and relationships, and he concludes regarding his laboratory rat, "We can be reasonably confident it is doing so by use of a cognitive or mental map, rather than by a sense of smell."

It turns out that turtles, not the brightest of species by most measures, can also learn a complex maze after only a few trials, proceeding along not just slowly—that is a given—but methodically as well, "visually scrutinizing each choice point," as the *Oxford Companion to Animal Behaviour* puts it. Chameleons also happen to be very good at navigating complex mazes and solving related situations known as detour problems. Astonishing? Not at all. In their natural habitat, chameleons are, according to the *Companion*, "frequently required to make detours among the branches of trees to come within striking distance of their prey."

And chimpanzees are also excellent with a mental map, although I doubt whether they could replicate the performance of the Clark's nutcracker. (Why not? Because they don't need to!) Young chimps and gorillas master object permanence even more quickly than human children do, but this is not as puzzling as it might seem at first glance, since young primate babies mature more quickly in most respects than do humans. They can move around in their environment after just one month, compared with eight or nine months for a human baby, so they have the opportunity to begin learning about the wide world at an earlier age. The chimp experiment that I read about most often was first set up by E. W. Menzel in the 1970s and has now been repeated by many other primatologists. The subject chimp is carried around a large outdoor space by one experimenter so the animal can observe a second experimenter hiding food in randomly selected sites. This tour of the area takes about ten minutes, after which the chimp is returned to the company of his or her mates, and all of them are released into the test zone. The movements of the test chimp are followed closely.

In a way this experiment resembles the famous traveling-salesman problem that continues to fascinate mathematicians, in which the idea is to find the shortest route that will take the salesman to every potential customer on his map. If there are a lot of customers, supercomputers are challenged by this task. The chimpanzees do not solve their particular problem perfectly, but they perform very well, retrieving, on average, about thirteen of eighteen items of food. More important, they do so efficiently, not simply following the route taken initially but utilizing shortcuts and hustling directly from hidden food to hidden food. Menzel concluded, "Especially since a novel set of locations was used on every trial, and the informed animal ran directly to hiding places that were not visible from the point from which their run commenced, the term 'cognitive mapping' seems as good a descriptor as any."

Other experiments, both in controlled conditions and in the forest, have confirmed Menzel's first tests. One of the more intriguing such tests utilizes a closed-circuit television. In the experiment, chimps watch on television as an experimenter hides somewhere in an enclosure. In effect, the television screen is a map. Can the chimp read this map? Yes. Released into the enclosure, most chimps proceed directly to the hiding human. They can also relate the contents of a "dollhouse" to the equivalent full-size room. As in humans, the chimp's sense of smell is considerably less well developed than vision and the sense of touch. Therefore no control for smell is needed in this experiment.

Are the chimps, the chameleons, the lab rats, the bees, and the birds mapping the terrain in the same way? Are they mapping the terrain the way we do? It's difficult to say. Bees seem to have a more limited distance than birds at which they can operate effectively. At several hundred meters, they get lost if they have to find a novel route. The nutcrackers, in contrast, can cache and retrieve their pine nuts over immense areas of forest.

ROTATION

A corollary of the mental-maps capability is the ability to recognize and manipulate mental images. Honeybees can recognize a mirror image of a flowerlike shape, proved by removing a target flower and substituting its mirror image and a choice of other patterns. The bees will always prefer the mirror image. The very idea that bees could remember images in this way was heretical as late as the 1970s. But it is a fact. Even more impressive, bees can perform a "mental rotation" of a two-dimensional object.

Pigeons turn out to be excellent in a variety of tests that require the manipulation of mental images. In one classic experiment, the hands of a clock displayed on a computer screen disappear and then reappear while moving at a nonconstant rate of speed. Pigeons are nevertheless able to estimate accurately when and where the disappearing hand will reappear. This is not easy to do, and the birds have been subjected to a battery of finely tuned tests that try to pin down how they're so successful. The best explanation to date: They consult some kind of mental imagery. Pigeons are also able to recognize images rotated any number of degrees the experimenter chooses. (This work was done by Nieworth and Rilling in 1987.)

What is really fascinating is that pigeons apparently do not do what human subjects do on these tests, which is rotate the image in the "mind's eye." (We know that humans do this "mental rotation" because the time required for us to solve the problem is directly correlated with the degree of rotation.) Jacques Vauclair, a specialist in this area, showed that baboons also excel in these rotation problems and apparently solve them as we do, by "mental rotation," because their times also vary with the degree of rotation. (Of course, their times are faster than ours by a factor of up to eight! Vauclair is not sure why this is, but he hypothesizes that we get bogged down asking extraneous questions, perhaps unconsciously.) Studies with dolphins indicate that they, too, adopt a humanlike mental strategy. The pigeons' response rate, on the other hand, is constant. It doesn't seem to matter to them how much the image has been rotated, so experimenters conclude that the bird is doing something different than we do, something prewired, presumably. Oh, and one more point: They're also about three times faster than we are on these tests.

SLOW BUT SURE

We think of elephants as dwellers of the bountiful savannas of East Africa, but a small number—about two hundred—live in the Namibian desert of Southwest Africa, one of the harshest environments anywhere on earth. It is startling to see these immense animals trudging slowly over baked desert floors and alongside barren sand dunes. We feel as if we're suddenly on a different planet—the wrong planet. But here they are. It is also startling to realize how big these elephants are—bigger, on average, than their counterparts elsewhere on the continent, although we might figure that the environment would dictate just the opposite. In fact, the largest African elephant ever measured—thirteen feet, ten inches—was found in this desert.

Where is the water around here? Often enough, the water is a long way off from the best feeding grounds, as much as forty miles away and several feet underground as well. If these elephants merely wandered around this desert in aimless fashion seeking both food and water, they would find neither and they would die. There would be no desert elephants of Namibia. But the elephants know where all the water is, where all the food is, and where all the best routes between water and food are. This knowledge is not instinct. They have learned the map of the region and passed it down through the generations. If we do not eradicate them with our rifles and our encroachment into their homeland, they will survive.

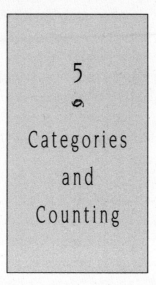

5

Categories
and
Counting

RAISING THE STAKES

In his book *The Others: How Animals Made Us Human*, Paul Shepard writes about the prodigious naming and categorizing habits of the few remaining tribal societies around the world. He quotes one anthropologist who estimates that such societies incorporate in their everyday working vocabularies the names for over a thousand plants and animals. Nor do these people need to know all these species for economic reasons, any more than most stamp and coin and beetle collectors do their collecting for economic reasons. We humans collect and categorize things for the sheer pleasure and ancient purpose of it.

Can animals establish categories or, as they are labeled by researchers, "learning sets"? We have seen how all kinds of animals use mental maps in order to get around the world and forage for food. This cognitive ability is so widespread, to me it appears to be something of an entry-level talent to the wide world of animal intelligence. Cognitive ethologists agree and raise the stakes; they look for learning which requires a degree of abstraction—a tougher proposition than working only with objects such as landmarks and food hidden under cups. If an animal can learn one category, can it then transfer this learning to the conditions in another category? In short, can this animal learn how to learn?

The answer is yes.

Let's begin a brief survey of what has become a mountain of evidence by looking at a set of experiments with macaque monkeys, generally considered by primatologists to be "middle range" primates in terms of intelligence. First, the monkey is trained by rewards to discriminate between two objects, say a ball and a box, and is then rewarded for selecting the ball. After this pair of objects is mastered—when the monkey has reached the point at which he always selects the ball because this selection produces a reward—a different pair of objects is introduced, and the monkey is trained, again by reward, to select one of the two. After he has learned always to select the same object, another pair of objects is introduced, then another, and so on. What happens over this span of trials is quite instructive: The monkey gets to the point that after dealing with several hundred different pairs, he is perfect. With any subsequent new pair, he picks the object for which he is first rewarded every time. Simple enough, perhaps, from our perspective, but the experiment proves that the monkey has learned what is expected of him and is able to generalize this learning in novel situations—with each new pair of objects.

A more complex test of this type is called the matching-to-sample, or MTS, test. In this experiment, one object is presented along with two or more test objects, one of which is identical to the sample. Color is a common criterion. A red ball, say, is presented in the company of one other red ball and one green ball. The idea is to pick the red ball. Food is used to reinforce the correct choice. If the experimenter so chooses, the "opposite" category can also be trained and tested for when the idea is to pick the different object, in this case the green ball. Primates are excellent at such same-or-different tests. Pigeons also learn this skill, but they are slower to pick it up.

The most difficult challenge of this type is the "relations between relations" test, in which the animal is "asked" whether a pair of red balls has the same relationship as another pair of balls, one red and one green. Such reasoning by analogy is reasoning of a high order. Children don't acquire this skill until past infancy, and when the relationship is subtle, this test can challenge adult humans. Young chimpanzees have no success at all with analogical reasoning, but adult chimps do, as amply demonstrated by Sarah, the main subject of the book *The Mind of an Ape*, by David Premack and Ann James Premack. Do the small and the large circle stand in the same relationship as the small and the large square? Sarah uses a symbolic chip, whose meaning she has already mastered, to answer yes. Do the half-moon and the same shape with a black dot in the middle stand in the same relationship as the "home plate" shape and the same shape with a black dot in it? Yes. Do the half-moon and the same shape with a black dot stand in the same relationship as "home plate" and the same shape colored completely black? No.

Amazingly to me—I am not sure how I would do on the test—Sarah is correct on about three-fourths of such tests. She does even better on what are called "conceptual analogy problems," some of which would challenge us humans. For example, after being shown a lock and key (Sarah knows the relationship between the two), she is shown a closed paint can and asked to select either a can opener or a paintbrush, both of which she is familiar with. This relationship is tricky, because either implement could logically be used with the can of paint, but only one stands in the same relationship with the can as the key does with the lock. Sarah correctly picks the can opener, not the paintbrush. In one trial, she was correct in fifteen out of eighteen similar tests. It is difficult if not impossible to see such results as indicative of anything other than intelligent thought.

Sarah also excels on the intriguing "conservation test," which stumps most children under the age of seven. In this challenge, two identical glasses are filled with identical amounts of water. Is the amount of water in each glass the same? Yes, five-year-old children say, and so does Sarah using her symbolic colored chips that mean "same" or "different." Next, the water in one of the glasses is poured into a narrower glass. Is the amount of water in this narrower glass the same as the amount in the other glass? Most five- and even six-year-old children answer no, because, they explain, the water level is higher. These children have not mastered the concept of "conservation" regarding water.

Yes, says Sarah, well over half the time. She understands and uses the concept of conservation. Or does she? The attribution of "conservation" to the chimpanzee has been challenged on a variety of grounds, all coming down to the charge that she is not doing what she appears to be doing. She simply must be doing something else. Why? Because she's a chimpanzee, not a human; a concept of categories requires language, and chimps don't have language. In short, we may have here a classic illustration of Roger Fouts's "rubber ruler": The interpretation of a given behavior depends on the animal involved.

THOSE AMAZING BIRDS

Professor John Pearce of the University of Cardiff, as noted earlier, works with rats, mazes, and mental maps. Very conveniently, he is also an expert in category tests, and his favorite animal in this regard is the trusty pigeon. His long-standing work with these birds and their remarkable ability to handle abstract concepts follows up on the groundbreaking work of Richard Herrnstein of Harvard University in the 1970s. It is utterly fascinating—and highly controversial—research.

In Herrnstein's categorization test, pigeons were first presented with dozens of pictures, one at a time. Some of these pictures had a tree somewhere in the scene, while the others did not. The object for the pigeon was to learn to select the picture with a tree. When it did so, it was rewarded with a bit of food. If it pecked at a picture that did not contain a tree, the bird was not rewarded. The pigeons learned very quickly to recognize trees—even if just a leaf or a branch or an aerial shot of a forest was showing in the pictures. The pigeons seemed to have learned to recognize not one particular tree but a generalized concept of "tree." To test this, the pigeons were shown a new batch of pictures with trees of all shapes and sizes hidden among other pictures of plants containing no trees. The pigeons caught on immediately, recognizing the trees almost every time.

Perhaps it is not surprising that pigeons can recognize trees. They would be in trouble if they could not! Are pigeons hardwired to know trees? To test this conceptual ability, John Pearce has been conducting experiments based on some fascinating findings from Japan by Shigeru Watanabe of Tokyo University. For example, can pigeons learn artificial concepts such as distinguishing impressionist versus abstract painting styles? Surprisingly, the researchers discovered that pigeons could indeed be taught to discriminate between

Picasso and Monet paintings. Moreover, when shown new paintings they had never seen before, the pigeons were able to classify them as impressionist or abstract.

Amazingly, Pearce has devised categorization tests in which pigeon performance is much better than human performance. In fact, categories that are almost impossible for Pearce's undergraduate students are easily solved by the birds. An example is a test with a series of abstract patterns flashed on a television screen. For the students, some of the patterns are followed by a tone. For the birds, the tone is replaced by a reward of food.

The students' performance on this test was miserable. (Perhaps he should have tried food instead of a tone.)

"Oh dear, that's not very good," their professor says on *Nature*'s animal-intelligence series to his embarrassed class. "I don't want to worry you, but my pigeons find this problem quite easy. For those of you who have failed to match the intellectual skills of my pigeons, the solution is the average height of the pattern shown on the video screen. When the average height is low, then a tone is presented. But when it is high—no tone." Most of the students didn't figure this out, but they did beat the birds when the challenge was to select the pictures in which the shapes were of equal height. The birds do poorly on this version of the test.

So what's going on here? Are the pigeons "thinking," as we are thinking on these tests? It's not clear, but the results do seem to indicate that pigeons are capable of learning "relatively abstract classificatory systems," to quote Jacques Vauclair. Many experimental psychologists have their doubts, however. After all, if they challenge Sarah the chimpanzee, they're likely to challenge a flock of laboratory pigeons.

The first and most obvious challenge to the results is the possibility that the birds are simply memorizing the pictures they have pecked and for which they have received a reward of food. While we amateurs in this field might think that this would require a highly unlikely display of excellent memory by a mere bird, pigeons can in fact memorize hundreds of pictures and remember them months later. This has been proved in many control tests performed in many different labs. Pigeons have excellent visual memory. In this case, however, there is a way to find out if the birds are just memorizing the pictures paired with food. Were this the case, they should score only at chance levels when presented with a new set of pictures. With a new set, they have not had a chance to remember the rewarded pictures. If, however, they really have internalized a category of "trees," then their initial score with this new set of pictures should be much better than chance.

May we have the envelope, please? The pigeon's score with new pictures is *much* better than chance, about 75 percent! They know what they are pecking at, and even some of their mistakes are perfectly understandable when, for example, the picture included a shape, such as a telephone pole, that might well have been a tree. Such control tests prove that the pigeons are not just remembering rewarded pictures, but have formed the concept of a tree.

Wait a minute, though. Maybe they have formed the concept *not* of "tree" but of "treelike shape." There is a big difference between the two. One is a feat of genuine cognitive or mental abstraction, the other a feat of visual acuity. Critics of the results point to the errors, such as the telephone pole, as indicating that the birds are working only with visual categories. It is correct that a telephone pole does look somewhat treelike, so this error might indicate that the birds are responding only to visual clues—"a small set of relevant features," as one observer phrases it—and not to any category we humans bring with us to the experiment.

Moreover, pigeons can discriminate at a much better than chance rate between happy and sad human faces. Do we really believe they are thereby demonstrating shrewd categorization instead of extremely subtle responses to visual clues? No, and John Pearce does not claim that they are. As he says regarding the trees, the birds could be responding to "a green blob" somewhere in the picture or to something else we humans might not pick up on. How else do we explain the fact that the birds do quite well judging between the paintings of Monet and Picasso? "One way," Pearce says, "is to suppose that when the pigeon sees a complex photograph, such as of a Picasso painting, he notices a number of salient features. Then the bird solves the problem simply by looking for those features in the other photographs."

Pearce does not say that his pigeons are budding Einsteins. They are capable of surprising performances, but he does not believe they entertain truly abstract thoughts or have an internal dialogue with themselves. They are one step "below" that level. Nevertheless, he adds, the results on his tests "suggest we must completely rethink how we view the acquisition of concepts." He theorizes that the tests with the birds and the undergraduates indicate that while we have two ways of thinking—the concrete and the abstract—the pigeons have only one—the concrete, based on the images in their brains. When odd categories like certain abstract shapes happen to be perfectly suited to the pigeons' talents, they beat humans. Otherwise, it's no contest. Furthermore, the pigeons don't even beat goldfish who learn to differentiate between simple shapes and these same shapes with a little bump on the top. Donald Griffin quotes Stephen

Walker, a psychologist at the University of London, as being surprised that "even a vertebrate as small and psychologically insignificant as a goldfish appears to subject visual information to such varied levels of analysis."

But Griffin asks:

> Why should this be surprising, when it is well known that fish can discriminate many types of patterns that signal food or danger? We should be on guard against the feeling that only primates, or only mammals and birds, have the capacity for learning moderately complex discriminations. For the natural life of almost any active animal requires it to discriminate among a wide variety of objects and to decide that some are edible, others dangerous, and so forth.

ALEX

We now meet Professor Irene Pepperberg of the biology department at the University of Arizona, Tucson, and her famous African gray parrot, Alex, with whom she and her students have been working for more than twenty years. Alex is unsurpassed among birds in categorization skills. He identifies—or "labels," as the experimenters put it— more than eighty objects. He identifies seven colors, five abstract shapes, and numerous materials. If Alex is presented with two identical objects and asked to identify the attribute that is different, he correctly answers "none" in understandable English!

Are his abilities the same as ours when we handle these tests? Pepperberg answers, "We don't really know. What we would say in a scientific way is that they're analogous." She estimates Alex's overall skills in these particular tests as equivalent to an ape's or a dolphin's, which in turn are roughly equivalent to a four- or five-year-old child's.

Pepperberg uses elaborate means in her testing to guard against "Clever Hans errors." In all the tests, Pepperberg, the official scorekeeper, sits with her back to the testing setup. She does not know the right answer. She simply reports what Alex has said as an answer. "For example," she explains, "if he says something like 'gree,' which could be interpreted as either 'green' or 'three' depending on what you think he should say, a student who knew that the correct answer is 'green' might say he was right, whereas I would say it was unclear and the answer would be discounted." A student trainer who has worked with Alex on a given set of skills would never be the one who tested Alex on those skills. This precaution against "expectation cuing" keeps Alex from thinking, "Oh, this is Jo, so we're going to do color tests today." Likewise, the bird is always tested in several different ways in the same session, so he can't figure out, "Oh, this is 'numbers' today. I'm just going to spout out my numbers." For example, he might be shown a green key and a blue key and asked to identify the quantity or what quality is the same about the two, what quality is different. He would be asked questions about color, shape, and material.

As with many primates and mammals tested in lab conditions, boredom can be a problem with Alex. It is not rare for him to say in the middle of a test, "I'm gonna go away," and then do just that. But when he's engaged, he's tough to fool. When he says the word for a certain object, he cannot be tricked easily. For example, if Alex says "wanna banana" and a nut is presented instead, one of three things will happen. He either refuses the nut in stony silence, refuses the nut and repeats his request for a banana, or accepts the nut and throws it at the conniving human being who had the nerve to try to trick him in the first place. The simplest, most straightforward explanation here is that Alex truly does have this banana "in mind." It's hard to come up with any other plausible explanation.

ONE, TWO, THREE, FOUR

Many psychologists have long believed that certain cognitive processes are absolutely dependent on language, or on some corollary of language, and that counting is one of these skills. But any number of carefully constructed tests with a range of animals pose a strong challenge to this assumption. In fact, rudimentary counting may be much more widespread in the animal kingdom than we had ever imagined. If this turns out to be the case, even the most committed doubter about the animal mind and consciousness will have to reexamine his or her position.

The most basic challenge to the idea that counting and language are inextricably linked is posed by the fact that babies, with no language whatsoever, have a rudimentary sense of number, if not of specific numbers. The fascinating textbook experiment here is to set up a little stage in front of a baby and place one toy on the stage. Then hide that toy behind a screen. Next, clearly show another toy also being placed behind the screen. Raise the screen and time how long the baby looks at the two toys before losing interest and looking away. Repeat the test until you have an average time—five seconds, say—that will serve as the baseline for this particular baby. Now introduce a trick into the experiment. Hide the one toy behind the screen, place the second toy behind the screen, then raise it to reveal an incorrect number of similar toys—just one, say, or four. Now measure how long the baby looks at this scene before losing attention.

Inevitably, the baby stares at this "incorrect" number of toys much longer than it stared at the "correct" number. Something has changed, and babies know it.

So babies without language have some conceptual sense of number. However, babies have the capacity for language, if not yet language itself. What about primates? It turns out that many primates have exactly the same kind of reaction to this experiment. They look much longer when the screen is raised to reveal an incorrect number of toys. They, too, seem to sense that there's something fishy going on here. They, too, seem to have a conceptual sense of number, mass, or amount.

On average, a full seven years is required for children to have a solid concept of number. By that age, they can count a small group of jelly beans and name the corresponding number. Hundreds, if not thousands, of experiments have been conducted on a wide variety of animals to determine whether they have a similar grasp of number and counting and if not, what stage of development they have reached. We should not be surprised to learn that the results of most of these tests are interpreted in many different ways.

In one experiment that will acquaint us with the complexities of the subject, rats are introduced into a box containing six identical "tunnels" lined up in a row. With training, the rats can be taught to locate without fail the fourth, say, of the six tunnels. The specific location of the tunnels within the box is changed from trial to trial, the tunnels themselves are changed daily so that no scent clues have been left behind from the previous trial, and visual clues from outside the box are controlled for. Still, the trained rat will select the fourth tunnel.

Apparently the rat can "count" to the fourth tunnel. But is this the concept of "four" that you and I have? Does the rat extrapolate from knowing about this fourth tunnel to knowing that it has just eaten four pellets of food or that this is the fourth one of these darned tests it has been given today? The debate rages.

The famous German ethologist Otto Koehler devised a similar experiment that he felt demonstrated basic counting ability—"thinking in unnamed numbers," in his phrase—by ravens. Koehler trained his birds to select an object based on the number of spots painted on it. It is important to note that these spots were not of uniform size or shape. They could be any size or shape; it didn't matter. Koehler's birds could be taught to unerringly select the object with any number of spots up to seven spots. Again, is this "counting" or something considerably simpler, a merely "perceptual" understanding akin to our human visualization of the count of a domino. Shown a domino, we don't really count the six spots on the double-three. We know without counting. Psychologists call this simpler action "subitizing" and many comparative psychologists believe that the animals in most of the classic counting experiments are actually subitizing, not counting. This is the belief of Professor Euan McPhail, psychologist at the University of York who serves in *Nature*'s animal-minds series as a reliable splash of cold water on any assertion of animal consciousness. (McPhail even brings up the point I alluded to earlier: If animals do have consciousness, do they therefore have souls, and if they have souls, is not heaven a very crowded place indeed?)

However, subitizing cannot be the explanation for the achievement of certain cormorants in China, whom Dr. Miriam Rothschild believes can count to the number seven. Rothschild, who is justifiably famous in natural-history circles, reports seeing the birds pull off this feat many times. These particular birds are raised like chickens by fishermen. Fishermen? Yes, because the birds have been helping them with their work for hundreds of years. Cormorants are superb divers for fish, but when they do so on behalf of the fishermen, a string tied around the neck prevents them from swallowing the catch. The bird returns to the surface with the fish in its pouch, and the fisherman takes it out. The unwritten agreement between fisherman and "fisherbird" is that the bird is allowed to keep for itself every seventh fish. After all, the cormorant, like all of us, needs some kind of incentive for all the hard work.

Sometimes the bird dives and returns without a fish, and this failure doesn't count. The bird gets to keep the seventh *fish*, not the fish caught on the seventh outing. How does Rothschild conclude that the bird is counting along with her and the fisherman? Sometimes the fisherman makes a mistake and fails to reward the cormorant after its seventh successful dive, directing the bird to go down again, with the string still around its neck. When this happens, according to Rothschild, the bird just sits there. It knows it has brought back seven fish, and the last one should be for itself. The fisherman says the Chinese words for "go on" to the cormorant, but if he doesn't take the string off, the bird is not going anywhere. Only after the fisherman realizes his error and rewards the bird with the seventh fish will the cormorant dive again. After seeing this scenario played out numerous times, Rothschild concluded that the bird was counting to seven.

This is, of course, anecdotal evidence in the extreme, and therefore grounds for dismissal, to many minds. The same cannot be said for Irene Pepperberg's numerical tests with her parrot Alex. Investigating arithmetical ability turns out to be one of Pepperberg's favorite subjects, and these tests are as stringently controlled as the others we have observed. In a typical test of the bird's numerical ability, Pepperberg places in front of Alex a tray of different objects of different materials (wood and wool) and colors (yellow and red). Alex is then asked, for example, how many yellow wood objects he sees.

The key to this test is the presence of the two criteria—"yellow" and "wood"—which precludes a quick perceptual grasp of the answer. Common sense tells us, and tests confirm, that a perceptual process produces more errors when the number in question is larger, because it's slightly harder to perceptually grasp five objects than two objects. On the "yellow-wood-objects" test, we humans score the same regardless of the correct answer. This demonstrates that we are *counting*.

The same pattern holds for Alex. He averages about 80 percent correct answers no matter what the correct answer is. Pepperberg reasons by analogy that this performance suggests that the parrot may also be counting, although she argues that parrots may have better subitizing skills than humans. She has also conducted experiments indicating that Alex transfers his concept of four objects on a tray to four notes played by a piano, but the crucial tests of this ability have yet to be carried out. She is now working with him on associating the spoken word "four," which he knows to associate with four objects on a tray and—here's the big catch—the written Arabic numeral 4. Pepperberg explains, "Eventually our idea is to present him, say, a green 3 and a blue 4 and ask him to tell us what color is the bigger number or the smaller number."

Tests similar to those presented to Alex prove that monkeys clearly understand differences in quantity, if not necessarily the numbers we give to those quantities. The test is simple. Marc Hauser of Harvard University is the experimenter who explains this work in the *Nature* television series. In clear view of the test subject, Hauser places two choice plums in one box and one plum in another box nearby; then he allows the monkey to go to one of the boxes and retrieve the food. About 90 percent of Hauser's monkeys go directly to the box with two plums. Or they go to the box with four plums versus just three. This is a distinction that infant humans do not make until they are three or four years old. After an animal has grasped the basic problem, Hauser adds a complication by mixing food and non-food items and thereby requiring the monkey to keep in mind not only number but the kind of object as well. Hauser explains, "In one experiment we would place two plums in one bucket and one plum and one stick or rock in the second bucket. In this situation, again, about ninety percent of the time they pick the two plums over one plum and one stick or rock."

These tests differ significantly from those of Irene Pepperberg in that they require the animal to keep in mind something it no longer sees. Hauser concludes that the monkeys are counting plums "in their mind's eye," and he is not surprised by these results. "Animals are constantly confronted with situations where they must evaluate the number of animals, or the number of pieces of food, so it is a natural task for them to be confronted with solving a simple arithmetical problem."

Perhaps no primate has been tested in counting skills more extensively than Sheba, the chimp who works with Professor Sally Boysen at Ohio State University. In one set of these tests, Sheba learns the correct relationship between one or two or three items of a favorite food, and cards with one or two or three black marks. If two jelly beans are presented, Sheba is taught to pick the card with two black marks. This is a fairly simple pattern-matching test, and Sheba learns it without problems. Then the test gets harder as the black marks on the cards are replaced by numerals 1, 2, and 3. Now Sheba is asked to match three jelly beans not with three black marks but with the abstract equivalent, the number 3. This is a test similar to that on which Irene Pepperberg is now working with Alex the parrot, although Alex does not see the four items before having to identify the Arabic number 4. Sheba the chimp masters it easily enough. Next, the jelly beans are dropped from the experiment and Sheba is challenged to master the equivalence between three black marks on a card and the numeral 3. She picks this up quickly as well.

Now a real counting task is presented to her. She is shown three dishes, each with either zero, one, two, or three jelly beans. The jelly beans are removed, and she is then asked to name the total number of jelly beans she has seen. She can do this successfully, up to the number six. Other chimpanzees in a number of different testing situations have also learned to match from zero to eight items with the correct symbolic numeral. Finally, and most impressively, Sheba's jelly beans are replaced by numerals 1, 2, or 3, and she is challenged to add up the total of the abstract numbers by selecting the correct abstract number. And she can accomplish this just as well as she can add the jelly beans.

ON THE OTHER HAND

When I want to enter a locked door and don't have a key, I knock. My dogs accomplish the same purpose by scratching on that door with a paw. When I'm hungry, I go into the kitchen, open the refrigerator door, and peer inside at the possibilities. My hungry dogs come find me, then lead the way to their feeding area of the kitchen. As the question is posed by Stanley Coren in his book *The Intelligence of Dogs*—and long before that, by Charles Darwin and his protégé, J. G. Romanes—if my pets behave the same way I do in a situation in which I am undoubtedly thinking, isn't my pet therefore thinking as I am thinking? If the chimpanzee Sheba sees five pieces of candy and then points to the numeral 5, isn't she therefore counting just as I would be counting?

The answer is . . . maybe, but maybe not, because reasoning by analogy in this way is fraught with pitfalls. It turns out that I owe much of my understanding of this issue to the psychologist Hank Davis, the critic who drew an analogy between Donald Griffin's books and Salman Rushdie's *Satanic Verses*. Davis is not a fan of cognitive ethology, and he explains his objections in his essay in *Anthropomorphism, Anecdotes, and Animals*. Specifically, he informs us of the common logical error known as "affirming the consequent."

The following statement is a good example: "If this is a good car, it will start on the first try." The sentence is correct, but the implication that starting on the first try proves that this is a good car is quite wrong and could cost me a lot of money. The car could be a lemon and still do this one thing right. With regard to counting, we say about ourselves, "If I am counting, I will point to 5," but it is not true that I point to 5 only if I am counting. There are a host of other reasons I could do so. Likewise, there might be several reasons Sheba does so.

It was Hank Davis who conducted the experiment in which the lab rats learned to choose the fourth tunnel, but he does not consider this performance *counting*. He argues that pointing does not prove counting, and he argues that Donald Griffin and other cognitive ethologists regularly make such "affirming the consequent" errors while assessing the performance of animals on various cognition tests. This is nothing less than the classic error of anthropomorphism, he states. In his view, the cognitive ethologists are saying, "If I, as a human being, am engaging in conscious thought, then I will behave in a sensible manner. Therefore if an animal behaves in a sensible manner, it is engaging in conscious thought." But the hidden assumption that only conscious thought produces reasonable behavior is dead wrong. Instinct, for one example, produces very sensible behavior. Davis concludes, "We do not know enough about the role of conscious thought in determining *human behavior* [my emphasis] to extrapolate to any other species."

As it happens—and we should not be surprised to learn this—Davis subscribes to the bold idea that conscious human thought in fact follows rather than precedes action. This is a provocative hypothesis, obviously, and there are even some narrowly focused experiments that lend it some credence. That subject is way out of our range in this book, but Davis's radical behaviorist leanings don't negate his warning. Sensible behavior does not necessarily mean consciousness lies behind it. The same behavior across species does not necessarily indicate the same cognitive processes. For example, if I were to get on my hands and knees and start barking along with my dogs, would I be truly barking in the sense that they are? No.

Regarding Sheba's success with numbers, the most popular alternative explanation I have read about argues that she has simply learned after arduous trial and error that when she sees the *shape* of the numeral 2 and the *shape* of the numeral 3, she should pick the *shape* of the numeral 5 if she would like a tasty reward—and she would, of course. This is a plausible explanation, we have to admit.

On the other hand, a fascinating aspect of the tests works against it. When performing counting tests, young children point at objects and count aloud. Chimpanzees cannot count aloud, but they do point and touch and move objects away from the others. Such "tagging" and "partitioning" gives every appearance of "counting" in the manner that children do. Sally Boysen concludes:

I think we have good evidence that the chimps have a solid understanding of the counting process. We've created a number of situations that require them to come up with novel and innovative ways of putting information together. Now, what this means in terms of how they encode that counting process, or what individual numbers mean to them, is something we can't measure directly, but it looks as though . . . they have an understanding of the number line and something about the process of ordinality . . . very similar to the capacities we see in children around the age of three or four.

By the way, Stanley Coren, author of *The Intelligence of Dogs*, is not a dog lover who believes his pet can handle algebra. He is a professor of psychology at the University of British Columbia—as well as a dog lover and prizewinning dog trainer. He tells the following story about a competing trainer who offered to show Coren the counting ability of one particular female Labrador retriever, Poco.

"Pick a number from one to five," this other trainer told Coren, who picked three. The trainer proceeded to throw three lures into the high grass, in different directions, at different distances. The lures were not visible to the dog, as Coren confirmed by getting down on his hands and knees to see for himself.

"Poco, fetch," the man told the dog, with no other apparent cues. She ran to the lure tossed out last, retrieved it, and returned to her trainer's side. He accepted the lure, repeated "Poco, fetch," and the Lab headed out and brought back a second lure. Commanded a third time, she retrieved the third lure. Commanded a fourth time, Coren writes, "the dog simply looked at him, barked once, and moved to his left side, to the usual heel position, and sat down."

The trainer's conclusion, and Coren's conclusion: Poco knew

three lures had been thrown, and she had recovered three lures. She knew there weren't any more because she had been counting. Of course, Coren knows all about the Clever Hans debacle from early in this century and earlier in this book. Could the dog be receiving subtle visual or oral cues, whether intentionally or inadvertently delivered? Yes, she could be, because dogs are extremely acute observers, visually and by undetermined means that might as well be ESP, as far as our own limited senses can determine. With this in mind, Coren tried in every way he could imagine to restrict the possibility of cuing, putting the generously cooperative dog through her counting paces for the next half hour. He enlisted the aid of a second bystander who wouldn't know how many lures Coren had tossed into the grass. This person certainly couldn't give cues to Poco. In the equivalent situation with Clever Hans, the poor horse was lost. But Poco nailed this trial, too. The dog always knew how many lures had been thrown and could not be tricked into retrieving a lure that had never been thrown.

But the fact that Poco refused to try to retrieve the lure doesn't prove she had been counting. Hank Davis is right about that. No one can prove that she was counting. But can Davis or the reader come up with a better explanation for this specific set of circumstances?

SOMEWHAT IRRELEVANT FOOTNOTE
FOR US DOG PEOPLE

Stanley Coren disproves an idea about dogs put forward by no less a savant than the esteemed Samuel Johnson, who compiled the first full-scale dictionary of the English language. "Did you never observe," Johnson asked rhetorically, "that dogs have not the power of comparing? A dog will take a small bit of meat as readily as a large, when both are before them."

When you think about this statement, it must be one of the sillier that Johnson ever made. Of course dogs compare—if nothing else, the size of other dogs. Is it purely coincidental that a dog is much likelier to move beyond the display stage and actually challenge a smaller dog than a larger one? I don't think so. Dogs know size.

Coren reports a test designed by Daniel Greenberg, the editor at that time of *Science and Government Report*, to refute the great Samuel Johnson. This experiment is easy to set up in your own home. Shape two balls of meat of noticeably different size and place them on the floor directly in front of your dog, one somewhat closer than the other. The dog will almost always go to the nearest ball of meat, regardless of size. Perhaps this was as far as Johnson took his observations. If so, he was not a good scientist. Next, take two more balls of meat of noticeably different size and place them some distance from the dog, say twenty feet, but the same distance in each case. Almost invariably, Coren reports and I can confirm (after admittedly limited research), the dog will run to the larger ball of meat.

6

Tools
of the
Trade

NOT SUCH AN EXCLUSIVE CLUB

If mental mapping is something of an entry-level mental talent for animals, and category formation one rung up the ladder, the use of tools has long been considered threshold behavior for true intelligence. In fact, it was widely believed for a very long time that humans were the only tool-using animals. After all, tool use implies a high order of concept formation, problem solving, adaptability, purposive thinking—the whole range of criteria cognitive ethologists look for in order to hypothesize intelligence and consciousness. No wonder Charles Darwin's report in *The Descent of Man* that he had viewed an orang use a stick as a lever was generally dismissed as another of his anecdotal, anthropomorphic, embarrassing errors that zoologists would rather not talk about.

One hundred years later, Jane Goodall still ran into the same bias when she reported observing a chimpanzee strip a twig of its leaves and stick the resulting stem into a hole with the clear purpose of withdrawing termites. "When I first saw this," she told *Nature* . . . at her Gombe research center in Tanzania, "I sent a telegram to Louis Leakey and he became very excited. [But] there was a sort of disbelief among many scientists, because at that time *we* were supposed to be the only tool-using and tool-making animal. Since then we've realized that the chimpanzees use many objects in many different ways and they modify them very, very frequently."

And not just chimpanzees. Since Goodall's revelation, many books and a large number of academic papers have been written on this subject of tool use among a wide range of animals. It turns out that the tool club is not nearly as exclusive as we once thought—or wanted to think, perhaps. Definitions are disputed, naturally. In the following discussion, I will use the strict language employed by the *Oxford Companion to Animal Behaviour*, which defines tool use as "the use of an external object as a functional extension of the body in attaining an immediate goal." Fair enough, although we should note for the record that the behavior, widespread among birds, of dropping a stubborn food item (forgive the anthropomorphizing) such as a clam on a rock in order to break it open, then swooping down for the meal, is a clever piece of work, whatever name you give it.

Certain female wasps dig tunnels and then stock them with paralyzed insects that will serve as food for the larvae. With the eggs laid and the food stored, the wasp seals the tunnel from the outside. And then some wasps have been observed using a pebble or twig or hardened clod of earth to tamp down the sealed entrance! Is this tool use? Yes it is, and the observations have been made by serious researchers, not just anthropomorphizing passersby! Certain ants use little pieces of leaf or wood to soak up fruit pulp or the fluid tissue of prey, and then transport this liquid food back to the colony. Tool use, however you cut it: truly remarkable behavior.

Of course, with these instances we run up against the old bias of viewing social insects as purely instinctive creatures. Right now we don't know if such behavior is strictly instinctive, but let's grant for the sake of the argument that it is. How, then, do we maintain the correlation with intelligence? Perhaps we don't. Euan McPhail and others believe that the surprisingly widespread use of tools casts doubt on tool usage as a barometer for intelligence. But why can't there be instinctive tool use as well as purposeful, intelligent tool use? There is no necessary contradiction here, any more than there's a necessary contradiction between the marvelous, instinctive navigation of the arctic tern and the less impressive but still somewhat intelligent navigation of the day sailor out for a sail around the bay.

When the crows of New Caledonia, the woodpecker finches of the Galápagos, and quite a few other species of birds hold twigs in their beaks to dig for grubs or other small insects, is this tool use? Absolutely. Is it instinctive? To some extent, yes, but birds have also been observed carrying the same preferred twig from site to site. If that's instinct, it's entrepreneurial instinct! One report cited in the *Oxford Companion* tells of a finch who was unsuccessful fishing for grubs with a forked twig, so it broke the twig above the fork and used the remaining single piece, with better results. Another report describes a young finch raised outside the nest (and therefore unable to learn from its parents) who "manipulated" twigs from an early age, instinctively. When hungry and confronted with food in a hole, this finch dropped the twig and tried to get the food with its beak. Unsuccessfully. Then this bird learned to use the twig for this purpose: instinct-plus, I would say.

Perhaps the most remarkable story of tool use and overall problem solving by birds—by any animal, when you get right down to it—is the incredibly smart behavior of Professor Bernd Heinrich's ravens at the University of Vermont. You almost have to see this performance to believe it, and we do see it in our *Nature* animal-minds series. However, the story actually began some years ago in Sweden, where the strangest thing was happening to a group of enthusiastic ice fishermen: Someone was stealing their bait and their catch. One Herbert Strandh of Habo wrote a letter to the editor of his local newspaper outlining the mysterious events. Early in the season he got good catches, but after a while his hooks came up empty, devoid of bait or fish. Other ice fishermen reported the same phenomenon. A law-abiding member of a law-abiding nation, Strandh couldn't figure this out, so he set up a stakeout. His letter continues, "A crow landed near the first hook. Then it walked over to the hole, took hold of the line with its beak and walked backwards until the bait was out and ate it up immediately, whereupon it went on to the next hook."

The crows were tried and convicted of stealing the bait and the fish! However, perhaps we shouldn't be too surprised by their "criminal" behavior. The crow is what ornithologists call a generalist, a reference to the bird's feeding habits. This is a category that also includes ravens. Crows and ravens have always had the reputation in both folk psychology and cognitive ethology of being highly adaptable and shrewd creatures. Their generalist lifestyle requires such flexibility—and their flexibility allows them to lead such a generalist lifestyle. Learning of the thieves of Habo, Sweden, Bernd Heinrich decided to find out just how shrewd and adaptable these generalists could be. At the University of Vermont, he devised a controlled experiment to study whether the birds were capable of *insight*. Using trial and error, they could attempt to solve the problem in several different ways—but only one way would work. He used the common raven as a substitute generalist bird in what strikes me as a classically well conceived, elegant experiment.

First, Heinrich raised a group of ravens by hand in an aviary, thereby isolating them from the full range of behavior they would normally learn in the wild. This assured him that they would come to his experimental setup absolutely cold, so to speak, with no conceivable direct learning to fall back on when applying themselves to a problem they had never encountered. Then he suspended pieces of meat on string hanging from horizontal poles in the aviary. Heinrich knew what the birds did not know until they tried and failed: The meat could not be snatched off on the fly. Nor could it be pulled up with one continuous pull on the string. No, this was a difficult challenge for any animal.

"In order to reach the food," Heinrich writes in the report of his experiment, "the birds needed to reach down from a perch, pull up on the string, place a pulled-up loop of string onto their perch, step up with one foot, place this foot onto the pulled-up portion of the string, release the bill from the string to reach down again, pull up on the string, etc., so as to repeat the exact cycle at least five times."

Then and only then would they win the piece of meat. Five ravens were the first subjects of this test. One solved the problem within six hours. Three of the four other birds finally solved it. One never did. Heinrich concluded what I believe any reasonable observer would conclude: that his birds were able to "see into the situation" before executing the behavior, which is simply too complex to be the result of any combinations of instincts. He also had the impression—impossible to confirm—that the four successful birds had not learned this behavior from each other, but had worked out the problem independently.

Another fascinating aspect of the experiment is what happened when the birds were startled while engaged in the task. In the natural world, a startled raven flies off while carrying with it whatever it happens to have in its beak. Among Heinrich's ravens, the ones who had not yet succeeded at capturing the meat flew off holding the string, only to have it jerked out of their beaks. This would be the predicted behavior. On the other hand, the birds who had successfully reeled in the meat let it drop before flying off, as if they understood that it was tied to the string and would be jerked from their grasp anyway.

Similar experiments have produced fewer "successes" than Heinrich observed with his ravens, but no one doubts the validity of his work. Other birds with more specialized feeding habits have never been able to solve the meat-on-a-string problem, but some do show apparently shrewd behavior. One example that has been written about a great deal is the green-backed heron. Standard operating procedure for this heron and other shore birds is to stand motionless near water's edge, poised to strike when a fish comes within range, but some shore birds also have an extensive repertoire of techniques to find or attract small fish more actively. The herons have been observed many times to toss onto the water a light object that will float—something like a crumb, berry, feather, insect, or leaf—and then grab any fish that rises to the bait. Some green-backed herons fish in this manner; many others don't. In some flocks, several birds will pick up on the trick; in others, only one or two birds. So this is not instinctive behavior, a point made even clearer by the fact that the herons who do fish use different techniques. Some toss the bait from a distance, then swoop down for the meal. Others toss the bait and stand nearby.

We might wonder whether the birds have learned this trick from watching humans, but in fact experimenters have never been success-ful at teaching herons how to fish with crumbs. The birds apparently pick it up on their own—or they don't. Of course, it is possible to explain these results as classic conditioning, from which perspective the bird learned from a lucky episode in which a dropped crumb was followed immediately by a rising fish. Without the lucky episode, the behavior would never be learned, and that's why it is so rare. But why discredit the bird because it takes advantage of a lucky accident? Or as Donald Griffin writes, "Is it reasonable to suppose that a heron develops this kind of behavior and uses it successfully without think-ing about what it is doing and looking ahead for at least a short time to what it hopes to achieve?"

He doesn't believe so, and neither do I.

TO EACH HIS OWN

When a sea otter living off the Pacific Coast dives to the seabed and returns with a stone, which it then balances on its chest while floating in the water and uses as an anvil for breaking open a mollusk, is this tool use? Without a doubt. And when the otter then holds this same rock in its "armpit" while diving for more mollusks, this is *really* tool use—you don't want to lose a good tool once you've found it! This behavior is not instinctive. Researchers at the Monterey Bay Aquar-ium have proved that young otters have to be taught, usually by their mothers, of course, to use a rock for cracking shellfish. When an orphaned baby otter is being raised at the aquarium, it has to learn "the old rock trick" and many other survival skills from its human "mother."

Like the birds, some mammals use tools, others don't. Primates are the chief achievers in this category. According to Vauclair's *Ani-mal Cognition*, at least seventeen species are incorrigible tool users. It is part of their daily life in the wild. Many arboreal primates throw branches from trees when pursued (often by human observers, hoping to have branches thrown at them!). Capuchin monkeys are superior tool users. They spontaneously use branches to drive others away, rocks to break open nuts, and sticks to reach for food. In lab tests, they will employ a combination of sticks to reach a peanut placed in the middle of a Plexiglas tube. Bonobos, the fourth and much lesser known of the great apes (the others are the gorilla, orang-utan, and chimpanzee), and sometimes called the "pygmy chimpanzee," are committed tool users, using leaves to scoop up water, sticks to reach objects or pole-vault over a moat, soft material to wipe their behinds. Frans de Waal writes at length about such tool use in *Bonobo: The Forgotten Ape.*

Still, it comes as no surprise to learn that chimpanzees might be the most proficient of tool users other than ourselves—after all, genetically they are our closest relatives in the animal kingdom, sharing 98.7 percent of our genetic material. Chimps and bonobos use tools, make tools, understand tools, and modify the same tool for more than one use, and they use more than one tool for the same purpose. In short, they have what could legitimately be called a tool kit, to use W. C. McGrew's neat phrase. And to use the British psychologist Richard Gregory's sharp observation, cited by the philosopher Daniel Dennett, such profligate tool use reminds us that tools not only require intelligence but confer intelligence.

Studies of several groups of Ivory Coast chimpanzees demonstrate both tool use and mental maps in the same situation. The goal for the chimps is the delicious meat of the *Panda oleosa* nut. The *Coula edulis* nut is easier to open and more abundant, but the *Panda oleosa* is prized. However, it is also very difficult to open. (Donald Griffin points out that the loud report that accompanies the cracking of this nut led early explorers to assume that some tribe was forging metal tools.) The chimps do so by using one stone to crush the nut against another stone or against some other hard surface such as a tree trunk. They also remember where the best tools are, and they use the tool closest to a given tree. In short, they utilize a workshop. It's important to note that although Panda nuts are common throughout West Africa, only the chimp population of the Taï National Park in the Ivory Coast have been observed eating them. As Sue Savage-Rumbaugh writes in *Kanzi: The Ape at the Brink of the Human Mind*, "This is a striking example of a *cultural* difference between populations." That emphasis on cultural is mine. Cultural differences among chimpanzees? Well, why not?

Savage-Rumbaugh continues, "Even more dramatic, however, was Boesch's observation of mothers actively teaching their offspring the skills of nut cracking." Boesch is Christopher Boesch, of the University of Basel, who reported the teaching behavior to Savage-Rumbaugh. She writes:

> Boesch told us how, on one occasion, he saw Salomé and her son Satre cracking Panda nuts. Salomé cracked most of them, and when Satre tried with a partially opened nut, he placed the nut improperly on the anvil. Before he could strike it with the stone hammer, Salomé took the piece of nut in her hand, cleaned the anvil, and replaced the piece carefully in the correct position. Then, with Salomé observing him, Satre successfully opened it and ate the second kernel.

On another occasion Boesch saw a different mother instruct her daughter in the correct way to hold the irregular stone hammer after watching the youth fumble the task for eight minutes. Mom finally came over, accepted the hammer from her daughter, carefully and slowly turned it to the correct position, cracked some nuts, and then handed the hammer back.

The next question seems obvious in retrospect, but it was quite bold at the time: Could apes learn to *make* stone tools? Could they follow in the footsteps of our cave-dwelling Paleolithic ancestors? (Archaeologists consider the different stone-making traditions as key distinctions between various early protohuman cultures. The first tools, found in South Africa, were made by Australopithecus and are dated about one million years ago.) In fact, the apes have not made stone tools in the wild, and have had no reason to, but could they be seduced into trying?

It's a longish story, and well worth the telling. Primatologist Savage-Rumbaugh teamed with archaeologist Nick Toth to find out whether the bonobo Kanzi could be taught to make stone tools at the Language Research Center in Atlanta. Two chapters ahead we will learn a great deal about Kanzi's famed language abilities, but right now let's find out what happens with the stone-tool-making endeavor.

Kanzi's goal was a tool good enough—sharp enough—to allow him to cut the string securing a box with food inside. He immediately understood what he needed to do and how he needed to do it, he quickly learned to discriminate between the good flakes and the bad ones, and he mastered—or seemed to master—the action necessary to produce them. (Like all the great apes, bonobos are at least three times as strong as a human of the same height, so the job was well within his physical ability.) But for weeks Kanzi was tentative about making the necessary hard blow.

Then one afternoon eight weeks into the project, Savage-

Rumbaugh was sitting in her office when suddenly she heard BANG . . . BANG . . . BANG and rushed outside to see what crisis had befallen the center. No crisis at all. There was Kanzi, fracturing rocks with solid blows. Kanzi soon learned to produce sharp stone flakes, but they were on the small side, about an inch long. Savage-Rumbaugh and Nick Toth made certain that the string was too tough for a flake this small, which would grow too dull before successfully cutting the string. Kanzi needed to make a larger, still-sharper flake.

What happened next surprised everyone, perhaps including Kanzi. Savage-Rumbaugh picks up the narrative in her book:

> One day during the fourth month, I was at the tool site with Kanzi, and he was having only modest success at producing flakes. He turned to me and held out the rocks, as if to say, "Here, you do it for me." He did this from time to time, and mostly I would encourage him to try some more, which is what I did that day. He just sat there looking at me, then at the rock in his hand, then at me again, apparently reflecting. I wondered what he was thinking, because he did seem to be pondering weighty matters as he gazed at the rocks. Suddenly he stood up on his legs and, with great deliberation, threw a rock on the tile floor with a tremendous amount of force. The rock shattered, producing a whole shower of flakes. Kanzi vocalized ecstatically, grabbed one of the sharpest flakes, and headed for the tool site.

That's where the food was tied up with the string. I'm sure there are skeptics who think Kanzi was in fact throwing out of frustration and got lucky. I trust Savage-Rumbaugh, who concludes, "There was no question that Kanzi had reasoned through the problem and found a better solution to making flakes. No one had demonstrated the efficacy of throwing. Kanzi had just worked it out for himself."

Surprised at Kanzi's shrewd success, Savage-Rumbaugh was then surprised that Nick Toth was disappointed, because he was approaching this experiment as an archaeologist. He had hoped to learn from Kanzi's efforts something about the development of the tool-making tradition of early man. Shattering the rocks on the hard floor wouldn't do this investigation any good at all, because that's not what our ancestors had done. So Toth talked his co-experimenter into trying to discourage the throwing technique. Okay, but how? Then another associate came up with the idea of covering the workroom with soft carpet, so that Kanzi would have to go back to "real" tool making. But the bonobo had other ideas. After trying a couple of unsuccessful throws against the carpet one day, Kanzi paused, "looked around until he found a place where two pieces of carpet met, pulled back a piece to reveal the concrete, and hurled the rock."

As Savage-Rumbaugh writes, "We have assembled a videotape of the tool-making project, which I show to scientific and more general audiences. Whenever the tape reaches this incident there is always a loud roar of approval as Kanzi—the hero—outwits the humans yet again."

When spring came, everyone at the research center moved outdoors, where there was no concrete. Kanzi got progressively better at making stone flakes the crude, old-fashioned way—the human way, that is. But then once again he came up with an advance especially suitable for someone with his enormous strength. One day he placed one rock on the ground, stepped back with another, took careful aim, and fired!

THE FAMOUS DANGLING BANANA

Jane Goodall's favorite tool story from her many years at the Gombe Reserve concerns Mike, who had always seemed to be one of the more intelligent chimps. Goodall says:

> He's the one who learned to use empty paraffin cans to enhance his charging displays and got to be alpha male. [At first, Mike] was a bit nervous of me and I held out a banana to him one day, and he quickly picked a little piece of grass and threatened me. One end of the grass hit the banana, and it was as though a light went on. Suddenly he'd realized he'd got the answer. Instantly he let go of the grass, reached out and picked up a piece of straw, [but] it was obviously "bendy" and he didn't even try to use it, [so] he dropped it, reached around, found a stick and hit the banana out of my hand. It was an absolute straightforward thought process from the moment the grass touched the banana to the moment he found the appropriate stick.

So it would seem, and so it would also seem regarding fishing for termites, but both behaviors have been challenged as indicating not much beyond the minimal adaptation of a natural behavior. Doubters point out that chimps strip the leaves from branches and vines all the time. They also poke objects into holes for no apparent reason. But the fact that certain "instinctive" behaviors are utilized in the termite fishing does not preclude the presence of insight. Donald Griffin has made this point many times. James L. Gould and Carol Grant Gould write in *The Animal Mind*, "indeed, having the wit to realize that something done in play . . . might solve a novel problem probably does qualify as insight." These two authors, by the way, are not easily swayed in the debate concerning animal minds. They believe that "the cognitive underpinnings of a behavior often seem to weaken as we learn more about the natural behavior of a species." Still, insight is insight, even if it utilizes natural behaviors. We might even ask if any insight anywhere, including our own, does not in some way rely on "natural" behavior—"human nature," in our case.

Although the Goulds' statement about insight among chimps pertains to termite fishing, they used it in the context of their discussion of Wolfgang Kohler's famous experiments with chimpanzees in the second decade of this century. Jane Goodall told *Nature* that her initial report of tool use by chimps in the wild was greeted with doubt. It turns out that hers was not the first such report, nor the first to be greeted by doubt. Wolfgang Kohler encountered such criticism much earlier.

From 1913 to 1920, he was the director of the anthropoid research station of the Prussian Academy of Sciences in the Canary Islands, in the North Atlantic. Actually, he was more or less stranded on those beautiful islands when World War I broke out in Europe. Kohler subsequently became famous as the founder of Gestalt psychology, but it was in Tenerife that he devised a simple set of experiments that shed a brilliant new light on the animal mind. Every author on this subject discusses Kohler's work at length, greatly aided by the film that Kohler made of his work with these chimps. He also wrote a classic book, *The Mentality of Apes*.

Of course, Kohler knew about Edward Thorndike's experiments with cats in the puzzle boxes, and he criticized their value. Those tests had "hidden" the answer, Kohler pointed out. There was no way the cats or any other animals could have known the correct sequence of mechanisms to push and pull, so therefore they had no choice but to use trial and error. By contrast, Kohler set up situations in which the elements of the answer were visible, just not "in place." (It was the different approach of these two behaviorist-oriented researchers that prompted Bertrand Russell to joke that the animals studied by American behaviorists behaved like Americans, "running about in an almost random fashion," and those studied by Germans behaved like Germans, "sitting and thinking." Even B. F. Skinner enjoyed the joke and acknowledged the point.)

Kohler's basic setup in Tenerife was simple. He placed a ripe banana suspended overhead on a string and out of arm's reach of the subject chimp. In most instances, the chimp in question tried to grab the banana by jumping, grew frustrated, walked off in a sulky mood, stopped and looked back, then looked at some of the items scattered around, finally put two and two together and moved back to the scene and used these "tools" to reach the banana. The "tools" were merely some wooden boxes and a stick. Some succeeded by stacking up several boxes, but not until the stack tumbled over a few times. For the *Nature* series, our producers reproduced this experiment at Burger's Zoo in Arnhem, Holland, and sure enough, once again the boxes proved difficult for the chimps to stack correctly. The actors take a lot of tumbles before final success. If you set aside your knowledge of the animals' presumed frustration, both Kohler's vintage footage and our new footage make for hilarious viewing. But the chimps do finally succeed.

One of Kohler's chimps, Sultan, became famous in books on animal thinking as one of the first who used a box and a stick to reach his banana. These experiments opened human eyes around the world, and Kohler saw these episodes as evidence that the animals were assessing the situation "as a whole" (from which we get the term "gestalt"). But the experiments also prompted doubters. No one argued that Kohler's chimps were not clever, but were they as clever as they seemed? Could this be another example of the logical error of affirming the consequent: "If the ape is thinking, he will use the boxes and the sticks to reach that banana. He does use the boxes and the sticks; therefore he is thinking."

Critics immediately pointed out that the chimpanzees never perfect the stacking of boxes. They seem never to catch on to the problems posed, and even after years they stack at random until they hit upon a configuration that will hold them up. Apparently they are not capable of getting systematic in their stacking. Other researchers have noted that chimps swing sticks almost automatically in all sorts of circumstances, and put sticks together and stack crates while playing around. So what was going on here was trial and error, though not of an obvious sort. Clever, maybe, but not what we want to call genuine insight.

Coincidentally, exactly the same objection was soon raised against another classic story from the annals of ethology, this one involving blue tits and milk bottles. Blue tits are the relatives of chickadees who became famous in England "between the wars" for learning to strip off the protective tinfoil cover of home-delivered milk and helping themselves to the rich cream that had risen to the top of the bottle. (Almost all milk was not homogenized in those ancient times, of course.) The birds seemed to demonstrate insight initially, and then imitation, but skeptics approached the blue-tit story from a different angle. They pointed out that one natural, instinctive behavior of this particular bird is to peel off the bark of trees in its search for grubs. "Peel" is the key word here, obviously. These skeptics went so far as to set up experiments demonstrating that blue tits will even peel back wallpaper. Time and again. Without reward. Could not the first blue tit have discovered the delicious cream by "instinctive accident"? And wouldn't other blue tits have followed suit because foraging birds often, if not always, flock to any promising new feeding site? In short, did England's blue tits and Kohler's chimpanzees in the Canary Islands demonstrate insight or something much closer to instinct?

Morgan's Canon proposes that we have to settle on instinct if insight is not clearly required. Scientists can't agree on the answer. To my mind, instinct is a much more reasonable explanation for the blue-tit behavior than for the chimpanzees' behavior while going after the dangling banana. I repeat the Goulds' perceptive statement in *The Animal Mind:* "indeed, having the wit to realize that something done in play . . . might solve a novel problem probably does qualify as insight." With the chimps, I would say it definitely does. I would also agree with the Goulds' next remark: "if we take a hard line and require complete, from-the-ground-up novelty before conceding conscious inspiration, then Kohler's pioneering work . . . does not provide much unambiguous evidence one way or the other. But by that standard few humans would get passing marks for cognitive prowess."

Touché!

I now feel obliged to pass along the following instructive experiment with humans, cited in the *Oxford Companion to Animal Behaviour* in the entry "Problem Solving." Test subjects are provided with two sticks and a string on a nail on the wall. They are then asked to hang a loop on another hook on the wall without getting closer than two feet. No problem. Almost all of us will use the string on the nail to tie the two sticks together, then use this jury-rigged device to hang the loop on the hook. Everyone gets an A on this test. But when the experiment is changed and the string is not just hanging on the wall but is now holding up a picture, most of us do not realize that the solution is to convert the use of the string from hanging the picture to trying the two sticks together.

In hindsight, simple enough, but apparently not in real time. This sobering result is a necessary caution to us when we're thinking about, and perhaps criticizing, animal behavior as a sign of genuine thinking and consciousness. It is easy to debunk such behavior, but when we stop to think about the overall situation, we realize that a lot of time and practice—years, in many cases—is required by humans to learn new skills, from tying shoelaces to adding two plus seven to playing a piano to hitting a ball with a bat. Even as adults we don't find novel situations any easier to fathom and control than animals do, relatively speaking. This simple test proves that point.

INTELLIGENT ENOUGH

Wolfgang Kohler's "dangling banana" experiments with apes have been replicated to a degree—with pigeons. Robert Epstein and his colleagues at Harvard came up with this clever permutation. First the birds were taught to push a box along a flat surface. Note that they were not taught to hop onto the box, just to push it around. Then they were taught to peck at a banana by standing on a box beneath it. Finally, they were put into a situation with a dangling banana and, off to one side, a box. The birds knew the two skills required—pushing one box, standing on a different box to peck the banana—but would they have the insight to understand that they could use the pushed box to stand on in order to reach the banana?

In every case, the test bird exhibited some momentary confusion when introduced to the setup, looking at the banana, then at the box. Epstein continues, "Then each subject began rather suddenly to push the box in what was clearly the direction of the banana. Each subject sighted the banana as it pushed and readjusted the box as necessary to move it toward the banana. Each subject stopped pushing when the box was in the appropriate place, climbed on the box, and pecked the banana."

Now the question is, Can instinctive behavior linked with learned behavior get a poor bird into trouble? The answer is found in the following experiment, as reported in *Animal Minds*. Pigeons were shown a light *for a few seconds* just before food was presented. The pigeons quickly made a connection between light and food, and when the light was again presented, the birds instinctively began to peck on it, even though this pecking behavior was not necessary to receive food. Their instinct was to peck, and peck they did! If a devious experimenter changed the rules of the experiment, so that pecking a shining light stopped the delivery of food, it took a while for the birds to stop their instinctive pecking and eventually learn that a light no longer signaled food. In fact, the pecking instinct got them in trouble because they would peck the light even though it *stopped* the food.

Likewise, we have seen how animals use landmarks for mapping purposes, but this reliance on landmarks can backfire. A sooty tern hen, for example, does not sit on her egg so much as she sits on the place where she *first* sat on her egg. There's a big difference, which experimenters have proved simply by moving the egg in the tern's absence—moving it just a few inches, in fact. When the hen returns, she sits on the ground where the egg had been, presumably judging this location on the basis of nearby landmarks like rocks. The hen will sit on this exact ground while looking at her egg right in front of her, fully exposed to the dangerous elements.

Many animals are susceptible to such counterproductive behavior, and to narrowly tuned behavior. Like all animals, including us, pigeons and terns give evidence of "behavioral prejudices," to employ the phrase from *The Animal Mind*. However, I was fascinated to learn that pigeons cannot be trained to peck in order to avoid a shock. They can be trained to hop onto a treadle in order to avoid this shock, but they cannot be trained to hop onto the treadle in order to obtain food. Do these results make sense? Yes, definitely. Pigeons eat by pecking, and they flee danger by jumping or by flying away. Ask them to switch these two instinctive behaviors—ask them to flee by pecking, so to speak, or to obtain food by hopping—and they are in trouble. The same behavioral prejudices hold for lab rats, who can be taught to jump in order to avoid a shock, but who cannot learn to jump in order to obtain food. Jumping for food is not in their innate repertoire, and no amount of learning can compensate for that lack.

A final example of behavioral prejudice involves Sheba, the counting chimpanzee at Ohio State University. In one set of Professor Sally Boysen's tests, she would place on a table two clearly unequal piles of M&M's. The rule of this game was that Sheba would receive the pile of candy she did not point to. So in order to obtain the greater number of M&M's to eat, Sheba should choose the smaller pile. Everything Boysen understood about Sheba's intelligence indicated that this challenge was well within her abilities. Under most conditions, she could understand and master a rule this simple almost immediately. In this case, however, Sheba never learned to point at the smaller pile of M&M's. She could not squelch that desire for the bigger pile of candy, even though it was never fulfilled.

(Before we start feeling smug, we should all remember the unsurpassed ability of human beings to engage in counterproductive behavior. Are examples from either private or public life necessary? I shouldn't think so.)

The bottom line is that every creature's mind, or brain—including our own, of course—is exquisitely tuned by and tuned to the needs of its particular world. There is no contradiction between the facts that a pigeon can perform admirably on certain abstract-categorization tests and then peck away to no avail in a different kind of test. The bird who pecks in vain would never encounter these conditions in the real world, where pecking serves the bird very well indeed—and where, presumably, the bizarre talent that enables it to distinguish Monet's from Picasso's paintings also serves it well. Rats get along fine without jumping for food. They thrive. Given half a chance, they take over. When interpreting tests of animal minds, it is necessary to remember the evolutionary and ecological perspectives.

If a seemingly more sophisticated creature does not exhibit the consciousness-implying behavior of a seemingly less sophisticated creature, does this cast doubt on the importance of that behavior as an indicator of consciousness? Not at all. What it does is remind us of the vitally important idea that will come up time and again: *All animals alive today are as intelligent as they need to be—and only that intelligent.* (E. O. Wilson, the godfather of sociobiology, proposed the following tantalizing corollary to this idea: In general, Wilson wrote, the male of the species is less complex than the female, "in a way that reflects their simpler, more selfish reproductive roles." Ouch!)

We intuitively understand that the remarkable senses deployed by many creatures are the gift of evolutionary pressures. For example, roaches are about a hundred thousand times more sensitive to surface vibrations than we are, which makes sense. They need this sensitivity. We don't, thank goodness. Many birds have remarkable eyesight, many predators remarkable senses of smell, and so on. As matters have evolved, they require these finely tuned senses. The same relationship with the environment holds for cognition/intelligence/thinking—use whatever terminology you like. All species have been shaped by the forces of evolution to meet immediate needs. The more a given species needs to be conscious of, the more it *is* conscious of. Either that or it becomes extinct.

One of the first investigators who thought in these terms was the royal gamekeeper at Versailles in the reign of Louis XV. Charles Georges Leroy published his observations in 1764, focusing on the different environmental pressures on predators—wolves, in this case—and their prey as the most likely explanation for the undoubtedly superior intelligence of the predators. Their "lifestyle" of cooperation required superior mobilization and coordination of forces. Meanwhile, their herbivorous prey had only to eat what was there. With this insight, Leroy was a century ahead of his time, maybe more.

But if the use of tools by birds is considered a sign of conscious thought, why do animals that we intuitively feel are "smarter" than birds—mammals, with their much larger and more structured brains—very rarely use tools? Even among the primates, only the great apes and capuchin monkeys, to our knowledge, employ tools, and not all of them. Others, living under identical circumstances, do not. Is a bird therefore "smarter" in some way than an orangutan or a dog? No. It's an "apples and oranges" question. The vegetarian food eaten by primates has been easily accessible throughout the ages, as far as we know, and their hands are excellent tools in and of themselves. Most of them have never needed other tools. Wolves and dogs don't use tools because as predators (by nature, at least, in the case of dogs) they haven't had to in order to eat. Other than a weapon or a trap, what device would help a dog or any other predator to catch fast-moving prey? Just as Leroy did with the royal wolves, we see the intelligence of dogs more in their handling of social situations and in their ability to negotiate a neighborhood.

Since we have certain birds who shrewdly use tools and other birds who are unable to modify maladaptive behavior, do we therefore have smart birds and dumb birds? Maybe we do, but what we mainly have is birds who know what they need to know. And as we've seen, every bird—every mammal, every animal, including humans—can be very smart and very dumb from moment to moment, as they (we) encounter situations that they (we) are adept at and then others that are foreign and therefore create trouble. The reason the classic laboratory animals—pigeons and rats and mice—are laboratory animals in the first place is that they are, in the real world, scavengers and therefore, by definition, versatile, adaptable, creative. Any scavenger should do pretty well on a properly set up laboratory IQ test.

These considerations demonstrate why rating animals on a scale of intelligence requires arbitrary choices on the part of the judges. In many ways, some birds are just as intelligent as some mammals, and in every case, it's safe to say, a given animal's highest intelligence will be demonstrated in its natural habitat, where it needs this intelligence. Some animals do much better on certain tests in their natural environment than on the same test in the laboratory. For example, chimps in the field are excellent at locating hidden food. We have seen the results of the test with a chimp riding around on the back of a trainer while another trainer hides food in nooks and crannies. In an indoor laboratory setting, chimps do much worse at this test. The same is true with dogs, who know where they've hidden their bones in the backyard but are not nearly so adept at remembering in a lab setting.

Why can Sarah and other chimpanzees solve the complex problems of analogical reasoning? This is not a trivial question at all. Many researchers consider it a pressing question. Clearly chimps do not need to solve them in their natural world in the forest—or do they? I quote Dorothy Cheney and Robert Seyfarth from *How Monkeys See the World:* "Socially living monkeys regularly appear to classify individuals on the basis of kinship or close association, and in many cases they seem based on characteristics other than physical similarity, such as close behavioral association or family membership."

Cheney and Seyfarth put forward the provocative hypothesis that "group life has exerted strong selective pressure on the ability of primates to form complex associations, to make transitive inferences, and even to judge causal relations, but primarily when the stimuli are other primates. Monkeys and apes are more likely to solve at least some types of problems if they involve social stimuli, like conspecifics, than if they involve objects."

This hypothesis was first broached by Alison Jolly in 1966 and then elaborated by Nicholas Humphrey. We will hear a great deal more about it later, because it makes special sense when thinking about the consciousness of our closest relatives, the great apes. These bonobos and chimps, as well as rats and birds, are pretty good at tests in our laboratories, but if you really want to see them or any other animal at their best, you have to observe them in their native habitat in the wild. One of playwright David Mamet's characters says, "The map is not the territory." Likewise, the laboratory is not life. Psychologist John Pearce:

Of course animals are "intelligent," but that says very little. It's rather like saying all animals breathe. The important questions are how do animals differ in their intelligence and how do they acquire their intelligence in the first place? So when I say to people that I'm studying animal intelligence, what I really mean is that I'm studying the way in which animals learn about the environments in which they live, and I'm studying the way in which animals solve the problems that they confront in their environments.

GRAND-PRIZE WINNER

This admonition—to think of intelligence in terms of the natural environment—holds especially true for the beaver. Imagine a beaver in a laboratory. It's a joke. I cannot leave this discussion of tool use and the broader issues of intelligent problem solving without dealing with what may be the most impressive example of problem solving in the entire animal kingdom (and is without a doubt the "largest" example): the beaver dam. In effect, the dam is this animal's tool, and the building of a beaver dam is an impressive technical feat, no matter how cold-eyed the observer.

The essential facts about beaver dams and lodges are well known. The first major description of the technology in the annals of American nature writing was written by Lewis Morgan, a native of England but on American soil a Renaissance man of the nineteenth century—elected official, lawyer, anthropologist, businessman, naturalist. Morgan wrote *The American Beaver and His Works*, a staunch defense, in the manner of Darwin and Romanes, of the "thinking principle" in animal behavior.

Beavers build dams in order to control the water level in the pond that is created behind the dam. The industrious rodents then build their lodge either in the pond or on the bank. In either case this lodge is protected from the high water that would flood it (in event of a flood, beavers open a hole in the dam) and from the low water that might leave the entrance exposed.

Cutting all the trees required for both the dam and the lodge is, obviously, an arduous task, and beavers go at it with ingenious organization. They clear roads, sometimes including installing ramps over immovable obstacles. They may build canals into the forest and float their logs to the construction site. They take advantage of available features such as fallen trees or large rocks. They use braces to shore things up when necessary. They can plug just about any hole. And they build dams hundreds of yards long.

The skills employed and the resulting features are so impressive that you wonder whether beavers can be *that smart*. The answer is probably yes and no. Some of the behavior required for dam building is innate. There is no doubt about this. All beavers instinctively saw down trees. They instinctively build little dams. Often they over-build, to the human eye, constructing dams that would hold back the Nile. They make mistakes. Sometimes one animal will saw on a tree at one level, his partner at another level. Sometimes a felled tree will catch in a second tree, and beavers apparently do not understand that felling the second tree would then yield a two-for-one benefit. Clever experiments by P. B. Richard have demonstrated that beavers react to the recorded sound of running water by piling up debris next to a loudspeaker. In fact, none other than Charles Darwin believed the beaver's sophisticated engineering to be the product of instinct, as he informed Lewis Morgan when the two men met.

On the other hand, beavers do not waste time building a dam if one is not necessary—if they live beside a lake, for example. They do not waste time digging a burrow into a bank that is not steep enough to provide a den above the waterline. If a suitable structure is available in a good location, they won't build a lodge at all. Beavers also seem to employ their basic behaviors in novel ways when necessary, just as we have seen in this chapter with birds and chimpanzees. Donald Griffin, the founder of cognitive ethology, is fascinated by beavers. Griffin cites P. B. Richard regarding what happened in one experiment in which drainpipes were surreptitiously and maliciously inserted into a beaver dam. Initially, the beavers in charge of this dam stuck mud in the dam itself near the drainpipe—that is, near the sound of the running water. Soon, however, they found the opening to the pipe, even though it was some distance upstream from the dam, and plugged it closed.

In another of Richard's mischievous experiments, he placed a pipe whose intake was well upstream and underwater. The entrance to the pipe was covered with a strainer. Eventually the beavers discovered this trick, built a platform directly beneath the opening of the pipe, and then plugged the strainer closed. If any experiment does, this one proves that for beavers, as Griffin writes, "adding of material to a dam is by no means a rigid response to this particular stimulus."

One final beaver story, a remarkable episode and a reliable one, reported by my friend of many years, Hope Ryden, in her book *Lily Pond*. Ryden had been observing one family of beavers for some time when one day she returned to the pond to find that vandals—humans—had torn a hole in the dam, which threatened to drain the pond within hours. Ryden and her companion discovered the hole in the morning, before the beavers had arrived for the day's inspection. In the animals' absence, they attempted to help the cause by piling stones in a semicircle around the hole. This structure did slow the outflow, even though most of the stones were below the surface. Midafternoon, right on schedule, the chief dam builder arrived at the site to inspect the dam. Immediately he went into action, and was soon joined by three other beavers who had been seldom seen at the dam site.

Somehow they understood that the most efficient immediate means was to work on the secondary dam that had been started, unknown to them, by Ryden and her friend. First the beavers tried to fit branches into the stone buttress. When this didn't work at all, they switched tactics and went to the bottom of the pond and the bottom of the wall, plugging the holes in the stone wall there and significantly slowing the outflow. Normally beavers stick mud and grass onto the upstream side of a dam after they have set in place the infrastructure of branches. In this case, they figured out that working below the surface was more important. It is important to note that by working underwater they were working *away from* the sound of the running water. No simple conditioning response going on here.

The animals worked all night, observed by Ryden. The following afternoon, when they emerged from their lodge, they did something Ryden had never observed before that day: Each carried with it a pole from the lodge with which to reinforce the dam. No inspection or memory "reinforcement" was necessary. The beavers remembered the crisis situation from the previous night.

The literature on beavers is extensive and replete with such examples of adaptability. As Griffin writes:

> To account for such reversal of their customary behavior . . . as the thoughtless unfolding of a genetically determined program requires that we postulate special subprograms to cover numerous special situations. . . . Such postulation of a genetic subprogram can always be advanced as an explanation of any behavior that is observed; but the plausibility of

such "ad hocery" fades as their number and intricacy increases. A simpler and more parsimonious explanation may well be that the beaver thinks consciously in simple terms about its situation, and how its behavior may produce desired changes in its environment . . .

Does the beaver have the dam in mind when it begins its very first labor in that direction? We do not know, but the Goulds write in *The Animal Mind*, "if beavers do not have a general understanding of the tasks they face, then the power of innate programming extends far, far beyond anything we yet have evidence for." Too far beyond anything we have evidence for. Innate programming will not explain a beaver dam.

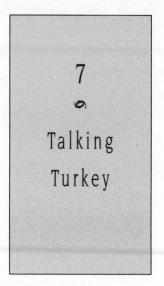

7

Talking
Turkey

ALARMING NEWS

Donald Griffin, the founder of cognitive ethology, believes that the
case for thinking and consciousness among animals rests on the three
pillars of versatile adaptability, which we (partially) investigated in its
many shapes and guises in the previous three chapters; evidence from
the neurosciences, the subject of a later chapter; and animal communication, the subject of this and the following chapter. Griffin put the
issue very simply in *Animal Thinking:*

> As civilized adult thinkers . . . our best—perhaps virtually
> our only—way of learning about other people's thoughts and
> feelings is through verbal and nonverbal communication.
> From these elementary considerations there emerges a very

simple but potentially potent point. . . . If non-human animals experience conscious thoughts or subjective feelings, we might be able to learn about them by intercepting the signals by which they communicate these thoughts and feeling to other animals. This idea is so basic that scientists, accustomed to dealing with complex issues, find it difficult to appreciate its potential significance. Nevertheless, the analogy to how we learn about other people's thoughts and feelings is so directly appropriate that we should make an effort to see where it might lead.

In his Harvard office, Griffin told me that he began thinking in these terms while arguing definitions of consciousness with the philosopher Thomas Nagel and other colleagues. Then he added, "So that's the one idea, it seems to me, that's original and constructive in this whole area."

That is an overly modest statement, to say the least, but focusing on the importance of communication is certainly a key "Griffinian" idea. In Charles Darwin's era, every creature's gestures, "body language," and vocalizations were generally considered to be little or nothing more than the spontaneous, essentially unconscious expression of emotions—excitement over finding food, or alarm about the sudden appearance of a predator, or an indication, perhaps a warning, of what the signaler was about to do next. In technical terms, this was called the "indexical" interpretation of animal communication. I much prefer Donald Griffin's facetious label. He called it the 'groans of pain" (or GOP) interpretation.

In the last years of the twentieth century, GOP is no longer tenable. If indeed a vervet monkey, for example, is just expressing an emotional state when it yelps at the approach of a predator, why would it matter whether there is an interested audience for this yelping? The animal's emotional state is presumably the same whether it is alone or with a crowd of other vervets. But the monkey emits alarm cries only if there is another monkey in the vicinity who might benefit from what the signaler "has to say." Ethologists label this phenomenon the "audience effect," and it's a dead giveaway that there's a great deal more going on with animal communication than was imagined a hundred years ago. Today the empirical evidence as established by literally thousands of experiments in the field and in the laboratory is too clear that animals are conveying not just emotion but also information.

What kind of creature intentionally conveys information? A thoughtful creature, Donald Griffin suggests, and many researchers agree with him. But is the lowly chicken, the most "consumed" bird on the planet, capable of meaningful communication? Could it be possible that a chicken is a thoughtful creature? Let's take a look, because we now know that there is a lot more to barnyard clucking than we ever suspected. When a cockerel sees an aerial predator such as a hawk, he issues a different alarm from the one issued after seeing a fox. Furthermore, a chicken who hears the "hawk" alarm scurries for cover while looking up, while the receiver of the "fox" alarm scans the immediate vicinity on the ground.

In order to make these findings, researchers equipped cockerels (golden sebright bantams, to be exact) with small microphones, because some of the calls are faint. They then rigged up phony threats, including models of large birds towed overhead on a set of wires—a contraption that replicated classic experiments by Niko Tinbergen in the 1950s. In one study, 400 "presentations" of the overhead hawk elicited 509 alarm calls for an aerial predator, zero alarms for a ground-based attack. So there's not much doubt that the chickens are issuing a specific, meaningful warning, and we have learned that many other birds also have different calls for different kinds of danger.

Further experiments will probably prove what experiments have proved with chickens: The audience effect is manifested in more than one way. The cockerels in these experiments are more likely to issue cries of alarm if there is a familiar bird nearby. With only unfamiliar birds in the vicinity, the cockerels cry in alarm no more than when they are alone—which is almost never. In effect, the cockerels seem to be looking after their own.

Chickens also have a "vocabulary" for conveying information about food. Apparently they name certain foods, or at least certain qualities of food, with special cackles. Careful study of sonograms is one proof of this hypothesis. Another is that nearby birds are more likely to approach if the indicated food is a preferred one, such as mealworms. In fact, one report hypothesized that the "gallinaceous" birds—pheasants, turkeys, and grouse, as well as chickens—have perhaps the richest diversity of food signaling of any animal. The audience effect also plays a role here: Cockerels call more often if a hen is nearby, much less if the nearby birds are other cockerels. (On the other hand, the male birds did not discriminate according to gender with their alarm calls; with alarms, they are more generous with their information.)

Careful experiments have discovered equivalent systems of alarms and responses among squirrels and meerkats and prairie dogs. We probably have no idea how many species have developed systems of differentiated alarm calls. Among the primates, the most widely written and debated alarm system is that of the aforementioned vervet monkeys, who live all across East Africa. If you have ever sat beside a water hole in East Africa and been mesmerized by the comings and goings and doings of a troop of monkeys with black faces, hands, and feet, you've probably been watching vervets. (It's worth remembering that apes, such as chimpanzees, bonobos, gorillas, orangutans, and gibbons, are genetically closer to humans than monkeys. Monkeys and apes together are the nonhuman primates.)

In the 1960s, vervets were reported to have separate calls for aerial predators such as hawks and ground predators such as leopards, and also for a third kind of danger, snakes. (All primates, nonhuman and human, are terrified of snakes.) These early reports of differentiated warnings raised doubts, not that the different calls elicit different reactions but whether these different reactions mean that the monkeys have any idea why they are reacting differently. Also, the monkey who issues the alarm almost always takes evasive action itself, so perhaps the other monkeys are imitating the action rather than heeding the alarm cry.

There were a lot of questions, and in the 1980s, Dorothy Cheney, Robert Seyfarth, and Peter Marler moved with their gear to the Amboseli National Park in Kenya to find some answers from eleven "social groups" of vervets. Three of the groups were studied continuously for eleven years. Cheney and Seyfarth write about this work in great detail in *How Monkeys See the World*.

An important part of their equipment was a series of hidden loudspeakers, which allowed them to issue bogus alarm calls and to study the resulting vervet behavior under relatively controlled circumstances. It would take several pages to lay out all the precautions and controls set up by the authors, including blind judging. Today these measures are standard operating procedure for any scientist working in the field.

To make a long story very short: Cheney and Seyfarth confirmed that the vervets do indeed use the three reported alarm calls—

"hawk," "leopard," "snake"—and three others as well, to a much lesser degree—"minor mammalian predator," "unfamiliar human," and "baboon." ("Minor mammalian" includes lions, cheetahs, and hyenas, who are minor in the sense that they rarely attack vervets; baboons will occasionally try to make a meal of a monkey.) The authors confirmed that the monkeys hearing the alarms are responding to the call itself, not to the behavior of the caller. They discovered a range of nuances with the audience effect. As with many other animals, solitary vervets do not make an alarm call, no matter how great the danger. Mothers give alarm calls at a higher rate when accompanied by their own offspring than by other offspring. Males give more alarms when accompanied by females than by other males. Intriguing but inconclusive tests suggest that vervets also respond to the predator calls of the superb raven, which, like many birds, has two different alarm calls, one for aerial, one for terrestrial danger.

Critics of vervet communication—those who say other researchers overinterpret these alarms and grunts—make much of the fact that vervets do not adjust their signaling based on the response of their listeners. (The same holds for cockerels in the experiments described above.) The critics argue that this failure of the communicators to modify their behavior is just one more indication of the limits of animals' language cognition. If animals do have a conscious intent to communicate in a way similar to our own intent, they would be responsive to the effect of that communication, as we are. Because they are not aware, apparently, they are not truly communicating.

Euan McPhail tells us, "What [animals] do is respond in fixed ways to a fixed set of stimuli, and what the animals detecting those signals do is respond, again, in a very inflexible way—a useful way, for their survival, but very much less flexible than the system we have." What is really going on, the critics say, is nothing more than classic stimulus-response conditioning, in which the stimulus comes in two parts—a predator and another monkey nearby. It's tough to disprove this rebuttal. As I've noted in several contexts, a behaviorist can always assert that an "undetected" or "misunderstood" stimulus is responsible for any animal behavior on earth, including our own. (Beware the phantom stimulus!)

Critics also suggest that the vervets' alarm cry means "Hide in a bush!" rather than "Hawk in the area!" or "Run up a tree!" rather than "Leopard on the prowl!" This might be correct, but so what? Either message is an effective communication of important information. Cheney and Seyfarth take great pains to consider all possibilities. They are not proposing that monkeys have sophisticated language capability. They acknowledge the limits of this communication, and one limit in particular really intrigues them. Vervets employ four basic social grunts. Cheney and Seyfarth ask, "Why stop at four?" Many times they saw mothers leave their young behind in vulnerable situations. They report one episode in which the left-behind youngster cried loudly for help when a group of baboons approached. The mother turned and saw the situation but could not call out "Follow me."

THAT BIRD AGAIN

Once again it's time for definitions—this time in order to draw the necessary distinction between communication and language. I take my definitions from Jacques Vauclair's *Animal Cognition* because these are readily understood by us amateurs and they make sense. Communication is the exchange of information between a sender and a receiver with some kind of specific code. Nothing more, but nothing less. Language is a system of communication that in addition *represents the world* to a receiver. At first glance the italicized phrase might seem uncomfortably vague, but I believe that everyone reading this book grasps the implication. Language is an immeasurably more powerful tool (and it is a tool) for dealing with the world than communication is. The alarm calls and social grunts of the vervet monkeys communicate on the basis of a code, but they do not represent the world in a broader way. They are not language.

For many linguists and behaviorists, this is all they need to know: Vervet communication is not language. Cognitive ethologists are happy enough to grant this point, but also feel that this communication tells us a lot about the mind, consciousness, and *Umwelt* of this monkey.

What about the chatty behavior of Alex, the gray parrot who has worked all these years with Irene Pepperberg? We have known for centuries that *Psittacus erithacus* and the other mimetic birds can mimic our words—they are the only creatures in the world capable of sounding anything like us—and they provide us with a great deal of entertainment in the process; the birds can be taught to say virtually anything, although some sounds are more difficult than others for them to pronounce. However, no one in the cognitive sciences, except perhaps Irene Pepperberg, had any idea that a bird could develop the talents for abstraction that we saw in the preceding chapter with Alex. And he was delivering his answers in spoken English, of course. Is this mere mimicry, informative communication, or true language?

In her efforts to find out, Pepperberg worked with Alex in a provocative social context, just as primatologists work with their animals in social settings, but for a somewhat different reason. Pepperberg wanted to keep Alex's attention by capitalizing on every parrot's manifest capacity for intense jealousy. He always worked with two trainers, and he was challenged to keep up with the second trainer in earning the attention of the first trainer—Pepperberg herself. She labels this the model/rival, or M/R, technique. One of her colleagues in California is using the M/R model with developmentally delayed children and also with autistic children, and it seems helpful in teaching basic labeling behavior. Another significant feature of Pepperberg's work with Alex is the complete absence of "extrinsic rewards"—rewards that have nothing to do with what he is learning at the time. Pepperberg feels that such rewards are just confusing. After identifying a cork, say, Alex gets a piece of banana only if he specifically asks for banana. If he asks for apple, he gets apple. If he doesn't ask for anything special, he gets the cork he identified.

Pepperberg acquired Alex from a pet store near Chicago in 1977, when he was thirteen months old. Either she or her students have interacted with him for eight hours of almost every day since then. The work has paid off. Alex has a hundred-word vocabulary, divided into basic categories: everyday objects, qualifying adjectives, simple actions such as "give," and concepts such as "none," "same," and "different." For twenty years, the community of language researchers has been arguing whether the famous chimpanzee Washoe was making up a new word when he signed "water/bird." In those same twenty years, Pepperberg tells us, Alex has coined exactly one new word: "bannery." She explains, "He was being trained on 'apple' and he had in his vocabulary 'banana,' 'cherry,' and 'grape,' and instead of learning the label 'apple' he insisted on saying 'bannery.' When you think about it, the apple is kind of like a large cherry and tastes a little bit like a banana. So this linguistic elision, as they call it, made sense."

Today Pepperberg is working with Alex on learning phonemes—the basic "pieces" of sound, such as *"aa"* and *"ee"* and *"th"* that we use to put words together. Can Alex be made aware of how he puts together his words? Pepperberg tells us, "We put the different bits of sound as [magnetic] refrigerator letters on a tray and we literally train him to identify the 'S' as the sound *'sss'* and the *'SH'* as the sound *'shh'* and the 'N' as *'nnn.'*

"When Alex has crossed the 80-percent threshold in this testing, Pepperberg says, "We're hoping that he will be able to look at, say, a 'K' and an 'OR' and another 'K' and be able to sound the word 'cork.' " Pepperberg does not presume that such a performance would be actual reading, but it would indicate that the bird understands "that his vocalizations are made up of individual bits of sound that can be recombined in novel ways."

"Does Alex possess language?" Pepperberg asks rhetorically. "No. Is it complicated two-way communication? Yes."

Or as Donald Griffin comments, "Pepperberg makes no claim that Alex has learned anything approaching the versatility or complexity of human language; but he does seem to have demonstrated some of the basic capabilities that underlie it. . . . In short, he gives every evidence of meaning what he says."

THOSE BEES AGAIN

I like this statement from Reuven Dukas's introduction to his book *Cognitive Ecology*, in which he quotes an article in *Science* by D. E. Koshland: "Anyone with a fly swatter knows that the flight information and landing computation of a housefly would elicit the admiration of any flight controller." Dukas cites the estimate that the fly's tiny brain must cope with a "visual information load" of about .5 megabytes per second. This assignment is a trivial matter for a 300-megahertz microprocessor, but quite a feat for a fly. We would all agree on that, but are we therefore inclined to credit this winged insect with cognition and consciousness? Most of us, no, because we tend to think of the invertebrates—animals without internal skeletons—as residing on the bottom rungs of the ladder of intelligence, however you want to define that word. Most of us draw the line somewhat "higher." But it is not true that there's nothing going on upstairs with these creatures. Insects—by far the great majority of all species, invertebrate or otherwise—exhibit startlingly bizarre but effective and adaptable behavior. The fly is just the beginning. Exhibit number one must be the famous dance of the honeybee, one of the most amazing and controversial behaviors found anywhere in the animal kingdom.

For centuries beekeepers had realized that their bees buzzed around on the honeycomb in a strange, agitated fashion. They also knew that a particularly nutritious and plentiful food supply of nectar and pollen would attract thousands of bees within a very short period of time: a remarkable, unexplained phenomenon. But no one was more surprised by the explanation that tied together these two observations than the discoverer himself, the Austrian zoologist Karl von Frisch.

Von Frisch had made his mark between the First and Second World Wars by proving that fish can hear, upsetting the received wisdom of the day. Then he demonstrated that honeybees have color vision. He was a terrific researcher, but he had studied these insects for many years before realizing what had been going on right under his nose, literally, all that time. Then again, his failure to see the truth is certainly understandable, because no one had any idea that bees or other insects—or any other animal—could possess such a system of communication. Color vision, okay, but the second most complex system of communication on this planet? To the astonishment of linguists, that's how von Frisch described the *Schwänzeltanz*, or "waggle dance," in 1946.

As is so often the case in science, serendipity played a major role in the discovery. Alas, the serendipitous event in this case was the Second World War. Prior to the war, von Frisch, a professor in Munich, had studied his honeybees the same way everyone else did, by placing food sources within a few steps of his hives, which he had outfitted with glass windows. It was only during the war, when his Munich laboratory was damaged by Allied bombing and he had to operate out of his country estate in the Austrian Tyrol, that von Frisch began to place food hundreds of yards away. Friends and students helped him tote his hives around that splendid countryside. They used—what else?—bells and cow horns to signal the arrival and departure of a subject bee, identified as such by the little daub of paint von Frisch managed to brush on a hovering insect. In Austria, von Frisch realized that the bees' agitated, buzzing behavior was much different when they were returning to the hive from a long distance than when they had dined just a few feet away. He and his students began a painstaking assessment of this behavior, and within a few years von Frisch was ready to publish his results and subject them to what he knew would be the harsh scrutiny of the scientific establishment.

Briefly put, von Frisch claimed that the agitated behavior of foraging bees returning from a significant distance was actually a carefully choreographed dance, described as the shape of a "figure 8" which has been flattened so that the two sections of the 8 meet not in a single point (as in the type used for this book) but in a line. You could also think of this flattened 8 as two ovals squashed against one another. Von Frisch labeled this line between the two ovals the "waggle run." He said that a returning bee positions his dance so that the angle between this "waggle run" line and the vertical axis of the honeycomb is the same as the angle between the food source and the position of the sun. If the waggle run is straight up, the food is directly in line with the sun; if the waggle run is straight down, the food is in the opposite direction from the sun; if the waggle run is 45 degrees right of vertical, the food is 45 degrees right of the sun; and so on around the compass. Furthermore, if one bee dances for an extended period in the hive, she compensates for the movement of the sun during that time by shifting the angle of her waggle run! What about the distance to the food source? After decades of further research, the means of designating distance are still not fully understood, but apparently this is achieved by some combination of the duration of the dance and other factors, including perhaps differences in the faint buzzing that accompanies the dance. But distance *is* conveyed, this we know, and every subspecies of honeybee around the world seems to have its own particular formula in this regard.

No wonder the world reacted with astonishment! (I don't exaggerate; von Frisch's report made news headlines everywhere.) This "dancing" explanation seems impossible, and it turns out to be only part of the story. Foraging bees do not normally dance following their flights outside the hive, but only dance if they have found an especially good source of food. How do they know this? The "house" bees in charge of unloading the nectar or pollen "tell" them, in effect, by the speed with which they do their own work.

Among the many bees competing to be unloaded, those with the richest nectar get the fastest service. Those with more ordinary fare to offer the hive have to wait and may even have to go find a storage cell on their own. (The house bees judge the quality of the nectar by the residue of the flower that clings to the hairs of the foraging bee. Von Frisch proved that bees are capable of discriminating between one test scent and at least 750 others.)

Any bee unloaded by the house bees within forty-five seconds of her return to the hive will usually dance. Bees who have to wait two minutes almost never dance. But this is not the end of the story either. The foraging bee also makes an independent assessment of the ease with which a source can be harvested, because only the foraging bee has this information. This assessment includes the distance factor. A good source several thousand yards from the hive is less likely to produce a dance than a lesser source only a hundred yards away. What's more, dancers directing other bees to distant sources stop dancing sooner than other foragers as dusk approaches, or during bad weather that would make flying hazardous. Incredible, but true. For their part, potential foragers who are reading the dance also seem to be making decisions. They don't necessarily fly off at the directions of the first dancer they encounter in the hive. And whether the hive needs nectar or pollen or water seems to be a factor in their decision.

I use the word "seems" because we don't know whether the bees' almost unbelievable behavior is in fact as goal-oriented as it "seems" to be. Von Frisch's work was challenged in the years to come by a host of commentators and researchers who suggested that the dance was really just some kind of cooling-off period after a long, hard foraging flight, and that information was conveyed by odor cues. They argued that von Frisch's claims for the directional and distance "value" of the waggle run was the figment of an overly active, hopeful, anthropomorphic imagination. Others, including Euan McPhail, are perfectly happy to concede that the dance is a means of conveying information, while denying that there is any conscious intention to do so. By way of provocation, McPhail adds, "The bees aren't intentionally communicating with each other any more than the flowers that attract the bees with their particular colors are communicating with the bees."

Setting aside the issue of interpretation, James Gould, one of the authors of *The Animal Mind*, happens to be one of today's leading researchers in this field, and his experiments are among the many that have subsequently proved that von Frisch was correct about the informative nature of the dance. (Von Frisch shared the Nobel Prize in 1973 with Konrad Lorenz and Niko Tinbergen.) Going back to "The Case of the Kidnapped Bee," it was among other things a clever scheme to trick foraging honeybees into conveying false information with their dances. They were thus recruiting bees to a feeding site that the forager had never been to. But within minutes of the dance, the targeted site, which had no food and no odor, was nevertheless swarming with bees. There is only one reasonable explanation for this result: These bees had heeded the instructions of the dance.

In another experiment, the Goulds trained a number of bees to fly to a feeding source on a rowboat in the middle of a lake. Initially they kept the quality of this nectar low, so that the bees would not dance when they returned to the hive. When the bees were considered thoroughly trained to come to this site, the quality of the nectar was increased, and the bees immediately responded in kind by dancing vigorously on their return to the hive. But here's the key question: Would the other foraging bees follow the directions to the middle of a lake, where there could not be any food, at least not in the "real world"? Or would they ignore the dance? They ignored the dance— at first. But over a period of time, as the Goulds positioned their boat closer and closer to shore, more and more bees heeded the increasingly plausible directions of the dance.

Totally remarkable.

A robot bee has recently been invented, which the Goulds describe as a "computer-directed collection of wood, tubing, and razor blades." This bogus bee has had some success in directing real bees to selected sites, opening up the possibility of a whole new set of experiments with very tight controls. It is important to note that the bees' dance is not a perfect system of communication. Recruited bees fly out of the hive in the right direction, plus or minus 15 or 20 degrees, and arrive at the right distance plus or minus 10 to 15 percent. Nevertheless, James Gould and Carol Grant Gould estimate that this simple dancing scheme can pinpoint with sufficient accuracy about a billion possible feeding sites outside the hive.

The success of the robotic bee, however, brings up the obvious problem in attributing conscious communication or language to the honeybees. How smart can the bees be if they're fooled by this mechanical device? Well, it is certainly correct that the dancing of the bees and the ability to interpret the dance is innate. Bees reared in complete isolation are perfectly good dancers. But as the Goulds argue, affirming the reasoning of Donald Griffin, who makes the same point in all of his writing, "the presence of an automatic or relatively simple response to a problem does not, in and of itself, prove that a creature is limited to that cognitive level. More challenging circumstances may bring out other strategies that call more of the creature's intellect into play." They then add, "We now know that much of the more flexible behavior that appears later in an animal's life is built upon patterns of analysis and response. . . . Being able to distinguish between the pragmatic programming success of natural selection and genuinely intelligent behavior . . . is essential to understanding the animal mind. . . . However, this distinction is often difficult or impossible to make."

Donald Griffin brings up yet another tantalizing, related question when he writes that the dance, and the interpretation of the dance in the hive, "sounds like rather complex behavior for genetically programmed robots." In recent years, researchers have learned that swarming honeybees also dance to indicate information about a possible new home, communication that is just as complex as the dance for food. It turns out that weaver ants have a system of head wags to direct their fellows to an odor trail that will lead to food sources, and a different set of gestures, when the entire body is jerked backward and forward, that indicate intruders in the nest.

If we think about the beehive and the ant bed as they relate to the law of parsimony and Morgan's Canon, we have to acknowledge the role of instinct in the social insects, but we also have to question whether this instinctive behavior might be too complex to issue from the nervous system in question. These insect species have simple neurological networks. Are there enough neurons, literally, with which to hardwire all the detailed behaviors for Plan A, Plan B, Plan C—all the plans that these social insects exhibit and require? As Griffin points out, the ability to move beyond instinct, to make simple decisions, perhaps generalizations, might be adaptively efficient and beneficial, given a certain level of complexity.

Meanwhile, the doubters still doubt the capacity of any insect or other animal for symbolic communication—a philosophical position, in effect. As Irene Pepperberg wrote in her essay in *Cognitive Ethology*, "By the mid-1970s, it appeared as though 'language' was to be defined as that part of human communication that animals were incapable of achieving." The entomologist E. O. Wilson said this explicitly in *Sociobiology* (the abridged edition): "With our own unique verbal system as a standard of reference we can define the limits of animal communication in terms of the properties it rarely—or never—displays." In short, critics of cognitive ethology seem interested only in what animal communication is not: human language.

The cave paintings at such places as Altamira in northern Spain and Lascaux in southern France are the oldest surviving examples of visual art. The fact that they depict mainly animals—such as this bison—shows what a crucial role they have played in human society from the very beginning.

Donald R. Griffin, the American scientist most responsible for the increasing acceptance of cognitive ethology as a valid subject for scientific inquiry. He proved that bats navigate by what he called "echolocation."

The famous Clever Hans with his owner, Wilhelm von Osten.

The honeybee, whose tiny brain consists of only 800,000 cells, is capable of extraordinary feats of navigation. And using the famous "waggle dance," a foraging bee can communicate the precise location of food sources to other members of the hive.

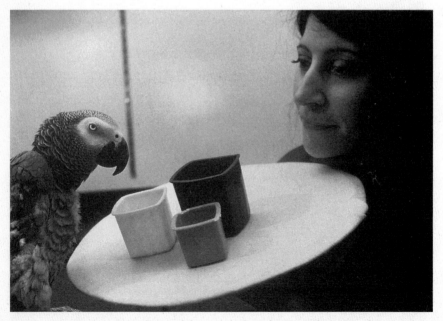

Dr. Irene Pepperberg with her parrot Alex, who, among his many other accomplishments, can tell her how many objects he sees.

TOP: Chimpanzees using sticks to extract termites—
a delicacy to them—from a big termite mound. Many
scientists did not believe Jane Goodall when she
reported this "tool use" by apes.

ABOVE: This raven may be thinking of a fish dinner.
Ravens in Sweden and Vermont learned to steal hooked
fish when ice fishermen left their baited lines
unattended on the ice.

RIGHT: Dr. Nicholas Dodman, the "pet psychiatrist," with
his patient Tasher, a neurotic cockatoo.

A beaver repairing its dam. Perhaps the grand prize winner of the animal kingdom when it comes to intelligent problem solving.

Temple Grandin, professor of animal sciences at Colorado State University, says she can think like a cow—in pictures. About half the cattle led to slaughter in North America spend their final hours in humane facilities designed by Grandin.

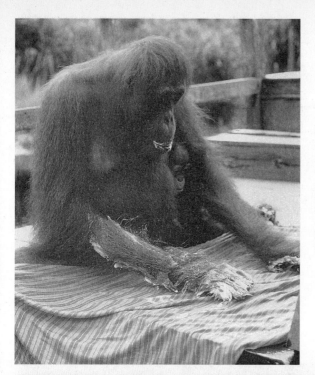

This orangutan at the Camp Leakey Research Center in Borneo seems to enjoy joining in to do the daily laundry. She soaps and rinses clothing enthusiastically, using techniques she has learned purely from observation.

Chimpanzees use tools extensively and teach their babies how to do it. This one has improvised a perfectly acceptable nutcracker!

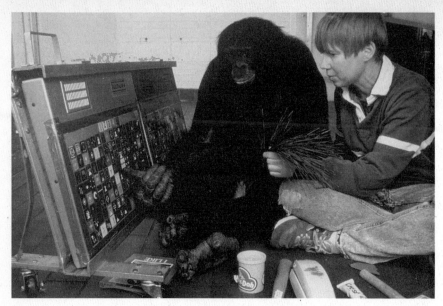

Kanzi, perhaps the world's most famous bonobo chimp,
at the Language Research Center in Atlanta.

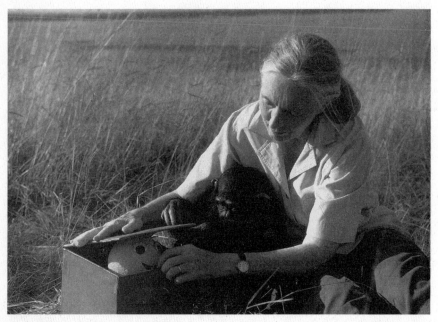

Jane Goodall's work with chimpanzees has been crucial to our understanding
of great ape behavior and intelligence. She campaigns fearlessly and effectively for the
chimp's right not to be separated from family and friends, caged, and tortured.

The desert elephants of Namibia must traverse vast areas of trackless desert to find
water holes hidden under the sand. They pass the locations of the
"secret water holes" from generation to generation.

Researcher Cynthia Moss was once
"trapped" in her Land Rover by a group
of young African elephants. "They flapped
their ears, shook their heads, and made
mock charges at me. I could only laugh
at them, it was so obvious they were not
serious." Moss writes about the need
for young elephants to play.

In Kenya, elephants gently examine the remains of one of their own.
"Although they pay no attention to the remains of other species, they always
react to the body of a dead elephant," writes Cynthia Moss.

The bonobo, our closest relative in the animal kingdom,
shares 98.7 percent of our human genetic material.

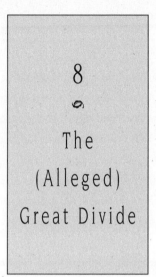

8

The
(Alleged)
Great Divide

TWO VIEWS

Is there any continuity between animal communication and human language, or are we confronted with an unbridgeable divide? Thinkers throughout the ages have been . . . well, divided. Aristotle found grounds for believing that there is a great deal of continuity up and down The Great Chain of Being. I cite this passage from *Historia Animalium:*

> in a number of animals we observe gentleness or fierceness, mildness or cross temper, courage or timidity, fear or confidence, high spirit or low cunning, and, with regard to intelligence, something akin to sagacity. Some of these qualities in man . . . differ only quantitatively. . . . For instance, just

as in man we find knowledge, wisdom, and sagacity, so in certain animals there exists some other natural potentiality akin to these.

But Aristotle drew the line at language and so arrived at his belief that we are the only rational animals. Descartes also drew the line at language. Darwin disagreed and saw continuity, of course, writing in *The Descent of Man*, "The difference in mind between man and the higher animals, great as it is, certainly is one of degree and not of kind." And supporting continuity, Jean Piaget argued that language is a "particular aspect of the general capacity for representation." Drawing is another aspect of representation; gesturing is yet another.

Certainly all species with anything like a nervous system operate pretty much the same at the cellular level. The differences between species are those of organization—and even organization is quite similar in closely related species—and sheer size of the brain. And yet, as Darwin observes, the difference between animal communication and ours is *so* great. Without any question, language is the defining aspect of our human identity, of who we are, what we think, and what we do. Many of us probably think of the chimpanzee in rough-and-ready terms as having a humanlike mind, "minus the spoken language." But this qualifying phrase may be crucial. Can we really imagine consciousness without language? It is difficult, but is it impossible? How do animals without language do anything that we would consider "thinking"? We just don't know. Many of us believe they do think, but it's impossible to picture the experience precisely, because by this point in our own natural history, everything we think of as part of consciousness has become embedded in language.

Is it possible that within evolutionary continuity "something happened" that pushed us humans across some kind of awesome

threshold? Do we humans have so much excess capacity in the fron-
tal lobe that the difference in degree becomes a difference in kind?
The stakes are high. As Donald Griffin points out, the only conceivable excuse we could have for denying consciousness to the great
apes and the cetaceans is on the basis of language. This "We have it,
they don't" declaration is precisely the position of Noam Chomsky
most famously, but also of many other linguists and philosophers
who argue that human language is *sui generis*, the product of a
uniquely human "language organ." Without language, Chomsky argues, the "smartest" animal may be capable of impressive accomplishments, but not true thinking. Nor consciousness, suggests Euan
McPhail. Animal communication is deemed as basically nothing more
than a series of possibly sophisticated signals.

I go along with the philosopher Daniel Dennett, who completely
agrees with Chomsky that language is indeed the *pièce de résistance* of
life on earth, the *sine qua non* of the highest reaches of consciousness.
But, Dennett argues, and the cognitive ethologists agree, the fact that
we might not be able to construe the workings of, say, a vervet monkey's brain as "thoughts," as we understand them, does not mean the
monkey is not thinking, and the fact that the vervet's system of cries
and grunts is not human language does not necessarily mean it's not
thoughtful communication. The animal may be thinking differently
with what amounts to a different language in a completely different
Umwelt, and we would make a mistake by expecting it to answer *our*
questions in *our* language.

APE LANGUAGE RESEARCH

The main battleground for this debate about the ultimate sanctity of
human language is ALR—Ape Language Research. It is on this
ground that the answers will be revealed in due course. The system-

atic effort to teach apes some kind of language goes back about seventy years, when A. W. Yerkes—the primatologist for whom the famous Yerkes Regional Primate Center in Atlanta, Georgia, is named—voiced the suspicion that apes had the ability to learn a gestural system. (Actually, the seventeenth-century English diarist Samuel Pepys might have been the very first observer with such hopes. He wrote in his diary entry for 24 August 1661, after seeing an ape in London, "I do believe it already understands much English; and I am of the mind it might be taught to speak"—about this Pepys was wrong—"or make signs"—about which he was right.)

In the last few decades, Vicki, Washoe, Nim, Koko, Sarah, Kanzi, Panbanisha, and a few others all have become simian celebrities. Vicki was the chimpanzee who learned a few vocal words of English in the early fifties, but that was all, and for good reason: Apes' "phonatory apparatus"—vocal cords, mainly—is poorly adapted for the purpose. When this fact of life became understood, attention shifted to the teaching of American Sign Language, ASL. Washoe and Nim, chimpanzees, and Koko, a gorilla, all were trained in ASL. Then Sarah, a chimp, was taught to manipulate symbolic plastic chips as her "words," and Kanzi and Panbanisha, two bonobos, were trained on a computer-based lexigram.

Today there is no question that a well-educated ape can learn and employ a large set of either sign-language gestures or another kind of symbol, and no question that he or she can tie them together into what are generally called "strings," in order to distinguish these sequences from grammatical sentences. Such a string might consist of the gestures for "apple/me/give/quickly." However, the interpretation of exactly what the apes are "saying" seems to be in the eye of the beholder. There are believers and there are nonbelievers. As I read the literature, the belief tends to drive the interpretation, as it so often does in many aspects of life. Those who are anxious, for whatever reason, to believe that the "language" skill is continuous between apes and humans see something beyond straightforward "communication" when they interpret this work. They see rudimentary syntax and understanding of the abstract nature of a word. They interpret the string about apples as a genuine grammatical request for an apple. Washoe made news around the world when she spontaneously signed the symbols for "water" and "bird" upon first seeing a swan, and her supporters claimed she had coined a new word for her vocabulary.

At least one trainer made no apology for her anthropomorphic modus operandi. Penny Patterson worked with the gorilla Koko in the most homelike setting she could devise and established as close to a parent-child relationship as she could between herself and her female gorilla. Patterson claimed that Koko had an IQ of 85 to 95 as measured on the Stanford-Binet test and a working vocabulary of five hundred signs, with another five hundred signs used occasionally. Patterson made no attempt to interpret Koko's signing through the cold eyes of the scientist, but rather through the warm eyes of the caregiver. Needless to say, her work was highly controversial within primatology, though there's no denying that Koko did sign a great deal and carry on "bilingual" conversations in which she responded to spoken phrases with sign language.

Critics of all these projects see intentional or unwitting cuing, as in the infamous Clever Hans episode, or mimicry, or straightforward "associative labeling." They point out that many signing "sentences" may actually mean, to the animal, "If I do this, then I get an apple." They point out that almost all signing by the apes is restricted to official training sessions, with not much impromptu use of the symbols; that an inordinate number of the signs and strings consist of requests for food; that any mistake is rationalized as a "novel meaning." (For example, Washoe used the sign for "flower" in reference to smoke. Did this indicate that for her "flower" meant smells, which is plausible, or that she had no idea what "flower" meant to her, because it didn't "mean" anything to her?) The doubters interpret the "apple string" as not much more clever than a dog's scratching on the pantry door behind which she has learned the kibble is stored: clever communication, but not language. And Washoe wasn't making up a new word. She was signing for "water" and then for "bird," that's all, and the same goes for other reported neologisms of other apes, such as "metal/hot" for a cigarette lighter, "listen/drink" for Alka-Seltzer, and "candy/drink" for watermelon.

In several sources I read about the following sentence from Nim:

"Give/orange/me/give/eat/orange/give/me/eat/orange/give/me/ you."

Here, the critics argue, is proof positive of what the apes are really doing: signing anything and everything they know in order to get something to eat, and in the process enticing their trainers into anthropomorphic overinterpretation. Therefore, said one of their more prominent leaders, the linguist Thomas Sebeok, turning the usual understanding on its head, "Facts do not convince me. Theories do." In the 1970s, one major researcher, Herbert Terrace, the trainer of Nim (short for Noam Chomsky), cried uncle and announced that he had been mistaken all along. He had now decided that the apes, including Nim, were not learning anything amounting to "language." What had seemed in person like thoughtful signings by Nim looked like rote gestures when viewed objectively on videotape.

In an article about the dance of the honeybees, James Gould wrote, "Especially in ethology, it is difficult to avoid the unprofitable extremes of blinding skepticism and crippling romanticism." This observation is doubly true for Ape Language Research. Looking back at the carnage of the last several decades, Donald Griffin believes that all the criticism was beneficial, because it helped researchers tighten their experimental protocols and controls. Penny Patterson's radical anthropomorphizing became still more marginalized, even as researchers came to acknowledge that the whole basis of language training is to anthropomorphize the ape by trying to induce him or her to see and relate to the world as we do, and to "talk" about it as we do. H. Lyn Miles, a professor of anthropology at the University of Tennessee and a language researcher herself who works with the orangutan Chantek, writes in *Anthropomorphism, Anecdotes, and Animals*, "How can you raise an ape in a human environment, provide human experiences and encourage human behavior, such as language acquisition or comprehension, to make the ape more humanlike, and then succeed in being nonanthropomorphic in your interpretations?"

Miles is right. It is impossible. As it happens, a great deal of research has been directed at comparing prelinguistic communication in human and chimpanzee infants, communication that is wholly dependent on the relationship with the mother. We should not be surprised to learn that there is a world of difference between the two relationships. The mother-child relationship among humans is much more visually oriented than it is in apes, where the contact is more exclusively tactile. There is much less of a teaching relationship between the apes. (However, Washoe's stepson Loulis picked up fifty signs from his stepmother, and only from his stepmother, because no signing was conducted directly with Loulis by humans.) Ape infants interact with human caregivers in a more "human" way than they react with their mothers—and we *interpret* this interaction in a more "human" way. How could we not? Miles adds, "The researcher may not intentionally distort the situation, but the situation itself makes it possible to use more anthropomorphic language when reporting it." She asserts that the best we can hope for is a "pragmatic anthropomorphism"—the idea we have encountered earlier, a variant on Griffin's "critical anthropomorphism." Some anthropomorphism is inevitable, by definition. We should accept this and account for it in our interpretations.

As the debate raged on, David Premack concluded that the inherent subjectivity associated with interpreting sign language could be avoided by using instead symbolic plastic markers of varying size and color. This was how he trained the chimpanzee Sarah, who eventually learned three basic categories of "words"—objects such as "apple," qualifiers such as "red," and actions such as "give"—and also a fourth category, "conditionals" such as "same," "different," and "if-then" (These are the same basic categories that Alex the parrot was taught by Irene Pepperberg.) If a blue chip stood for a red object, Sarah nevertheless identified the object as red. She understood the symbolism. Sarah knew that half an apple stood in a "same as" relationship with a half-filled container of liquid. She understood that "open" could be used in conjunction with a can of food or a box of toys. These tests proved that Sarah had incorporated a level of abstractness in her understanding of what she was doing. This had been difficult if not impossible to demonstrate with the sign-language approach, but with Premack's protocols and controls, it was difficult to deny.

Eventually Sarah understood the difference between these two strings:

If/Sarah/take/apple/then/Mary/give/Sarah/chocolate

If/Sarah/take/banana/then/Mary/no/give/Sarah/chocolate

KANZI

One day many years ago, Sue Savage-Rumbaugh saw a chimp perform a 360-degree flip at the top of his enclosure. Neat trick, she noted, and without really thinking she then made a little loop with her finger. The chimp had never seen this gesture, to her knowledge, yet he immediately understood her request that he do another flip. Savage-Rumbaugh writes in *Kanzi*, "I was so taken aback by the alacrity with which he understood what I meant that I simply stood there, rooted in place, staring at him transfixed."

That moment led to the work that eventually placed the bonobo Kanzi at the forefront of the ALR debate. First, however, Savage-Rumbaugh had to reconcile her own doubts on the subject. In her early years working with primates at the University of Oklahoma, she became known among her colleagues as "the unbeliever." Like Herbert Terrace, she had grave doubts about what was really going on, even though she was impressed by David Premack's work with Sarah and the plastic "words." She wondered whether the whole approach of her predecessors might be misguided. These women and men had concentrated on training their charges to produce words. She decided that *comprehension*, not production, was the key cognitive ingredient in language acquisition. But it was precisely the animal's comprehension about which she harbored such doubts. Asked a question such as "What would you like to do?" most primates in the studies she knew would sign more or less at random.

"Do apes have language?" is the wrong question, Savage-Rumbaugh decided. "Do apes understand words?" is a better one. For her part, she would focus on understanding what a word meant to her subjects, not on their ability to produce "strings." Could an ape talk about "banana" in some context other than requesting a banana for lunch? As she writes in *Kanzi*, "It is not obvious that this distinction has been seriously dealt with by other ape-language researchers." And perhaps the best way of all to find out about true understanding would be to determine whether one ape could tell another ape something it did not know. (Here we recognize Donald Griffin's insight that communication within a species is the best possible window on thought and consciousness.)

In short, Savage-Rumbaugh decided to start fresh with the chimpanzees Austin and Sherman at the Language Research Center at Georgia State University in Atlanta. Convinced of the importance of embedding teaching in social situations, as it is with human children, she set out to establish a middle ground between a controlled and an "enculturated" setting: pragmatic anthropomorphism. And she would use a system of lexigrams, following in the footsteps of David Premack and his use of plastic chips. It is important to understand that these lexigrams were not representative icons. Each shape was completely abstract and arbitrary. Moreover, the location of the lexigrams on the panel was shifted after each work session, to assure that Austin and Sherman were learning the symbols and not their location on the board.

As always, the work was time-consuming and frustrating. Whatever apes are learning, they are not doing so at nearly the rate of children. On average, they learn a few words a month, while children can learn dozens of new words a day. With Sherman and Austin, a pattern set in: frustration followed by the proverbial light going on. The favorite example of most of the commentators I've read is the situation in which one of the two chimps was shown food being deposited by a trainer in one of several containers, while the other chimp was in control of the tools for opening those containers—one tool per container. Without the keyboard, the two passed the correct tool at no better than a chance rate. With the keyboard, would Austin, say, who had seen the food placed in the box, sign to Sherman for the correct tool? Yes. Would Sherman understand the request and pass that tool to Austin? Yes. But, again, this comprehension did not come immediately. When one of the apes was frustrated by the other's failure to get it right, he would gesture through the window, try to get his partner to concentrate on the keyboard, and repeatedly hit the request button on his own keyboard.

After many weeks of training, "the light went on," and when it did, the two chimps incorporated this use of lexigrams into their daily lives. To all appearances, they were soon playing games with each other via their personal keyboards. This should be no surprise, because as I stated earlier, the use of tools (words are tools par excellence) not only identifies but confers intelligence. For the same reason, it shouldn't be any surprise that chimps who have had language training do much better than chimps without this instruction on the abstract-reasoning problems such as "key" is to "lock" as "screwdriver" is to "paint can." Animals with language training understand the "conservation" test involving glasses of water almost immediately.

In 1980, in the middle of Savage-Rumbaugh's work with Austin and Sherman, B. F. Skinner and associates published what amounted to a parody of her work, featuring two pigeons named Jack and Jill, whom the Skinner team had trained to mimic Austin and Sherman's performance in certain narrow circumstances. By definition, these behaviorists could not countenance the "intentionality" Savage-Rumbaugh was proposing for her two chimps, but she knew that neither of Skinner's two pigeons would have been able to use the label from the peanut-butter jar, spied lying on the floor, to signal the other one about a meal, and to do so spontaneously. That was the level of intentionality and abstraction Austin and Sherman were demonstrating.

That was also the level that Kanzi would surpass. Kanzi is a bonobo, a "pygmy chimpanzee," which happens to be a very misleading phrase. (Bonobos are about the same size as chimps, but with longer arms and legs; also, they stand upright.) These are by far the least studied of the great apes, but they may well be the most intelligent. In their native habitat in central Zaire (their *only* native habitat), they are much quicker to pick up nuances of human expression than chimps are. They are much more vocal in the wild than the other great apes. They look at each other and at humans with a very level, considered gaze. As everyone who has ever observed them agrees, it is almost impossible not to anthropomorphize regarding their emotions and behavior, even more so than with chimps. Frans de Waal writes in his book about bonobos, "Whatever the implications for language, it is impossible not to be struck by Kanzi's obvious intelligence." It is impossible to look at the picture of this animal on the cover of Savage-Rumbaugh's two books and not think of him in terms of his intelligence. (*Kanzi: The Ape at the Brink of the Human Mind* was published in 1994. *Apes, Language, and the Human Mind*, a more academic book co-authored by a philosopher and a linguist, was published in 1998.)

Kanzi was not the first of the great apes to be tutored with a system of lexigrams, but he was the first who used the system spontaneously, after growing up in the company of his adoptive mother, Matata, who was learning lexigrams. Without any human prompting, Kanzi became adept at working with the symbols. With Kanzi (and with Austin and Sherman, for that matter), hitting the correct button when shown an apple would not be nearly enough to count as genuine comprehension. They would have to use the lexigram for "apple" in the absence of an apple, and they would have to use the word to convey information to a third party.

Kanzi also does extremely well with vocalized words—even when heard over earphones, in testing situations, so there is no chance of inadvertent cuing. Not only can he pick up specified objects, he can follow simple spoken directions such as "Put the ball in the bowl" or "Carry the bowl to the refrigerator." In her book, Savage-Rumbaugh details the laborious process she and her associates followed while working with Kanzi. In one study, 13,691 utterances with a vocabulary of about a hundred "words," generated over one five-month period in 1986, were studied one by one. After nine years of working with Austin, Sherman, and Kanzi with the lexigram keyboards, Savage-Rumbaugh wrote an academic paper for publication. It was turned down by the major journals. One cited "over-enthusiastic over-interpretation." Finally, however, the paper was published in a volume of "conference papers," and immediately it received wide publicity.

Many observers believe that Kanzi and the other apes are indeed exhibiting a "protogrammar" of limited means, roughly equivalent to the development of a two-and-a-half-year-old infant human, and that they do give solid evidence of being able to communicate simple thoughts, desires, and even intentions.

To my mind, the most recent work with the apes demonstrates clearly that they are not just "signaling" in clever ways. They are, by necessity, working with simple ideas. But is this enough? Certainly not for those critics who maintain that nothing short of full-fledged human language counts as any kind of thoughtful or conscious communication. In the effort to defend human "specialness"—and our language *is* special, there's no debate about that—they denigrate the now well-established and extraordinary abilities the apes do have.

THE REAL TEST IS THE REAL WORLD

Frans de Waal has mixed feelings about language research with the great apes. On the one hand, he writes, "The apes in these studies are so well attuned to people, so willing to interact, so used to the way we relate to our surroundings, that all sorts of questions can be addressed that are impossible to answer with apes who view us as strangers with strange habits. . . . Kanzi's flint-making is an example of an experiment that might not have worked with an untrained subject."

On the other hand, de Waal has concerns not with the anthropomorphism but with the anthropo*centrism* of the whole Ape Language Research enterprise, with the approach that says, "Let's see how much like us they are." De Waal believes we might learn more about the primates by studying their communication with each other in the wild, not with human trainers in the lab. In *Bonobo: The Forgotten Ape*, he writes, "Kanzi's wild counterparts wear no earphones, yet they may well listen more carefully to one another than we dare assume." He wonders whether Kanzi's "striking command [of spoken English] may actually be better understood in terms of social cognition." In the wild, bonobos engage in complicated, rapid-fire exchanges, back and back, back and forth, especially during aggressive confrontations—which are relatively rare, by the way, especially when compared with chimpanzees. (As de Waal writes elsewhere, chimps resolve sexual issues with power; bonobos resolve power issues with sex. It is no exaggeration to say that sex manifested in almost every conceivable way is the social glue for this species. The authors of the *Kama Sutra* have nothing to teach bonobos.)

De Waal describes these vocal confrontations:

> They seem to be trading information about emotions and intentions. The calls are quite variable. . . . A spectrographic analysis . . . indicated that they changed in quality over the course of the encounter but remained similar to each other (a process known as vocal matching), as if the two males gradually converged on a solution to their predicament. . . . I hold it possible that what chimpanzees do by means of visual displays of strength and determination, bonobos do by means of a more "languagelike" exchange of information about internal states. It is not that they are talking the issue over, but there is a certain dialectic and coordinated quality to their vocal contests that is absent in the chimpanzee.

Just as the bonobos will never understand our language in all its richness, so we will never completely understand theirs, in all its richness. Cheney and Seyfarth's research with the vervet monkeys uncovered an array of vocalized communication beyond the alarm calls we've already considered. Vervet mothers recognize the vocalizations of their offspring, and they recognize also the vocalizations of the offspring of other specific mothers. A complex set of grunts is a vital social lubricant among the vervets. Cheney and Seyfarth have pinpointed four of these grunts, each used in narrowly defined situations. They write, "When a monkey hears a grunt, he is immediately informed of many of the fine details of the social behavior going on, even though he may be out of sight of the vocalizer. . . ." Reviewing this research, Donald Griffin writes, "Although these experiments do not indicate just what meaning the grunts conveyed, they do show that they were not interchangeable."

Similar experiments have confirmed such purposes among other primates: one kind of cry when meeting family members, another when meeting a highly ranked individual in the troop, and so on. The wedge-capped capuchins of Venezuela combine their calls into pairs, triplets, and quadruplets, which seem to reflect "intermediate" emotional states. It seems quite likely that they make similar discriminations among foods. Cheney and Seyfarth write in conclusion, "The vocal repertoires of non-human primates, when assessed by the animals themselves, are far larger than scientists initially perceived them to be. . . . Primates make subtle acoustic discriminations when distinguishing between calls." The key words in that statement are "when assessed by the animals themselves." It seems likely that all sorts of communication are being transacted among animals, almost always without our knowledge and understanding. Elephants communicate with infrasound (extremely low sound waves beneath our range of hearing), but we didn't learn this until 1983. We are only beginning to understand the significance of chemical communication with pheromones and other molecules between human beings. As Donald Griffin said to me, "Who knows what thoughts and feelings are being communicated and exchanged in the chemical domain?"

The most intriguing story I know of that illustrates the mysteries of animal communication comes from Cheney and Seyfarth, who in turn are reporting a study by Emil Menzel, in which this pioneer introduced one of six young chimpanzees into an outdoor enclosure and showed him either a hidden source of food or a stuffed snake.

This chimp, called the leader, was then reunited with his fellows outside the enclosure, and there was no indication whatsoever that the leader had communicated his important knowledge of the situation to the other chimps. Mainly they played and wrestled in the manner of all young chimpanzees. Nevertheless, the moment this gang of six was allowed into the enclosure, they headed straight for the food, if this was a "food" experiment. They knew not only that there was food but where it was, and sometimes the other five chimps preceded the leader who had the direct knowledge. If this was a "snake" test, the group emerged into the enclosure with "piloerected fur" (a technical term, I guess, but we get the picture) and approached the danger zone with extreme caution, sticks at the ready.

This experiment strikes me as so amazing I'm surprised I didn't read about it more often. According to the school of thought that debunks thoughtful communication among animals, any kind of communication outside that enclosure about specific facts inside the enclosure is probably impossible. But those chimps do communicate, even if we never learn how they do.

One final, somewhat technical, thought on this issue. Donald Griffin and others have pointed out that English and German are two of the very few human languages in which word order is the key element of syntax, but much of the work in linguistics has been done by native speakers of these two languages. Could this be the reason such emphasis has been placed on syntactical rules as key elements required of any purported animal language? The vast majority of the thousands of languages around the world are "inflected" languages, in which word endings or different word forms are the dominant element in revealing syntactical meaning. ("He," "his," and "him" are vestiges of inflected use in English.) Could Kanzi and the other primates be taught even better with some kind of inflected language? Could we be asking our questions in a more effective way?

DOLPHINS ET AL.

Dolphins have brains that are considerably larger than those of the great apes. We should, therefore, expect them to exhibit real talent in the language area, and they do. In *Nature*'s animal-minds television series, we follow the work in progress conducted in Hawaii by Lou Herman and his associates with bottlenose dolphins. Herman's dolphins understand the all-important difference between "Take the Frisbee to the surfboard" and "Take the surfboard to the Frisbee." They have no problem with "right water, left basket, fetch" (which means "Take the basket on your left to the stream of water on your right") and "left water, right basket, fetch."

A traditional complaint leveled at language experiments with all animals has been the charge that almost all the training involves "imperative" sentences, in which the animal is instructed to do something, or, in the case of the apes, instructs the trainer to do something (provide food, mainly). This complaint was addressed and answered in the work with Kanzi, and it is also addressed in the work with these dolphins, who carry out instructions without complaint, but also answer questions.

"Is there a ball in the tank?" The dolphins answer by pressing one of two paddles, which mean, depending on the experiment, "yes/present" or "no/absent." They have little trouble with these tests. A no answer to the question about the ball proves that the animal both understands the nature of the question and holds in his mind a mental picture of a ball. One day Herman instructed the dolphin "hoop, Frisbee, fetch," but there was no hoop in the pool at the time. Herman expected a no response, but the dolphin elaborated on that response, in a way, by fetching the Frisbee and taking it to the no paddle. Herman paused for a moment and then agreed, "Yeah, that's right." The dolphins respond successfully to novel sentences. One of Herman's more adept animals, Phoenix, scored at a rate of 71 to 87 percent on sentences of two or three "words," and 60 to 68 percent on sentences with three to five "words." (When considering these scores, remember that the chance rate is very much less than 50 percent, since the dolphins have a large variety of actions to choose from.)

All the marine mammals—including whales, sea lions, and otters—have relatively large brains. Those with which such work is practical, including some of the smaller whales, have been the subject of language studies, and all have given evidence of comprehension roughly on a level with the great apes'. One of the more successful set of lessons was conducted with the California sea lions Rocky, Bucky, and Gertie. After two years, the female Rocky, who received the most intensive training, comprehended ten signs for objects, five for modifiers of color and size, and five for actions, such as touching and placing. Twenty signs altogether, with which Rocky correctly responded to 190 different combinations.

It has been pointed out that the sea lions and the dolphins could perform well on these tests by following just two basic rules. "So what?" Donald Griffin asks. Following those two rules might still require genuine thinking. The fact that they and the great apes can follow any syntactical rules at all overthrows centuries of ingrained prejudice that they are not capable of any use of language whatsoever. Griffin writes:

Two is significantly greater than zero. Furthermore, if dolphins and sea lions think in terms of these rules, they must be capable of thinking in correspondingly complex terms about the relationships between the signals and the actions or objects for which they stand. It would be unwise to allow our preoccupation with the quantitatively unique capabilities of human language to obscure the fact that these experiments reveal at least part of what the dolphins were thinking.

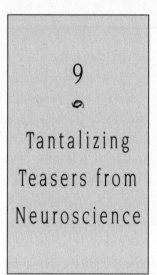

9

Tantalizing
Teasers from
Neuroscience

MIND OR BRAIN OR BOTH OR NEITHER

I have no idea what "mind" really is, and I don't believe anyone else
does either, but I do know what the brain is (unlike Aristotle, who
believed it was the organ that cooled the body's circulating blood).
Somehow thinking and emotion and consciousness are caused, or
mediated in some way, by the chemical and electrical activity within
the brain and the central nervous system. Or maybe consciousness is
nothing but this chemical and electrical activity. That could be, according to a lot of modern researchers, for whom Cartesian "dual-
ism," as it became known, is totally out of the question. There is a
school of thought that mind must be some kind of "epiphenomenon"
that somehow results from the activity of our brains and has no subsequent influence on behavior. It is a state of the nervous system,

that's all, an "emergent property" or an "intervening variable." I've read about these three concepts, and I assume dozens of others are batted around in the ivory tower. All I know is that no philosophy in the world can erase the fact that it definitely feels like something to walk around with this "epiphenomenon" in my brain.

I wonder whether there's not a worthwhile analogy with the famous wave-particle duality in particle physics and quantum mechanics. Looked at in one kind of experiment, a photon of light behaves like a wave. Looked at in another, it behaves like a particle. The two explanations seem to be mutually exclusive, but there's no getting around or unifying the experimental results. Physicists have decided to accept this duality as a mysterious fact of their lives (if not of our lives), and to move on to other problems. Couldn't the same perspective be valuable in the mind-body problem? In *Mind Matters*, Michael Gazzaniga, president of the Cognitive Neuroscience Institute, makes just such a suggestion. He thinks of the mind as the "interpretive" state and the brain as the "fluctuating physical-chemical state," and one is just as real as the other.

In any event, cognitive ethologist Donald Griffin explicitly states that the defense of consciousness for animals does not require the defense of an ineffable, nonphysical "mind." Brains can be conscious, too; brains can have emotions, too. As I've stated, one of the three main pillars of cognitive ethology, in Griffin's mind, is the evidence from the neurosciences. So let's talk about brains and chemicals for the rest of this chapter.

NOT A LOT OF DIFFERENCES

I must admit I didn't understand a great deal of Jeffrey Camhi's textbook *Neuroethology*, but I did catch these two sentences, which I take to be a conclusion of much of the research reported in the book: "It is clear that all animals face similar behavioral problems, such as obtaining mates, food, and shelter and avoiding predation. Moreover, the neuron signals in the brain that produce behavior appear to be nearly identical in all animals." Even at a higher level of structure, the activity in another mammal's brain and in mine is just about the same, when each of us is engaged in similar mental or emotional "behavior." The latest and most detailed experiments using EEGs and ERPs and PET scans and all the other amazing tools are on the way to demonstrating this.

In the *Nature* series about animal minds, we observe the high level of activity in the hippocampus of the London cabbie as he sees in his mind's eye a particular route through the city; the hippocampus of the lab rat is also the most active part of its brain when it is consulting its own mental map of the radial maze. Experiments show that damage to the hippocampus in any species has harmful effects on whatever spatial-memory abilities that particular animal does happen to have. For example, lesions in the hippocampus of black-capped chickadees (this organ in seed-storing birds is about twice as large as that of other birds) do not disrupt food-storage activity or color memory, but they do reduce the accuracy of retrieval. The birds' mental maps are damaged. Homing pigeons with analogous lesions orient themselves homeward initially without problem—but then they never get home!

After reviewing the highly technical literature in the field, Donald Griffin writes, "The behaviorist interpretation of such data is simply that the experiments have monitored electrical activity correlated with information processing, but that this tells us absolutely nothing about . . . conscious thinking." Nothing is proved, and Griffin doesn't claim it is. His point is that similarities of animal and human brain activity certainly do not diminish the possibility of comparable conscious thinking and emotional life. The neurological similarity is reason enough to take the idea seriously.

Here are two other reasons. In human beings, the left hemisphere is mainly responsible for language, nor is it coincidental that most of us are right-handed, because the right hand is controlled by the left side of the brain. This correlation between the use of tools, the language faculty, and the brain's now famous left-brain/right-brain lateralization has been considered uniquely human. It is sometimes cited as proof of the "We have it, they don't" boast regarding human language. But this assumption of unique lateralization may well prove to be incorrect. Intrigued by the studies reported in the previous chapter about the important role that subtle changes in alarm calls, food calls, and other vocalizations play in primate communities, neuroscientists have conducted experiments to determine whether primates also exhibit left- and right-brain biases. These studies do find tentative evidence of lateralization. Most primates turn out to be right-handed.

REM (rapid eye movement) sleep is implicated in human dreaming. Now we know that most if not all warm-blooded animals also have REM sleep. (If invertebrates dream, we will never know by analysis of REM sleep, because their eyes don't move rapidly or in any other way; they are fixed.) Do animals dream? It seems so, based on REM analysis plus the signs of dreaming every dog owner has observed when a sleeping pet starts groaning and churning its legs. And if you have ever mischievously wakened an apparently dreaming dog, the results are amusing: The dog reacts as we do when startled out of a deep sleep or dream. A moment is required to figure out where it is—if it has not bitten you already! (Let sleeping dogs lie, and all that.) Michael Gazzaniga reports in *Mind Matters* about the

work of the French researcher Michel Jouvet with REM sleep in animals. Jouvet concludes that dreams for animals are rehearsals for "essential, genetically driven response patterns such as . . . fight-or-
flight responses."

However, there is a rear-guard action under way (Euan McPhail
is a charter member) that denies that REM sleep necessarily has anything to do with dreaming, because babies give evidence of having
just as much REM-like sleep as adults—more, in fact—but what do
babies have to dream about? McPhail also notes that animals born at
an earlier stage in their maturation—rats without their eyes open, for
example—spend almost all of their first days on earth in REM sleep.
But are they dreaming? It's an open question, asserts McPhail. I suppose it is, but I can also see how a baby would have a lot to dream
about just two hours after its hair-raising entry into this alien world!

SIZE MATTERS

The human brain has grown—or, more accurately, evolved—from
the bottom up, literally. At the bottom near the brain stem are the
areas that control emotional life. All mammals have an amygdala and
a hippocampus and an olfactory lobe—known collectively as the limbic system. Reptiles and amphibians also have the amygdala and the
olfactory lobe. These are the "oldest" areas of the brain, and they are
centers of emotion in all creatures. The amygdala might be thought
of as our radar for danger. Activity here triggers fear, the most basic
of all the emotions, and stimulates the heart to pump adrenaline.
When a hiker rounds the corner and stumbles upon a dozing rattlesnake sunning in the path, the amygdala in each animal is chiefly
responsible for the fear-based response in each case. Scary pictures
alone will bestir the amygdala in humans, as PET scans prove. If

Freud was anywhere close to correct . . . well, we won't get into Freud, but we can all agree that the emotions wield great power in all of us.

On top of these ancient structures evolved the cortex, which controls muscle movement and learning, and the neocortex, seat of the highest functions of the brain, the highest levels of learning and abstraction. And the neocortex has the important job of mediating the raw emotions pouring out of the limbic system. Only mammals have a neocortex, and comparative-anatomy studies demonstrate a direct correlation between the importance of a given sense to an animal and the size of the neocortical area devoted to that sense. In the rat, cat, and monkey, significant areas of the neocortex are devoted to sight, hearing, touch, and movement. In the human being, by comparison, these senses are controlled by a much smaller proportion of the brain. For better or for worse, we now have other things on our minds.

Neuroscientists agree that there is a close correlation between brain size as related to body size and the complexity of cognitive activity. When it comes to brains, quantity counts. Beavers, compared to muskrats, for example, have a relatively large brain for a rodent. On the other end of the mammalian scale, there is a threefold difference in brain size between the human being and the chimpanzee (about the same relationship as holds between the chimp and the hedgehog, as primitive a mammal as there is).

While we humans have trillions of nerve cells in our brains, some worms execute their very basic game plan with fewer than a hundred nerve cells altogether. We do not know of a minimum size below which consciousness is "physically" impossible, but many scientists and laypeople assume there must be some such threshold. The presence of a "spinal cord" with a big bunch of cells—a brain—at the anterior end is implicitly considered necessary for higher cognitive abilities. This would be bad news for the invertebrates, which by definition do not have a spinal cord, except that the supposition is simply wrong. As Donald Griffin writes, "Experimenters have demonstrated that the central nervous systems of crustaceans, insects, and cephalopods organize and modulate information in ways that are quite comparable in complexity and precision to those of vertebrate brains."

Some invertebrates, like the arthropods, a group that includes the insects, have a centralized cord of nerve tissue, but it's in the stomach, so to speak, as a system of paired ganglia (bunches of nerve cells). We know that the social insects in particular are capable of what appears to be adaptive behavior. It has been argued that the honeybee's brain of about eight hundred thousand cells simply is not big enough to maintain the cognitive function that would be necessary to support a "conscious" foraging dance. But Griffin points out that one could argue just the opposite: that the brains are not big enough to support all the complex hardwiring (the ROM, in effect) necessary to program the array of apparently adaptive responses of which these bees and other social insects are capable.

Right now, we simply do not know the extent to which brain size constrains a given behavior, but we do know that the common housefly can perform aerial wonders with its tiny brain. We do know that the "mushroom body" in the bee's brain—the region generally thought to be the center of whatever learning the bee accomplishes in its brief lifetime (about three weeks)—gets larger as the bee matures and performs more tasks around and *outside* the hive. I emphasize "outside" because it is the older bees who are foraging outside the hive. Is it a ridiculous stretch to wonder whether these foraging bees require increased learning capacity while dealing with their mental maps, foraging choices, and dances?

(The ganglia setup of the insects even offers certain advantages that we spinal-cord possessors lack. For example, a cockroach participating in an experiment can learn to lift a leg from water in order to avoid a shock even with its head cut off. This handy learning takes place in the ganglia. However, it's only fair to us vertebrates to note that no one, to my knowledge, has ever proved that we, too, could not learn this same trick under the same decapitated circumstance!)

An even bigger problem for the supposition that invertebrates fall below the line of thought or consciousness is posed by the cephalopods. Squid and octopuses have brains containing between one and two hundred million nerve cells—by far the largest brain among the invertebrates. It is a basic tenet of biology that these cells are doing something worthwhile. Stay tuned.

In earlier chapters we have seen evidence of considerable cognitive powers on the part of birds, even though we tend to think of birds as less intelligent than mammals. These experiments of cognitive powers are confirmed by anatomy. Comparing brain size relative to body size—the necessary qualification—the largest bird brains are larger than the smallest mammal brains, and there is considerable overlap between avian and mammalian brains all the way "up the scale" until we reach the primates. It is true that bird brains do not have a cortex of any apparent significance, and since this part of the brain is considered the seat of learning, its absence would not seem to bode well for them, but scientists have determined that it is the striatal areas in bird brains that perform the equivalent functions. Irene Pepperberg, the trainer of Alex the parrot, one of the world's most intellectually impressive birds, pointed out to us that the size of the striatal area relative to the rest of the brain varies greatly across avian species. And sure enough, parrots, crows, and jays—which are among the smarter birds, however you wish to define "smart"—have relatively "humongous" striatal areas, to use Pepperberg's adjective.

PET PSYCHIATRY

Nothing is proved, but the evidence is mounting that a brain is a brain is a brain. There are crucially important differences in sheer size, but there also seems to be continuity up and down the line. Regarding the emotions, there can be little doubt. The Cartesian idea of the animal as a mere mechanism without feelings was always ludicrous, and one reason we can now be more certain of this is the evidence provided by psychopharmacology. *Medical treatments that work for human beings work for dogs and cats and birds as well.* In my view, this is a profoundly important development.

One of the leading experts in the field is Dr. Nicholas Dodman, professor of behavioral psychology at Tufts University School of Veterinary Medicine, director of the Behavior Clinic, and a much-in-demand pet psychiatrist. One of the more laid back of the new cognitive psychologists and a charming Englishman, Dodman told me that he acquired his interest in animals from his mother, the "Dr. Dolittle of the neighborhood," who took care of all the wounded animals. Mrs. Dodman felt that the only way to get to know animals was to live as closely with them as possible, when they would act differently and naturally. Her son told me, "I would go home and she would be standing in the kitchen and some wild bird would swoop through the back door and perch on the kitchen table. She would say, 'That's my friend.' It was clear this animal did not fear her and they had some kind of relationship."

Early in his academic career, Dodman wrote papers in which he used a phrase such as "the animal appeared anxious," and he would be asked what he meant. Well, he said, this creature was vocalizing, pacing, and hyperventilating in a situation that might well be expected to promote anxiety. Then Dodman's professor would ask how he *knew* this was "anxiety," because anxiety is a feeling that we could never prove in an animal. In effect, Dodman was being charged with "affirming the consequent," the logical error we have discussed earlier regarding counting. An animal who's anxious will pace and hyperventilate, but this behavior doesn't prove anxiety. No, it doesn't *prove* anxiety, but can we really imagine any other reason an animal living in a situation that would promote anxiety in humans would vocalize, pace, and hyperventilate just as we would? I don't believe so. Only willful blindness could deny this correlation. Dodman agrees, but he told me that he also had another argument in hand when dealing with those early critics. He would reply to their doubts, "Well, how about this: give it an antianxiety drug and it's less anxious."

Can we imagine any reason other than anxiety that an animal who appears anxious responds to an antianxiety drug? Not really, and even Dodman's doubters go along. As he points out, they debunk an animal's body language as evidence of an emotional state, but they accept beneficial response to medicine.

Dodman told me about a paper published in 1992 by a psychiatrist suggesting that dogs as well as humans can have obsessive-compulsive disorders. To Dodman, this issue is a "no-brainer," but the paper by a mainstream psychiatrist at the National Institutes of Health in Washington gave increased credibility to the idea that animals and humans share the same disorders. He told me about the first time he met with Klaus Miczek, editor of the *Journal of Psychophar-*

macology, and Dr. John Ratey, who teaches psychiatry at Harvard Medical School. Independently the three doctors were using the same cocktail of medications for their most aggressive pets, lab animals, and human beings, respectively. It was an exciting moment for the pet psychiatrist.

By now in this culture we are familiar with the term "alpha male"—the aggressive guy who tries to lord it over everyone else in his quest for dominance. There are plenty of alpha-male dogs and cats, and the brain chemistry in each case is practically identical to the analogous chemistry in hard-driving men. One of the chemicals in question is serotonin. Animals—including us—with especially low levels of serotonin are prone to aggression, and they are likely to win the ensuing aggressive encounters. With the animal's dominance reinforced, serotonin levels increase for the time being, all is well, and aggression decreases. When the serotonin levels start to fall again, the likelihood of aggressive behavior increases. This is a simplified picture of complex events in the brain, but as Dodman writes in *The Cat Who Cried for Help*, "it's almost as if dominant animals are serotonin junkies and need to engage in an aggressive encounter to get a fix."

The cat in question in the book is Ashley, who had manhandled his owner so successfully that he was left at home when the owner went alone to keep the appointment with the pet psychiatrist. But Dodman didn't need to see the cat. The owner's descriptions of biting, nipping, tantrums, and ambushes were quite enough to give a picture of "a fairly confident and determined cat who liked to get his own way. . . ." Dodman handed this owner an "aggression questionnaire" usually reserved for dogs. Ashley the cat scored quite high. Dodman then suggested a series of behavior-modification tricks for Ashley and the Prozac-like drug Anafranil, which elevates serotonin levels in the brain, thus reducing the impulse for frequent aggressive encounters. "I have had several aggressive cats become quite placid within a few days of starting Anafranil or Prozac," he said.

"Well, I feel we should try the medication," the cat owner replied. "I just don't feel safe in my house anymore." The drug worked. The drug almost always works.

Sometimes, however, the cause of aggression is not so much alpha-male behavior as anxiety. So it was with Stormy, who had been on the verge of driving his housemate (a cat named Penny) crazy with his unprovoked attacks. Of course, Penny had started the problem in the first place by attacking her sister Yoshiko, a new arrival in this particular household of felines. Penny despised Yoshiko, Stormy took a liking to Yoshiko, so, predictably, in the resulting triangle Stormy and Penny became sworn enemies. The conflict smoldered for over a year, then escalated when Stormy inflicted serious bodily damage on the smaller Penny, not once but twice. The cat's vet had prescribed Valium, which worked well enough for eight days before a dangerous reaction set in. The vet then referred Stormy and his owner to Dr. Dodman, who recommended BuSpar, "a designer drug virtually devoid of side effects, toxicity, and addictive potential, and it is an extremely effective treatment for anxiety. It also has antiaggressive properties." Stormy calmed down, and order was restored to the household.

It turns out that psychopharmacological treatment for cats with emotional and/or severe behavioral problems is perhaps even more common than it is with dogs, because dogs are more "amenable" to training and retraining than cats are. With cats, the medicine is often the only recourse. When the problem is "inappropriate elimination," as it is euphemistically called—the number-one behavioral problem for cats—the solution again may be BuSpar, or it may be conditioning, because this is one stress-related disorder amenable to conditioning in cats, or it may even be something simpler, like removing the plastic stair runner from beneath the litter box. (Most cats hate those things, or any other thick plastic.)

In the companion *Nature* television series to this book, we interviewed Dodman with Tasher the cockatoo, an anxious bird who plucks out her chest feathers in a manner that can only be termed an obsessive-compulsive disorder, exactly analogous to trichotillomania in people, in which the individual seeks just the right hair, each one a little bit different, then plucks it and inspects it, and sometimes chews the bulb. Parrots do the same thing with their feathers.

The disorder is not all that rare in psittacines, which are nervous and needy birds in the best of times. Irene Pepperberg's parrot Alex tends to pluck his feathers when Pepperberg is out of town. The more she is in town, the better Alex looks. "That's just the way it is," Pepperberg says simply, and she interprets feather plucking as "an artifact of captivity." In one Dodman study of psittacines, all thirteen birds with obsessive feather plucking improved under Prozac. The area of the brain that seems to "control" such disorders is the striatum, which is, as we have seen, well developed in birds. And again, serotonin levels are implicated in this disorder. Prozac works, in Dodman's phrase, like oil on troubled waters. In the end, four of the thirteen birds in this study completely "refeathered." (Unfortunately, it can be dangerous to medicate birds because of their naturally high metabolic rate; so Dodman gives the average parrot a dose only one-tenth as large as the normal human dose.)

Another of Dodman's patients was Sympathy, a dog who was shot by a policeman two years before arriving at Dodman's clinic. Ever since, she had been terrified of policemen, police cars, police dogs, and sirens of any sort. If Sympathy were human, she would be diagnosed with post-traumatic shock disorder. Behavioral therapy would not work with Sympathy, but Prozac helped a great deal. Today when a police car passes on the streets of Boston, she walks as closely as possible to her owner, but she does not panic.

Dogs (and to a lesser degree cats, who are more solitary by nature) are susceptible to separation anxiety and codependency relationships, what Dodman calls the "Velcro syndrome." As with people, this problem results from dysfunctional early experiences. A typical case would be a puppy weaned from its mother too early, then stashed in a cage in a pet store for weeks or even months. "When they find a loving owner, they bond to them like glue," Dodman says of such dogs. "The relationship is more intense than it should be because they're so needy. And the situation gets worse with time, as every separation compounds the one before." Dodman does not shrink from using the terms "panic" and "terror" to describe the feelings of such a dog when the owner leaves the house and the door closes. Serious household destruction is usually the result, and people often misinterpret the dog's destructive behavior as sheer maliciousness and vindictiveness for being left alone. To prove that this is not the case, Dodman suggests that any family in such a situation videotape the dog when it's left alone in the house. We observe just such behavior in our animal-minds *Nature* program. What we see is anxiety and destructive behavior and the clear evidence of a "dog who loved too much" (which happens to be the title of one of Dodman's popular books).

"Counterconditioning" helps these animals, beginning with the simple distraction of a tidbit when the owner leaves the house. Dodman works closely with the owner to set up an appropriate regimen of "systematic desensitization," in which fears are peeled away, one by one. In the case of Max, a golden retriever abandoned by his first owner and painfully attached to the new owner who found him wandering in the woods, this distraction is a bone stuffed with peanut butter. For a moment, at least, the dog experiences a pleasant emotion, directly the opposite of the one he has been feeling at these moments. After a few sessions, Max seemed to forget that he was alone, or even came to enjoy being alone as long as he had a bone filled with peanut butter. Eventually Max could be left alone with just a few toys, and his howling ceased. This kind of psychotherapy works with dogs, and it works with children—a provocative fact, to say the least.

The toughest cases for Dodman to solve are those in which the unwanted problem stems from "natural" behavior. The prime case in point is the dog who chases cars, a reflection of his natural predatory behavior. The dog locks onto this modern-day prey and loves every moment of the chase, even if he doesn't succeed (and with cars, it is a good thing he doesn't). It's a very difficult habit to break. Many pet disorders, especially eating disorders, stem from the fact that the pet's life, comfortable as it is, is not its "natural" life. Dodman suspects a component of depression in many overweight house pets. There's also the fact that the animals do not need to burn any calories to obtain food, as they would in the wild, or even outside in the neighborhood. The answer for this condition is a combination of a leaner diet and a richer environment—as part of what Dodman calls the "Get a Life Program."

TOO MUCH LIFE

Our pets acquire their emotional problems without our intentional help. In the laboratory, cruel experimenters can easily induce all manner of psychiatric disorders in their animals. Intending to test memory, a researcher at UCLA trained a group of rats in a traditional maze, then spiked the food so that the rats got sick, not immediately, but hours later. After this much time had elapsed, would the rats put together cause and effect and avoid that food in the future? Yes, they would. Furthermore, they acquired a phobia regarding that entire section of the maze, which they wouldn't go near. As Michael Gazzaniga notes in his entertaining book *Mind Matters*, humans have exactly the same response to a restaurant that has caused us food poisoning. We never return to that place.

Other experiments, some of them cruel, demonstrate that animals can easily be driven into a highly stressed-out state by the random infliction of pain, especially pain about which they can do nothing. In tests with two sets of rats exposed to random shocks, the subjects who could stop the shock by turning a wheel were better off and developed fewer stomach ulcers than the ones who received the identical shock of the same duration but couldn't do anything about it. The shock was the same in each case, but the feeling of being able to do something about it made a big difference in the "mental health" of the two groups.

Gazzaniga reports studies of large organizations confirming that the same principle holds for people: Upper-level management, with more power to control events, feel less stressed out than middle managers. Of course, the upper-levels also make more money, which might be a factor in their well-being. When a fish is snared on the hook, its body is flooded with endorphins, the same "natural painkillers" that flood my own body when I experience pain. Does the fish feel pain? Alas, the inference from biochemistry suggests that the answer may be yes, even though anglers (including myself, most definitely) have always hoped and perhaps believed that this is not the case.

In the wild, certain animals are excellent at inducing stress in each other, with no help from humans at all. Dr. Robert Sapolsky of Stanford University has done extensive research with the baboons of East Africa, who have too much spare time on their hands—at least in the case of the alpha male, who successfully makes life miserable for almost everyone else in his troop. He may attack physically or he may silently harass any other potential "couple" by simply being nearby at all times. His dominating presence alone is usually enough to make the other male slink off and leave the female alone. The other animals in the group end up with excess amounts of the gluco-corticoid hormones—just as humans do who are suffering from too much stress.

GOOD FEELINGS, FOR A CHANGE

Encountered one-on-one, sheep are not sheep as we know them by reputation. To know a sheep is to know an animal with quite complex behavior and good memory, according to Keith Kendrick, a neurobiologist at the University of Cambridge. He knows that a sheep can remember more than fifty members of its flock, that a ewe who has selected a favored male experiences a surge of dopamine in her brain when shown a picture of that male, and that looking at a picture of a preferred kind of food triggers brain activity in a sheep analogous to the activity in my brain when I look at a picture of cherry-vanilla ice cream. The seat of that activity in both cases is the hypothalamus, the area of the brain most activated by pleasurable self-stimulation. Do we have any good reason, or any reason at all, for presuming that the sheep looking at the picture of choice grass does not feel something like the sense of pleasant anticipation that I do while contemplating the ice cream?

Likewise, grooming among primates and some other animals floods their systems with dopamine. Smiling in humans—and perhaps in other animals as well, if we could read the expressions correctly—is grooming at a distance, in effect. And Dr. George Losey of the University of Hawaii has discovered that the little wrasses that clean tiny organisms and other parasites off other fish are allowed to do so only because the action "tickles" the larger fish. With good tickling, the fish will stay parked for hours, but given bad stimulation they will bite the offending cleaner fish (or the offending fake fish, if we're talking about one of Losey's experiments). One fish practically lifted itself out of the water in an effort to rub against a piece of wire just above the surface. As far as Losey is concerned, "The sea is not full of cold fish at all. They're out there having a darned good time. They get tickled during the day, they get sex in the afternoon . . . they have a lot of pleasure."

No one can say that emotions are chemical states and nothing but these states in the brain, yet there's no doubt that they are mediated by the chemical states in some way. Lab rats can be seduced into pressing a lever just about endlessly if the action results in either the direct injection of endorphins, such as dopamine, in the brain or the electrical stimulation of the hypothalamus, which then releases the dopamine. Dodman believes that this is strong evidence that emotions in animals are essentially the same as the emotions we feel. Or we could put it this way: Wherever it's found in the animal kingdom, dopamine is dopamine.

And oxytocin is oxytocin, as we learn from Dr. C. Sue Carter at the University of Maryland, who conducted an ingenious study of the prairie vole. Oxytocin is the hormone that seems to play a key role in the experience of pleasure we feel during sexual activity. It is released in the brain of all mammals at these pleasurable junctures. It also plays a key role in mother-infant bonding, indicated by its presence at elevated levels at the time of birth and when nursing. Oxytocin is a "relaxing," antistress hormone and, apparently, much more. Think-ing about these matters, Carter hypothesized that the hormone might also be instrumental "earlier" in the behavioral cycle that eventually leads to sexual activity and childbearing. The term "emo-tional glue" sometimes used in reference to human couples doesn't mean much to biologists, as Carter points out. She wanted to investi-gate the biochemical underpinnings of this "glue." Specifically, she wanted to find out whether the same biochemical glue that underpins sex and maternal bonding in people and voles—oxytocin—also un-derpins pair bonding.

The prairie vole is a good subject for studying this hypothesis because it happens to be a socially monogamous species. Such behav-ior is quite rare among the rodents, as we might not be surprised to learn. I should also point out that social monogamy is not the same thing as sexual monogamy. Marriage among humans is an institution of social monogamy, but it does not guarantee sexual monogamy. Adultery happens. The same holds for these voles, but promiscuity doesn't matter to Carter, who is interested in the initial and perma-nent pair-bonding behavior.

At her laboratory in Maryland, Carter introduced a young, un-paired female vole to a male and allowed her to spend one hour with him. Under normal circumstances in the wild, this one hour is not enough time for the female to "make up her mind" about this poten-tial lifetime mate. In the wild, she'll go back and forth between candi-dates, vacillating, undecided, for about twenty-four hours. Her decision is indicated when she begins spending almost all her time with one of the males, and she may even become aggressive with the "loser." In effect, female prairie voles go through puberty in a twenty-four-hour period. Prior to meeting their first strange male, their reproductive hormones are suppressed.

So one hour is not nearly long enough unless the prepubescent female is injected with oxytocin prior to the meeting with the male— any male. In this case, bonding and mating will almost certainly follow within the one-hour time constraint. Carter concludes that the hormone biases the female vole in favor of whatever male she meets immediately following the injection.

Clearly, oxytocin precipitates bonding, and Carter's work also confirmed that its absence prevents bonding. If the natural release of oxytocin in the female was blocked by biochemical means, she would not bond at all, no matter how long she was kept in contact with a male. This one hormone cannot be the whole story, Dr. Carter says, but it must be a major part of that story.

She is careful to note that oxytocin "works" only if the hardware (the neural receptors) are present upon which oxytocin can act. If you give this hormone to a rat, for example, this rodent does become somewhat more social, but it does not become monogamous like the prairie vole. Give the hormone to a different kind of vole that is not monogamous, and this vole does not suddenly become monogamous either.

Carter concludes:

When a young prairie vole male meets a female, they go through a very dramatic hormonal shift which might have some of the same features as humans "falling in love." We don't know, we don't have measurements of "love" in prairie voles, we only have measurements of pair bonds and attachments. . . . It is particularly difficult to study "positive" emotions. Most of the research on [animal] emotion deals with "negative" emotions such as fear and anxiety. The work we're doing with prairie voles is a bit unusual. It allows us to focus on positive emotional experiences that animals have.

It also provides evidence that even the lowly prairie vole may be experiencing emotions not totally unrelated to our own at crucial moments in its life. Could the prairie vole actually "fall in love"? Apparently some people find this possibility alarming and "dehumanizing." I don't. I have no problem giving any animal its due.

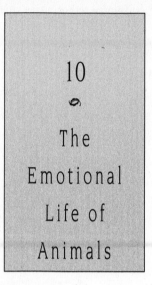

10

The Emotional Life of Animals

CAN THERE BE ANY DOUBT?

Hormones are not emotions. Even behavior is not emotion. Only emotion is emotion. The biochemical evidence for animal emotions is compelling, but it is not ironclad proof that animals feel emotions as we do. When we speak of anger, we do not have a shortage of serotonin in mind; when we humans dream of love, we are not imagining a dose of oxytocin coursing through our brains. We mean the subjective feeling of anger, the feeling of love. When we have those feelings, biochemistry and "behavior" are utterly beside the point.

Dr. Marian Stamp Dawkins, Oxford zoologist and author of *Through Our Eyes Only? The Search for Animal Consciousness*, has come to believe that the weight of evidence is on the side of consciousness for animals, but she admits we cannot prove that animals have these subjective feelings, and she warns against our natural tendency to accept at face value the body language and behavior we do see. The dolphin's "smiling" visage just happens to be the way its head is shaped. The chimpanzee's biggest "grin" is actually an expression of alarm. (Editors in the era of the early manned space program might not have known this when they featured cover photos of "grinning" chimps emerging from their capsules after an orbit or two.) And is a charging lion "angry," or just charging? "Just charging" is more likely. The lion's only object in attacking the wildebeest is eating. It's not personal. We humans can certainly attack one another without anger. Millions of soldiers throughout the ages have been killed by millions of other soldiers who were not angry. When we think of one-on-one aggression, anger usually plays a role, but not always. One sibling can strike another not out of anger but in trying to establish dominance.

So we do have to be careful about matching hormones, body language, and even behavior to emotions. On the other hand, we have plenty of other clues that the correlation is highly likely. One is that animals incontrovertibly *anticipate*. This might not seem like an important point, but it is. The early experiments proving that animals experience anticipation helped undermine the strict behaviorist agenda, which had little room for such a "phenomenon." Rats were supposed to hustle through the maze and accept their food at the end. If they were tricked and there was no food . . . well, there was no food. The rat was not expected to act surprised when the reward turned up missing. But a rat does act surprised in this situation, and it was difficult for behaviorists to explain, because such surprise implied not only memory, which was acceptable as a factor in conditioning, but also anticipation and disappointment, which were not. (The first experiments in this regard were conducted by Edward Tolman, whom we have met as the early-twentieth-century investigator who had doubts about behaviorism all along, but felt constrained by the dogma until later in his life.)

Marian Dawkins writes about a "remarkable" series of experiments with humans and rats conducted by Michel Cabanac, a Canadian physiologist. "His experiments," Dawkins writes, "show that the physiological and behavioral [responses] are so similar that the leap of analogy we would have to make to assume that conscious experiences are also similar is reduced to the barest minimum."

In the experiments, Cabanac charted the reactions of humans and rats to sweet substances. Humans graded a series of such solutions on a scale running from +2 for really good to −2 for really bad. Then he plotted changing attitudes toward the same solution depending on circumstances, such as hunger, thirst, or a prior sweet drink. And these attitudes did change, as we would expect. Then the rats took the same test. Since they couldn't report on their opinions, Cabanac judged their reactions based on how much they drank of each solution under the different circumstances. Plotted on a graph, the results were astonishing: The subjective experience of pleasure/no pleasure reported by the human subjects matches almost exactly the quantity of the solutions drunk by the rats. Dawkins argues that this is a powerful justification for drawing an analogy between the conscious feelings of pleasure experienced by both groups of subjects. Of course, it is possible, as Dawkins states, that we with our conscious feelings just happen to react in the same way as rats who are nothing but little machines. But is this plausible?

Pain is not an emotion, but it is another clue to emotion. Strictly speaking, pain is a warning that what's going on in the immediate world right now is dangerous to good health; we should take immediate action to alleviate the condition causing the pain. Given this obvious and undisputed function of pain for *Homo sapiens*, it strikes me as absolutely remarkable that Descartes, and many others with much more technical knowledge than he had, could argue that animals do not feel the pain. If pain is not felt, then it's not pain and it doesn't serve its purpose. But it does serve its purpose. When I accidentally step on my dog's tail or her foot, she howls bloody murder. What could provoke those howls if not pain? So it seems to me that we are perfectly justified in concluding that pain is, therefore, very much felt by my dog.

If this logic isn't totally scientifically airtight, too bad. (Or—with apologies to Monsieur Descartes—*quel dommage*.) From my layman's point of view, sometimes common sense is quite enough, thank you very much! It is also true that the experience of pain is mediated by culture. For example, rhesus monkeys inflict severe wounds on each other when fighting, and respond to those wounds as we would, by screaming. But very quickly these outward signs of distress disappear and the animal is utterly quiet. In mating season, one rhesus may go so far as to rip out an opponent's testicle. The wounded party will scream bloody murder for a while but then, remarkably, he will be seen mating later in the day. Many observers have drawn a similar conclusion regarding childbirth, which has evolved into something of a long ordeal in Western culture, but only a day's—or an hour's— absence from the fields in many other cultures.

We know that animals can carry pain in the form of "emotional" scars for a lifetime. This is the downside to the extraordinary effectiveness of the amygdala at inducing fear and prompting the necessary evasive action. The situations triggering such reactions can leave deep-seated, apparently lifelong scars. For the *Nature* series on animal minds, we visited Keiko, the orca, or "killer whale," who starred in the movie *Free Willy*. In September 1998, Keiko was released into a "sea pen" off the coast of Iceland after living—surviving, I should say—for almost two decades in a small oceanarium in Iceland, another in Canada, a dinky local amusement park in Mexico City, and for two and a half years at a much better facility at the Oregon Coast Aquarium. "Lethargic" would be a fair, objective description of Keiko's behavior when he arrived in Oregon. Can anyone truly believe that this wonderful, very family-oriented animal has led a life as full and rich as it would have been swimming with his mates in the vast depths and expanses of the oceans?

Jane Goodall has seen and tried to help all too many young chimps who have come to her Gombe center after unknown traumatic experiences in childhood. One of these chimps hits himself over and over and over, all day long. Another, La Vieille ("The Old One"), has lived at Gombe now for many years, yet she is still afraid to leave her enclosure, so deep are the scars she brought with her. Anyone with an open mind who looks into the eyes of this creature sees the buried sadness. Those who doubt are bluntly dismissed by the famous primatologist: "I cannot imagine how anybody could possibly imagine that animals don't have personalities, feelings, emotions, and that their minds don't work very much like our own minds, especially chimps. . . . I know they're capable of suffering."

Goodall asks why shouldn't we infer emotion when this inference seems warranted, just as I infer your anger or sadness when the situation makes this emotion not only plausible but likely? She bases this judgment on almost forty years' experience living with chimpanzees. When one of the chimps at the Gombe center jumps up and down and squeals in apparent pleasure in just the way a human child does, Goodall believes we should conclude that this pleasure is not just "behavior" but that it is felt as pleasure by the chimpanzee as well. When a young chimp reacts with alarm at a new pop-up toy, just as a human infant might, we should draw the conclusion that the chimp is alarmed. Goodall knows whether a chimp's face is expressing pure relaxation, anger, sadness, or embarrassment. She says bluntly, "I defy anyone who knows anything about children to watch a small chimpanzee and not realize within a very short space of time that that child has exactly the same feelings, emotions, fears, despairs as human infants."

Anything less, to Goodall's mind, is simply "illogical," and certainly men and women who work professionally with animals have no choice but to see and carefully read the emotions of their animals. Correct judgment can be a matter of life and death with dangerous animals, and it is often the difference between success and failure with others.

Animals get bored and distracted. For professionals working with them, anthropomorphism, if that's what it is, regarding emotions is sheer pragmatism. This does not mean, however, that these professionals understand the emotions of their animals as they would understand the emotions of their friends. With Irene Pepperberg's parrot Alex, the presence of powerful emotion is unmistakable, but often Pepperberg does not quite know what to make of them, or how to define them. Her model/rival protocol, which I explained earlier, is based partially on the renowned ability of this species to become jealous, although when she's being carefully scientific, Pepperberg doesn't use the term "jealousy." But she does know that if she cuddles another bird, Alex is likely to attack, or try to. When she sees in the morning a certain puffy-feathers, slit-eyes look, she knows she will get bitten if she makes a wrong move with her hand. But whether this is the bird's anger with her or frustration over something else, she does not know. But it's not all trial and tribulation with

Alex; sometimes in the morning he has a certain relaxed posture, indicating that a productive lesson is in the offing.

SHE KNOWS FEAR

Temple Grandin, professor of animal sciences at Colorado State University, thinks in pictures, not in words, and she may therefore come much closer than the rest of us to understanding how animals really do see and feel about the world. In fact, she almost considers herself a member of a unique species, the autistic. In her essay "Thinking Like Animals" in *Intimate Nature: The Bond Between Women and Animals*, she writes, "Autistic emotion may be more like an animal's. Fear is the dominant emotion in both autistic people and prey animals such as deer, cattle, and horses. My emotions are simple and straightforward; like an animal's my emotions are not deep-seated. They may be intense while I am experiencing them but they will subside like an afternoon thunderstorm."

Knowing that autistic children often seek the confines of a couch beneath the cushions, knowing that therapists use deep pressure to soothe autistic children, she inferred that cattle, specifically, would be soothed by soft pressure applied to wide areas of the body. She already knew they would be panicked by yelling and poking and prodding. She knew that curved chutes at the slaughterhouse would be more comfortable for the animals than straight ones, because the curve would hide from view the commotion at the end. She knew that blood horrifies people but is of no concern to cows. Instead they worry about abrupt motion that may indicate a predator; they worry about "high-pitched noises, disturbances of the dirt . . . a shiny reflection, or anything that appears to be out of place."

Today about half of all the cattle in North America spend their final hours in facilities designed by Grandin, author of *Emergence:*

Labeled Autistic and *Thinking in Pictures*. Perhaps the reader is wondering what I wondered when I first encountered her ideas. Grandin replies:

> I am often asked how I can care about animals and be involved in their slaughter. People forget that nature can be harsh. Death at the slaughter plant is quicker and less painful than death in the wild. Lions dining on the guts of a wild animal is much worse in my opinion. The animals we raise for food would never have lived at all if we had not raised them. . . . It is important that our relationship with farm animals is reciprocal. We owe animals a decent life and a painless death.

While some people doubt the subjective nature of animals' emotions, others wonder whether their emotions are perhaps *more* powerful than our own, because they are less mediated by all the abstracting and rationalizing going on in the adult human's neocortex. Or perhaps that is another way of saying that animals' emotions may be more childlike and unrestrained.

No emotion for animals or more emotion? If that were the choice, I'd have to believe the latter.

PLAYING AROUND

In general, it seems to me, researchers tend to focus on the "negative" emotions of animals, probably because more of us are inclined to agree that, yes, a lot of animals experience fear and anger. We tend to be a little more possessive of the positive emotions of pleasure, happiness, and joy, but maybe we don't have good reasons. After all, play is widespread in the animal kingdom, especially among mammals and birds. But is play really a manifestation of pleasure? That depends on how you define the word, and this turns out to be a tough one, of course. One author has compiled a list of thirty-nine definitions! One of the more restrictive analyses I read suggests that play is simply the result of low levels of "arousal" (not sexual arousal, but overall arousal). When bored, we play in some way. This does not sound very exciting, but such a definition actually bodes well for animals, because only a thinking being is capable of boredom. The oyster, we presume, does not get bored. A lot of other animals do.

When I see my three beautiful Labradors racing around upon arriving at our cabin in the woods, I see pure joy. Here these wonderful creatures can run off the leash and swim in the stream to their hearts' content.

Elizabeth Marshall Thomas, author of the bestseller *The Hidden Life of Dogs*, tells the story of a young dog of her acquaintance who had been given to an inactive, elderly couple. They already owned an inactive, elderly dog and did not have the energy to keep up with the newcomer. The young dog had company, technically speaking, but no one to really play with. One evening Thomas saw this dog on a snowy hillside near his house, running in a circle with his nose to the ground, then stopping to burrow, then taking off again in the circle, then returning to the same spot for more burrowing. Six times the dog ran the route in this manner, "alert, excited, tail high and waving, nose to earth." In the beginning, Thomas figured some little rodent was the prey, but after the repeated loops she began to wonder and investigated the site, where she found no rodent hole, no rodent, nothing whatsoever. The dog had been playing make-believe, Thomas decided.

Any number of times I have watched one of my dogs stalk, presumably, some ferocious prey. A field mouse? A squirrel? Often this fearsome prey turned out to be a leaf. Somebody was playing make-believe, which, unfortunately, is not always the case, as my dogs' encounters with countless skunks and two porcupines attest.

With dogs, the invitation for another dog or a human to play is the familiar "play bow": forelegs flat on the ground, rear end high in the air, mouth wide open, tail waving like mad. This posture is unmistakable to us as well as to other dogs. In fact, the purpose of play may well be the development of social skills, but wouldn't it be nice if it had no developmental purpose whatsoever? After all, kittens play in the most charming ways, and cats are basically solitary predators.

A more accurate point might be that play behavior is a rehearsal, under relatively safe conditions, for the real thing—life as an adult. (Is play anything else for children?) Play is, developmentally speaking, serious business; play fighting is one of the most common forms of play. This plausible and attractive theory was first developed by Karl Groos in the late nineteenth century. By this definition, play exercises all the cognitive and motor functions the creature is, or will be, capable of: thus the kitten's instinctive stalking, sudden changes of direction, and bursts of speed. Experiments with rhesus monkeys—experiments that cannot be condoned—have proved that animals raised with everything they need except playmates inevitably grow up to be dysfunctional adults.

In general, the species we tend to think of as "smarter" are the ones that play—animals with "a budget for exploration and self-stimulation," as philosopher Daniel Dennett quips in *Consciousness Explained*. These are mammals and birds. Off the coast of western Australia, dolphins surf the giant waves with apparent abandon. They are the only dolphins in the world known to do this. What possible reason could there be for this behavior other than the sheer joy of it? And why haven't other dolphins "discovered" this form of play?

Spinner dolphins frolic in the wakes of large power boats, but they haven't been observed surfing natural waves.

One of Jane Goodall's first discoveries at the Gombe center was the chimpanzees' fondness for raiding her camp for new toys; another early discovery was the compatibility of puppies and chimps as playmates. I have seen a wonderful picture of a young bonobo playing blindman's buff. There's no question that's what he's doing. Kanzi, the lexigram-trained bonobo in Atlanta, once hid from his increasingly worried trainer while flattened out on the bed covered with blankets—motionless—for twenty minutes! Then he burst forth in high spirits. Pure devilment—pure play, let's face it. And bonobos and chimps are famous for playing games of make-believe.

In *Elephant Memories*, Cynthia Moss's fascinating book about the 680 elephants living in the Amboseli National Park in Kenya, she writes about being "trapped" in her Land Rover by a group of young elephants who "rumbled, flapped their ears, shook their heads and made mock charges at me. I could only laugh at them, it was so obvious they were not serious." A seriously angry elephant is an unmistakable elephant; these kids were playing.

Birds are harder to observe playing, but they do, and it's no surprise that among the main avian players are the usual suspects in this book: parrots, ravens, crows. Parrots play with objects while lying on their backs. To all appearances, crows and ravens get a kick out of teasing gullible dogs. At least, they do so over and over and over again, with nothing to gain by it. Miriam Rothschild tells us about her magpie who enjoyed mimicking ducks in order to get her dogs to fly out of the house in an attempt to catch them. The bird would preen mightily after this successful hoax. Paul Shepard tells us about the hawks he observed while working as a seasonal park-ranger/naturalist at Crater Lake National Park. These birds were circling around each other, the higher one dropping a wad of lichen to the lower one, who would catch it with his talons, circle above his mate, and drop the lichen to him. Around and around they went. Shepard watched this game for several cycles before one of the hawks changed the game by flying over and dropping the lichen to him! (When Shepard told this story to a famous ornithologist who was also working in the park that summer, the man snorted, turned abruptly, and walked off. A behaviorist, no doubt.)

We have seen some of the amazing things honeybees can do, but do they also play? This is not a notion that comes to us naturally, but on sunny afternoons young worker bees a couple of weeks old venture forth from the hive for some simple loop-the-loops near the front door. Over the next few days they will venture farther from the hive, probably getting the hang of their navigational and mental-mapping skills, including calibration with the sun. Sounds like rehearsal play to me, but if this is indeed the point, it is not all that successful, as the Goulds point out in *The Animal Mind:* Honeybees suffer a 50-percent attrition rate on their first official day of foraging.

SINGING GORILLAS
AND THE HIGHER EMOTIONS

In the wild, gorillas sing. They especially like to sing after a fierce thunderstorm has ended, the sky has cleared, and the rain-forest air smells sweet. Their singing is not of the Pavarotti quality, but it definitely sounds like singing and it surely sounds as if it is coming from a happy animal. They do not sing in captivity as a rule, but Michael, a resident at the California Gorilla Foundation, listens to Luciano Pavarotti for hours on end. He can hardly contain himself while tapping to the rhythm, utterly transfixed. Only the most jaded of observers would doubt that Pavarotti's singing makes Michael happy—just as it does millions of other fans.

Sue Savage-Rumbaugh tells the following story about her star pupil with the lexigrams, Kanzi. The bonobo's stepmother, Matata, had been away from Kanzi's quarters on breeding leave, which was successful. Now she was due to return to the laboratory while in the family way. Kanzi had done very little with the lexigrams before Matata's departure, but he had made great strides in her absence. What would happen now? Keeping the two separate "for the sake of science" seemed difficult in terms of practicality and cruel besides, but Savage-Rumbaugh was worried that Kanzi would lose interest in his language studies with his stepmother back in the picture. She decided to reintroduce the two, then keep them separate for a few days, and assess Kanzi's frame of mind.

On the afternoon Matata arrived, Kanzi returned home from a long, hot day in the forest. Savage-Rumbaugh immediately informed him that there was a "surprise" waiting in the colony room. Kanzi expected food, naturally. Savage-Rumbaugh replied, "No food surprise. Matata surprise. Matata in colony room." Savage-Rumbaugh picks up the story:

He looked stunned, stared at me intently, and then ran to the colony room door, gesturing urgently for me to open it. When mother and son saw each other, they emitted earsplitting shrieks of excitement and joy and rushed to the wire that separated them. They both pushed their hands through the wire. To touch the other as best they could. . . . I hadn't the heart to keep them apart any longer, and opened the connecting door. Kanzi leaped into Matata's arms, and they screamed and hugged for fully five minutes, and then stepped back to gaze at each other in happiness. . . . If we've lost him back to the world of the bonobos, so be it, I thought to myself.

But all's well that ends well. Kanzi gestured for his lexigram keyboard and indicated "open." If anything, Matata's return inspired him to greater glory with his lexigrams.

Grief in animals may be the hardest emotion to understand, at least in my experience. When my golden retriever Jenny died, her four-year-old daughter, Mink, looked and sniffed at Jenny's body and clearly did not have the slightest idea what to make of it. When we took Jenny's body outside to the grave we dug behind the house, Mink acted as though she had lost her mind. She ran and ran around and around the yard, over and over again until finally she dropped from sheer exhaustion. When we came back into the house, Mink would not leave us for a moment—pushing up against the legs of one of us no matter where we walked. Apparently, however, her grief, her realization, did not hit her with its full force for two or three days, when she just stopped eating, lay down, and paid no attention to anyone or anything. This went on for about two weeks, when we decided we had to get a puppy for Mink.

When the new puppy, Maggie, a tiny yellow Labrador arrived, Mink exhibited only mild interest in her, and we worried that this was not going to work—until the next morning. During the night these two bonded, became inseparable, and remained that way until Minker died many years later.

Unlike dogs and many other animals, primates appear to show their grief immediately—especially if it is a mother who has lost a newborn. One of our most moving *Nature* films ever was about a group of Japanese macaques that had been filmed over several years by Japanese researchers. Our star was Mozu, and we called the film "Mozu the Snow Monkey." During the filming, one of Mozu's relatives gave birth to a stillborn baby. The mother would not leave her dead baby; in fact, she would not let go of it. She carried its little body everywhere.

At night she would climb up into a particular tree, hold the dead baby in her arms, and scream. It was the most bloodcurdling scream I have ever heard. She did this for three days and three nights. On the fourth day, she put the body of her baby on the jungle floor and disappeared into the jungle herself.

Joy is a higher-order emotion. So are compassion and empathy. To us laypeople, these terms "compassion" and "empathy" are closely related; in the minds of some ethologists, however, they are critically different. Compassion they think of as straightforward fellow feeling, while empathy suggests a higher order of identification with the feelings of another. But how could a creature show compassion without a sense for the feeling in the other creature that merits this compassion? That's too fine a line for me.

We have all heard stories about dolphins coming to the rescue of struggling human swimmers, stories we have every reason to believe because dolphins often help their own in similar straits, pushing an ailing fellow to the surface to breathe and holding the creature there for long periods of time. Clearly dolphins must feel empathy for other dolphins, and apparently for humans as well.

In *Bonobo, The Forgotten Ape*, Frans de Waal tells a series of remarkable stories about these primates that can only be interpreted as showing compassion and empathy. One features the famous Kanzi on videotape helping his minimally trained sister, Tamuli, deal with spoken English. When Tamuli hesitates when asked by Savage-Rumbaugh to groom her brother, Kanzi takes her hand, puts it between his chin and chest, and stares at her with a questioning gaze. In another story, a mother sucks water into her mouth and delivers it to her whimpering two-year-old. She does this three times. In the Milwaukee Zoo, an elderly male bonobo named Kidogo suffers from heart disease and has a great deal of trouble getting around. With one exception, the rest of the bonobos go out of their way to help this patriarch, and sometimes when the one misanthropic five-year-old tries to tease him, another bonobo steps in to protect the old ape.

Jane Goodall has seen many cases of adoption among wild chimpanzees, even adoption by adult males. Her favorite among these tales was the adoption of a sickly infant named Mel by rough, tough, twelve-year-old Spindle, who let the youngster ride on his back, cling to his belly, and climb into his nest at night. Spindle even rescued Mel from hazardous encounters with sexually aroused males, encounters that earned Spindle rebuffs for his troubles. But he endured them for the sake of Mel. Goodall says there is no doubt that Spindle saved Mel's life by adopting him. Even La Vieille, emotionally scarred for life, apparently, cared for a young orphan even needier than La Vieille herself. And Goodall describes the mourning of the seemingly healthy male chimpanzee Flint when his mother Flo died. He sat with the body for hours. He became more withdrawn by the day. And within a month he, too, died.

A Denver, Colorado, television station videotaped this next story, and it soon became known around the world. A great African bull elephant was down on his side and either unwilling or unable to stand up. Elephants will always die soon if they cannot stand up. In this case, even a large crane was unable to pull the elephant up onto four legs. But, as it happened, a group of smaller, Asian elephants was led past the downed African elephant.

These Asian elephants immediately approached their "cousin" and prodded him into standing up, then supported him until he had the situation under his own control.

Empathy? Grief? These are emotions that other animals do not share with humans?

Of course, one could interpret all these situations and many others besides as something less than meets the eye. Behaviorists and quasi-behaviorists hold that all empathy is, at root, just as selfish as everything else we do. Even humans, much less other animals, are altruistic because we expect something else in return ("reciprocal altruism") or because it feels good to be altruistic.

Fine. If this is your argument, who can refute it? As Mr. Spock might have said, it is not *susceptible* to refutation. But I would argue that *whatever* compassion and empathy are with humans, so they are with chimps and bonobos and dolphins and dogs—and a host of other animals that humans have loved.

Stories of compassion *across* species lines are not rare either. I have already related the remarkable story told by Jeffrey Masson in *When Elephants Weep* about the dog and the lion—a friendship that was ultimately broken up, alas, by the suddenly mature lion.

In 1984, the famous gorilla Koko made headlines when her pet kitten, who was called "All Ball," slipped out a doorway and was run over by a car. Koko cried when Francis Patterson informed her of the death. Three days later, Koko signed "cry" when asked if she wanted to talk about the kitten. Five years later, when shown a picture of herself and All Ball, she signed "that bad frown sorry inattention." (Before the unexpected death of All Ball, Koko had signed "trouble, old" when asked why gorillas die, and she signed "comfortable hole bye" when asked where gorillas go when they die.)

De Waal relates an amazing story about the seven-year-old bonobo Kuni and an injured starling in the Twycross Zoo in England. The keeper was worried that the bonobo meant the bird harm, but in fact Kuni went to extraordinary lengths to try to get the bird airborne once again. At one point she climbed to the highest point of the highest tree in the vicinity and, hanging on to the tree with both legs, unfolded the bird's wings, one with each hand, and threw it aloft. No luck; the starling plummeted to the ground, whereupon Kuni took up guard duty—apparently successfully, because by the end of the day the bird was gone.

Jeffrey Masson interprets the infamous Clever Hans episode as an instance of amazing empathy across species—empathy by the horse, who could seemingly read the most minute of inadvertent cues from its teacher. Hans would be the one who could teach us something, if only we had the physical senses to receive his messages. Masson argues that the mutual love of dogs and humans is prima facie evidence of the extraordinary empathy of each species for the other. Otherwise, how could there be such love? We don't feel such emotion for trees or for insects or for hamsters that we do for horses and dogs and cats. Maybe our intuition and our empathy "know" something that we don't. It is a powerful argument.

Cats, although currently the most popular pet in America, *are* different from dogs, and cat lovers say, "Amen!" Some pet lovers love both cats and dogs; some hate one and love the other. As with religion, it is best in polite society not to engage in a discussion about the relative merits of cats and dogs. In his book *Dogs Never Lie About Love*, Masson relates the story of a German ethologist who argues that while we chose dogs—wolves, at the time—for domestication, cats chose us, while remaining true to their independent nature. The cat is *domestic*, according to this line of reasoning, but not truly *domesticated*. Those of us who like cats tend to think of them as little lions and tigers and cheetahs and love the wildness and independence in them. It's all part of their great attraction.

A RECIPROCAL RELATIONSHIP

For centuries, animals have been considered good medicine for ailing humans. Paul Shepard believes that "animal-facilitated therapy" began with the Quakers two centuries ago in England, where the inmates of an insane asylum lived with a garden, rabbits, and poultry. In James Serpell's *In the Company of Animals*, an excellent book about just what the title says, Serpell reports the results of a study in Australia regarding the effect of the mere presence of a gentle dog in a nursing home for the elderly. For the "experiment," two groups of residents were set up, one with whom the dog would live for six months, one that would carry on as it always had, without a dog. The difference in the mental health of the residents at the end of the test period was extraordinary. The residents who lived with the dog were healthier and happier. Serpell acknowledges that this test does not qualify as hard science. As with most of the studies in this area, this one could be criticized for its lack of strict protocols—the staff members assessing the success of the project were in favor of it in the first place. But there have been many other related studies, and I have not read of one that did not come to a similar conclusion.

A particularly surprising result obtained in Maryland showed that pet owners had a significantly better chance of surviving heart attacks. At some point, if there is any justice for animals, anecdote may become evidence.

A series of tests conducted at the Johns Hopkins Medical School in the 1970s demonstrated the reciprocal benefits humans can provide to dogs. Serpell spares us the details, but the gist of the experiments was the measurement of heart rate and blood pressure in dogs subjected to electric shocks. Unsurprisingly, the presence of a petting human lowered the rate of increase in these two indices by 50 percent. The presence of a human combined with training to anticipate the shock prevented the dogs from exhibiting any measurable stress, at least as measured by heart rate and blood pressure. (Serpell labels these experiments "ethically disturbing." I would call them unconscionable.)

The single most amazing such story I have ever heard about—a story that would make anyone pause and wonder—is from the anthology *Intimate Nature: The Bond Between Women and Animals*. The author is Fran Peavey, "writer, environmental activist, and peacemaker." Here is what she says:

> One day I was walking through the Stanford University campus with a friend when I saw a crowd of people with cameras and video equipment on a little hillside. They were clustered around a pair of chimpanzees—a male running loose and a female on a chain about twenty-five feet long. It turned out that the male was from Marine World and the female was being studied for something or other at Stanford. The spectators were scientists and publicity people trying to get them to mate. The male was eager. He grunted and grabbed the female's chain and tugged. She whimpered and backed away. He pulled again. She pulled back. Watching the chimps' faces, I began to feel sympathy for the female.
>
> Suddenly the female chimp yanked her chain out of the male's grasp. To my amazement, she walked through the crowd, straight over to me, and took my hand. Then she led me across the circle to the only other two women in the crowd, and she joined hands with one of them. The three of

us stood together in a circle. I remember the feeling of that rough palm against mine. The little chimp had recognized us and reached out across all the years of evolution to form her own support group.

THE SECRET LIFE OF ELEPHANTS

At birth, the brain of almost every mammal is already about 90 percent of its adult weight. Humans are exceptional, with a brain at birth only about 25 percent of adult weight. Elephants are right behind us, with brains about 35 percent of adult weight. As Cynthia Moss writes, they have "a lot of mental and physical development ahead of [them]." So it stands to reason—and there is plenty of evidence as well—that elephants may have as rich an emotional life as any creature on earth. Moss, however, is not interested in comparing the family life of elephants with our own. She looks at elephant life for its own sake.

Moss, whom I consider a kindred spirit and friend and for whom I have the greatest admiration, describes a chaotic meeting between two large groups of elephants, complete with "earflapping, rumbling, screaming, trumpeting, clicking of tusks together, entwining of trunks, spinning and backing, and urinating and defecating." This went on for four or five minutes. Describing another greeting later between two other groups, Moss writes in *Elephant Memories*, published in 1988, "Above all, the sounds of their greeting rent the air as over and over they gave forth rich grumbles and piercing trumpets of joy." The author concludes:

> After 18 years of watching elephants I still feel a tremendous thrill at witnessing a greeting ceremony. Somehow it epitomizes what makes elephants so special and interesting. I have

no doubt even in my most scientifically rigorous moments that the elephants are experiencing joy when they find each other again. It may not be similar to human joy or even comparable, but it is elephantine joy and it plays a very important part in their whole social system.

Like Cynthia Moss, Joyce Poole has studied elephants for most of her professional life. In fact, Poole was a student at Moss's camp in Kenya and has written her own book on the elephants of Amboseli—*Coming of Age with Elephants*—and she, too, is in awe of the greeting ceremonies. She has even concluded that the family life of an elephant may be richer emotionally than our own, and she explains this as a result of the incredibly close matriarchal society of female elephants: "Imagine being born into and living with a family until the day you died, living with your sisters, your aunts, your grandmother, your mother, never straying more than ten meters [away]. When anything happened that threatened that family, or anything joyful happened and you came together as a unit and screamed and yelled and sort of threw your arms around each other—that's what it's like living in an elephant family." With elephants, the maternal bond gives every indication of being just as strong as with people, and lasts a lifetime as well, but only with the females.

Males eventually go off on their own and may never return. For about eight months a year, they hole up in a bullpen, almost literally, "hanging out with all the other males," as Moss explained to me, getting fit, building strength for musth season. (Some scientists conclude that musth is the male equivalent of the female estrus, or heat. It is marked by a secretion from glands in the male elephant's temporal region.) Since a mature female may bear a calf only every fourth year or so, and there are probably only a few mature females in any one family, the male would be "wasting a lot of his time," reproductively speaking, by sticking with just one family. He is better off trying to become the big alpha male for a large territory, in which case he could father as many as a hundred calves in those four years—evolutionary permission to be as promiscuous as possible.

In her book *Elephant Memories*, Moss describes the heartrending efforts of a family of female elephants to save Tina, who had been shot in the lungs by poachers. When the confrontation with the men ended, the elephants turned to the downed animal. (One elephant had already died with a bullet in the brain.) "Her knees started to buckle and she began to go down," Moss writes, "but Teresia got on one side of her and Trista on the other and they both leaned in and held her up." Teresia was Tina's mother. "Soon, however, she had no strength and she slipped beneath them and fell onto her side. More blood gushed from her mouth and with a shudder she died. Teresia and Trista became frantic and knelt down and tried to lift her up. They worked their tusks under her back and under her head. At one point they succeeded in lifting her into a sitting position but her body flopped back down." Other elephants tried to stuff grass into Tina's mouth. "Finally . . . when [Teresia] got to a standing position with the full weight of Tina's head and front quarters on her tusks, there was a sharp cracking sound and Teresia dropped the carcass as her right tusk fell to the ground. She had broken it a few inches from the lip well into the nerve cavity, and a jagged bit of ivory and the bloody pulp were all that remained."

"They gave up then but did not leave. Tina's family buried her with leaves and earth in the shallowest of graves. They stood vigil through the night, then began to move off. Teresia was the last to leave," Moss writes. "She reached behind her and gently felt the carcass with her hind foot repeatedly. The others rumbled again and very slowly, touching the tip of her trunk to her broken tusk, Teresia moved off to join them.''

On one other occasion, Moss witnessed what appeared to be the beginning of a burial ceremony—the elephants had broken off branches and palm fronds and placed them on the carcass—before a spotter plane flown by park rangers swooped down and inadvertently interrupted. Moss learned that the myth of an elephant graveyard is just that, a myth, although there are certain locations with good food and water that attract ailing elephants and might therefore have more than their share of bones. She suspects the myth arose following the discovery of enormous piles of bones remaining from the slaughter of an extended family of elephants. In southern Africa, one tribe killed entire herds by building a ring of fire around them. Although the graveyard is a myth, Moss believes that the animals do have a concept of death. She saw too many episodes like that between Teresia and her daughter.

She writes:

Although they pay no attention to the remains of other species, they always react to the body of a dead elephant. I have been with elephant families many times when this has happened. . . . They stop and become quiet and yet tense in a different way from anything I have seen in other situations. First they reach their trunks toward the body to smell it, and then they approach slowly and cautiously and begin to touch the bones, sometimes lifting them and turning them with their feet and trunks. They seem particularly interested in the head and tusks. They run their trunk tips along the tusks and lower jaw and feel in all the crevices and hollows in the skull. I would guess they are trying to recognize the individual.

Joyce Poole adds that elephants often greet one another by putting their trunks in the other's mouth. She believes that this behavior is related to the behavior with bones, when, as Poole says, "They're very, very quiet. Terribly quiet. In fact the only thing you hear is the clank of bones and the sounds of the elephants exhaling, and the reason they're exhaling is so they can take in another deep breath so they can smell the bones." Poole believes it is very possible that elephants do recognize the bones of family.

Anyone who has worked with captive elephants has stories confirming the old cliché that an elephant never forgets. Many involve a particular keeper who has dropped out of involvement with an elephant for a decade or more, maybe even for two decades. The moment this keeper returns to the scene, the elephant reacts favorably or unfavorably to the memory, as the case may be.

The elephant behavior with bones is so predictable that wildlife photographers and filmmakers can easily "bait" a scene by bringing in bones from another site. Perhaps none of this should surprise us, because the tightly knit, matriarchal society of elephants can be devastated by the loss of the matriarch and never recover its cohesiveness. Moss has seen a mother wander lethargically at the rear of the family for many days following the death of her calf.

How ironic it is that many times Moss has witnessed elephants go out of their way not to kill a human, despite every kind of thoughtless, mean provocation. "At times," she writes in *Elephant Memories*, "it was actually difficult for an elephant not to step on or run over someone but they always swerved or backed quickly to avoid doing so." She adds that this behavior is not necessarily out of consideration for us. Elephants are not predators, after all. They are herbivores, not carnivores. They have nothing to gain in the wild by killing an animal. On the other hand, elephants can definitely be dangerous in captivity, because, Moss explains, the human-elephant relationship in captivity is one of dominance, with the human the dominant creature. If the elephant sees the opportunity to even the score, it will. In fact, the elephant, male or female, actively seeks any opportunity to redress old grievances—which the elephant does not forget. This is why several keepers around the world are killed every year—one of the highest per-capita fatality rates for any occupation.

An elephant does not need to tusk or stomp in order to kill. From time to time they have killed cattle weighing a thousand pounds with one swipe of the trunk. They well know their immense strength. The danger involved in working with elephants, and the direct correlation between this danger and the dominance relationship, has led to the theory that dominance should be avoided in the first place. The elephants should be treated as equals at all times. Common sense, we might think, but many keepers are reluctant to give up the old way, even though someday they may pay for it with their lives.

And equality is all elephants ask for. Just think of what damage they could do, as the largest land animals on earth, if evolution had molded them to think of themselves as superior to all other living creatures.

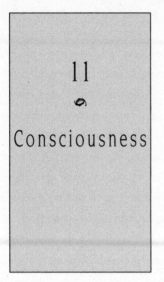

11

Consciousness

THE SELF-CONSCIOUS EMOTIONS

The primary emotions considered in the previous chapter—fear, anger, pleasures of all sorts—are simple, powerful, and shared, I believe, by many animals. This is the parsimonious, the least embellished conclusion (although behaviorists would not agree). However, the secondary emotions of embarrassment, guilt, and shame are considered by psychologists to indicate a higher order of consciousness. Apparently these emotions require, on the part of the person or animal, a sense of "what I look like" to someone else. In turn, this seems to require a sense of myself and a sense that others might have an opinion about me. In short, only creatures with both "other-consciousness" and "self-consciousness" would seem to be "capable" of embarrassment and shame. Otherwise, why and how would a creature care about another's opinion? Thus these are called the "social" or "self-conscious" emotions.

Most animals give no indications of experiencing shame or embarrassment. No matter what a creature might be capable of in terms of thinking and in experiencing fear and pleasure, we do not really expect most animals to be self-consciously embarrassed about anything. At least I don't look for it from a diamondback rattlesnake or from a largemouth bass. No matter how complex the social organization within a beehive, we do not picture the forager bee who has returned empty-handed, so to speak, to be ashamed of herself—but it is unlikely that we would be able to tell for sure.

We do not have easy answers concerning birds either. Irene Pepperberg is pretty sure that when Alex the parrot says, "I'm sorry"— which he does quite often, and with good reason—he is not really sorry at all. He will use the phrase to defuse what he correctly reads is her annoyance at his behavior. Pepperberg, however, does not sense any genuine embarrassment and contrition, and the bird will repeat the annoying behavior almost instantaneously. These birds are extremely self-centered. All in all, Pepperberg puts Alex at the emotional level of a two-and-a-half-year-old child—maybe a three-year-old on his good days. She laughs when reporting that the standard books on raising parrots warn that to have one is to have a young child on your hands for the rest of the bird's life, which can be forty or fifty or even more long years.

Neuroscience tells us that embarrassment and shame are the emotions of the neocortex. Every mammal has a neocortex sitting atop its brain, but the structure is not necessarily large, and most mammals show no evidence of the self-conscious emotions. When the nineteenth-century horse Clever Hans made a mistake, was he embarrassed before his audience? I doubt it. Most of us draw the line for the self-conscious emotions quite high.

Dogs? According to Jeffrey Masson, trainers of guide dogs say that old dogs who become incontinent do seem to be embarrassed. Most dog owners have seen "submissive body language" in pet dogs after some "elimination mistake" that certainly appears to be embarrassment and shame. My own dogs seem to be embarrassed after refusing to come when called or when scolded for "stealing" food, as well as with the other problem.

Not everyone agrees with me on this, but I think cats, too, become embarrassed from time to time. When they are scolded for whatever reason, usually completely deserved, they slink off to a hiding place and often will not be heard from for hours. Perhaps the emotion they are feeling is anger, not shame. Who knows? Certainly cats *do* appear to be capable of pride when dropping dead birds and mice at your feet!

Embarrassment, guilt, and shame serve as regulators of social life. That is the standard assessment, at any rate, as demonstrated in the work of Dr. Michael Lewis, of the Institute of Child Development in New Jersey, and others. Children first show signs of embarrassment about the age of two. By this age, infants have the sense of themselves, of others, and of rules and expectations. In the *Nature* animal-minds series, we see this demonstrated in a test rigged for a little boy to fail. When he does, he responds with the "collapsing" body language psychologists associate with shame: head and neck slumped, face turned away to hide from the eyewitness. (Pride invokes just the opposite body language: shoulders up, chest out, head high, arms flung overhead.) Then we see Indah, an orangutan living and studying at the Think Tank at the National Zoo in Washington, D.C., learning language with a lexigram keyboard. If the keyboard is rigged for In-dah to fail, she exhibits the rudiments of the classic collapsing body we see with the small boy: throwing her arm over her head and ducking to the side.

"Kanzi be bad now."

Thus did our favorite bonobo signal his caretaker Sue Savage-Rumbaugh one day before promptly swiping his half sister Panban-isha's banana. But does Kanzi really feel bad? Savage-Rumbaugh was curious and set up a simple trial, the equivalent of a test that has been tried on children for many years. Using the lexigram keyboard, she informs Kanzi that certain new toys are very fragile, and that he must be careful when playing with them. Unknown to Kanzi, of course, these toys have been rigged to break. They do so when Savage-Rumbaugh is watching through a one-way mirror. When the toy breaks, Kanzi reacts as every human child reacts. First he looks suit-ably embarrassed. Then he glances around to see if anyone witnessed the transgression. Then he tries to put the toy back together. Unsuc-cessful, he finally hides it under a rug.

In humans, the artistic and religious impulses, which we believe are at least as old as the earliest cave drawings, are in some ways self-conscious emotions. Certainly they require self-consciousness of a high order. Jane Goodall reports that chimpanzees sometimes make threatening gestures against thunderstorms, a report interpreted else-where as a "proto-religious" behavior. She has witnessed chimps re-acting to waterfalls in ways that, again, are impossible not to anthropomorphize about. Goodall says, "I ask myself [whether] per-haps it was feelings of awe like this which led to the early primitive, animistic religions."

One day at Gombe one of Goodall's assistants was seated on a ridge watching the sun set over Lake Tanganyika. We can readily imagine how beautiful this scene was. Soon two chimpanzees climbed the ridge, where they greeted one another and the student and then sat down in silence to contemplate the blazing colors of the sunset. There have been other reports of chimps watching sunsets. Perhaps some readers snicker at these stories, but I fail to see why. Many of the primates are, like humans, trichromats: We see three main colors—red, green, and blue. If you and I see the sunset in the same way (and of course there is no proof that we do, if you want to be pedantic about it), then there is every reason to believe that a chimpanzee is also seeing the same sunset in the same glowing colors that we are. Many other mammals, including cats and dogs, are dichromats, "missing" one of the three primaries, and there is no reason a sunset shouldn't be a pleasant experience for them as well. Most of us have seen drawings by primates, abstractions pleasing to the eye and, of more significance, abstractions that are obviously pleasing to the artists themselves.

One of my most prized personal possessions is a gentle, pastel abstract painting by "Mary the Painting Elephant," an abandoned circus Asian elephant who lives at Riddles Elephant Sanctuary in Arkansas. During a live broadcast on Arkansas Public Television, I stood next to Mary and her easel as she composed this work, using her trunk to hold the brushes, while she splattered water colors all over my new suit as well as her canvas. No matter. I fell in love with Mary, and if the way she tousled my hair with her "painty" trunk is an indication, I think she liked me a little bit, too.

DEGREES OF CONSCIOUSNESS? WHY NOT?

The "higher" emotions allow us to ease into the subject of consciousness by way of the back door, because the front door is so impregnable! After all, consciousness is what it's all about! Thomas Nagel's famous question "What is it like to be a bat?" implies that it's like anything at all. If it's not, then the bat is just as Descartes said, a machine made of nerves and muscles. Does it feel like something to the bat to be the bat? To the elephant to be the elephant? To the bee to be the bee? The line between those animals for whom it is like something and those for whom it is not is consciousness. Everything discussed so far has been a prologue to this question, in effect, and I am convinced that we have good reasons for inferring from our own experience that consciousness in animals is *something like* our own consciousness. I feel certain that it feels like something to be the elephant, certain that it feels like something very different to be the bat, and I believe it might well feel like something to be the bee—but I cannot *prove* it.

Many of us intuitively have doubts about bees because of the instinct factor, but nowhere is it written that an animal, human or otherwise, cannot be conscious of an instinct. Sneezing is one of Donald Griffin's favorite examples. Sneezing is entirely reflexive on our part, yet we experience it quite clearly! Breathing is an instinct. Language is an instinct, in effect, but we experience language quite consciously. One could continue this list indefinitely. Therefore an animal's life does not have to be primarily a matter of versatile or even voluntary behavior in order to be a conscious one.

If indeed consciousness arises from the activity of the myriad neurons in the brain, what difference does it make if this activity is instinctive or learned, simple or complex? Perhaps none at all—an argument that garners support from an unexpected quarter. As we have seen, Celia Heyes is an agnostic at best on the question of animal minds. In her daily life she, like all of us, is guilty of folk psychology and acts on presumptions of consciousness, but as a professional she thinks it is quite possible that no animals other than the human being possess consciousness. She definitely believes there is no way of ascertaining whether they do or not, and she discounts all inference arguments as loaded with pitfalls. And yet this consciousness-doubter agrees when Donald Griffin argues against the intuitive connection we draw between complexity and consciousness. As Heyes told us for our animal-minds television series, "Sometimes I may be gazing at a blank wall and I'm conscious of seeing the wall and of seeing the color of the wall. . . . The thinking is very simple, but I am just as conscious of it as I am when I'm thinking complex things."

Nowhere is it written in stone that consciousness is an all-or-nothing deal. Maybe it's like the dimmer switch, to employ Oxford psychologist Susan Greenfield's useful analogy: dimly held by some species, a little more brightly by others, and on up the scale. In fact, degrees of consciousness are what we perhaps should expect. This is a vitally important point. Those who hold doubts about consciousness and emotions for animals must explain how it is that these attributes arrive in the natural history of *Homo sapiens* like a bolt of lightning, with no precursors in the animal world. Such "overnight success" simply does not make much sense, intuitively or biologically.

It is certainly true that there is an enormous difference between the human mind and any animal mind, between our language and any animal communication or language. Even Darwin, a staunch proponent of continuity of the species, was puzzled by how great the difference is between us and all the others. But our position on the pinnacle does not negate the need for precursors. As Allen and Bekoff write in *Species of Mind*, "We believe that arguments about evolutionary continuity are as applicable to the study of animal minds and brains as they are to comparative studies of kidneys, stomachs, and hearts."

Ironically, perhaps, partial and damaged consciousness offers an excellent means of getting a better grip on the subject. The phenomenon of blind sight is a case in point. In Chapter Three, we looked at this rare phenomenon as an example of what cognition without consciousness might be like. It can also be used to illustrate partial consciousness. Briefly put, blind-sight victims have a large blind spot in the field of vision, as a result of some sort of injury to the part of the brain known as the visual cortex. When both the left and right visual cortices have been damaged, the individual is completely blind. Yet some of these individuals can nevertheless perform quite well on tests involving the identification of simple shapes and flashes of light. They see, apparently, and they report on what they see, but they have no consciousness of doing so.

One such individual is Graham "Y," who appears in our broadcast as one of Dr. Larry Weiscrantz's patients at Oxford University. After a boyhood injury, Graham lost sight in his right field of vision. He made adjustments and went on with his life; unable to obtain a driver's license, he rode bicycles everywhere. Then it was discovered that this young man has blind sight. He "sees" certain rapid movements and flashes of light, but others he doesn't see—or so he's told, because he has no sense of seeing any of them. "It is very bizarre," Graham says. On tests set up to discover his color vision, once again he scores quite well, especially with the color red, although he has no sense at all of seeing red. "I find it just as bizarre as you do, to be quite honest," he repeats. What does it feel like? "Nothing."

Animals can also have blind sight, which is not surprising, since the brains of mammals, particularly, have essentially the same structure as ours. Dr. Nicholas Humphrey spent years working with the monkey Helen, whose visual cortices were not functioning. Yet Helen learned to see, in a way. But then if a stranger came into the room, she became blind once again, or at least stumbled into things as if she were blind. Humphrey thinks of blind sight as something akin to extrasensory perception. He says, "They have the information, they don't know where it came from, and they find that very peculiar indeed."

Other researchers conducted an important series of tests on a monkey who was, like Graham, blind in his right field of vision. This monkey was presented with two sets of green lights, one in the left field of vision, one in the right. He was trained to touch any light that was illuminated, and to touch a separate blue light if *none* of the green lights was lit. The results of the test confirm our expectations regarding blind sight. When a green light on the left, his "good" side, was lit, the monkey touched it. When a green light on the right was lit, the monkey touched it *but also touched the blue light*. He saw the green light on the right, but he was not aware of seeing it, and therefore touched the blue light as well. He was conscious of the light in the left field of vision, but not the one in the right field. Some comparative psychologists believe that this test comes as close as any ever conducted to demonstrating animal consciousness in a controlled laboratory setting.

In the previous chapter, we looked at Temple Grandin's sympathy with the emotions of animals. Grandin is autistic. Whatever the exact nature of this illness, autism definitely produces an inability to perceive and deal with the world at large in the "normal" way. Autistic individuals do not synthesize their perceptions into an organized and coordinated picture of the world. As Grandin told us, she has all the emotions, but they come and go quickly. As someone else put it, the autistic's life is not a rich, Tolstoyan novel, but something more like a minimalist short story. The autistic person has a different kind of consciousness from the rest of us. Although Grandin does use words, and very well, she thinks in pictures, not words. A cow also thinks in pictures, not words, and you will never convince Grandin that both she and the cow are unconscious.

CONSCIOUSNESS AS ADAPTATION

Donald Griffin writes, "If we postulate the presence of simple thoughts, a great deal of animal behavior can be understood as a consistent adaptive pattern." He told me in his Harvard office, "Animals seem to be conscious of things that are important to them. 'That is something good to eat,' or 'That is something dangerous to get away from,' or 'That's a female of my species that's attractive to me,' or 'That's a baby that needs help or needs food.' Those are the sorts of consciousness that seem likely."

The philosopher Daniel Dennett suggests that this capacity for generalization might evolve when the list of behaviors required of a species becomes unwieldy for "if-then learning." As he summarizes the situation, all individuals in all species "learn through evolution"—through inherited hardwiring. Then surprisingly many species, including simple invertebrates, find themselves compelled to learn in a second way, what Dennett refers to as Skinnerian fashion—conditioned learning à la Skinner's behaviorism. Some select species are pressured by evolution to learn in yet a third way, by using information in an inner environment (the "mind") in order to draw conclusions about the outer environment. Here we have consciousness, pure and simple, and as the philosopher Karl Popper puts it (quoted by Dennett), consciousness "permits our hypotheses to die in our stead."

This is a witty and elegant phrase, well worth a moment's consideration. I think of a hungry lioness hunkered behind a mound, considering a grazing buffalo thirty yards away. A buffalo is no wildebeest. A buffalo is a different matter altogether, one of the most aggressive and dangerous animals in Africa, and the lioness understands this. Yes, she is hungry, and so are her cubs, but no, she is not that hungry and not that good a mother—not that dumb a mother. She will let her hypothesis die in her stead. She strolls away. Or think of all the fantasizing we humans do in moments of fear or anger. Pretty horrible thoughts, but most of the time we do not act on them.

Why can the great apes solve complex problems of analogical reasoning and achieve what they do with symbolic chips and lexigrams—talents they would not seem to need in the wild? The answer is one of the keys to this whole inquiry, really. The apes are smart enough to solve our abstract problems because they do in fact need to solve the equivalent practical problems in the course of their own lives in the wild, where programmed instinct and "Skinnerian" conditioning would not be nearly enough to see them through the day successfully. Consciousness quite possibly arose when social animals (a category that could include certain insects, don't forget) reached the point at which they were required to understand the intentions of the other animals. In Darwinian terms, consciousness would thus be one final, vitally important, and beneficial adaptation. And so animals would be "natural psychologists," to employ the term first employed by Nicholas Humphrey, while elaborating on the hypothesis of Alison Jolly.

The same point was made more colorfully by the primatologists David Premack and Guy Woodruff, who wrote that they were less interested in the ape as a physicist than as a psychologist. And two more primatologists, Dorothy Cheney and Robert Seyfarth, write in *How Monkeys See the World*, "group life has exerted strong selective pressure on the ability of primates to form complex associations, to make transitive inferences, and even to judge causal relations, but primarily when the stimuli are other primates. Monkeys and apes are more likely to solve at least some types of problems if they involve social stimuli [from members of their own species] than if they involve objects."

We noted in the last chapter, on animal emotions, how the intensely close, matriarchal society of the elephant clearly facilitates deep emotional reactions and bonds. Jane Goodall says that the patriarchal society of chimpanzees applies pressure to develop a different set of social skills, including the recognition of individuals and the accurate assessment of relationships that are always in flux, with chimps moving in and out of the group on a daily basis. We would be extremely naïve or willfully obtuse not to acknowledge that handling such a complex society requires some commensurably complex social skills. Goodall says, "They watch each other very carefully, they pick up tiny little intention movements, they intently look at one another's faces and seem able to read the expression, and it's just very clear from the way the chimpanzee reacts, what he does or doesn't do, that he understands perfectly well the intention of the other."

In his book *Chimpanzee Politics*, Frans de Waal tells the story of the two mothers, Jimmie and Tepel, watching their children playing. When the playing gets rough and mild admonitions do not quell the outbreak, Tepel gently prods a resting female, Mama, and points in the direction of the quarreling kids. Mama is a high-ranking matriarch unrelated to the others. De Waal writes, "As soon as Mama takes one threatening step forward, waves her arms in the air and barks loudly, the children stop quarreling. Mama then lies down again and continues her siesta."

De Waal contends that Jimmie and Tepel were concerned about starting conflict between each other as a result of conflict between their kids, so they called in the third party, Mama, to restore order. This is an illustration of what has become known as a "social tool."

Another example of the adaptive use of a social tool is the well-known behavior in which one female primate will "present" her rear end to a ranking male while threatening another female at the same time. Her idea is to enlist the male's help, perhaps to the point of inducing him to attack the other female. All too predictably, perhaps, the male is often taken in by this ploy.

There is literally no end to the stories of social intelligence involving primates. It is their—our—defining trait. One day in Georgia, Sue Savage-Rumbaugh was hiking through the woods with the bonobo Panbanisha and some dogs. (Panbanisha is the half sister of Kanzi, whom we already know well.) Suddenly the dogs stopped in their tracks and began growling at some threat in the trees. Panbanisha and Savage-Rumbaugh soon spotted the source of the dogs' concern: a large wildcat perched on a limb. Both the bonobo's and the human's hair instantly stood on end, and the two exchanged a telling glance of apprehension before immediately heading to safety. Back at the lab, Kanzi, his stepmother Matata, and another ape, Panzee, all understood immediately that something frightening had happened outside. They stared out the window, making the soft "whu-uh" sound that registers unusual events. Panbanisha vocalized, and the other chimps responded in kind. Savage-Rumbaugh spoke to Kanzi and Panzee in English, and "both of them listened with rapt attention and huge round eyes. At appropriate points during my recounting Panbanisha embellished my tale with bonobo 'Waa' vocalizations, as though to add her own emphasis."

In the days that followed, Kanzi and Panzee were obviously concerned whenever they approached the area in which the big cat had been seen. By what means and to what extent, we may never know, but they had understood the gist of the scary situation. Of this there is no doubt, not to Savage-Rumbaugh. She acknowledges that one such episode doesn't prove much, but when such episodes happen all the time—which they do, in her experience—she is left with no alternative but to conclude that highly effective and complex social interaction and amazing communication is taking place.

Elizabeth Marshall Thomas, author of *The Hidden Life of Dogs*, tells us in that book about a visit to Baffin Island with a contingent of Canadian scientists. Their appearance disturbed the local pack of wolves, and the young wolf and his mother who first saw the human beings retreated to their den and howled. An hour later, all the wolves had congregated and were howling in a haunting chorus. For wolves, Thomas speculates, howling is equivalent to our choral singing. It's a means of bonding and of communication—"perhaps to express their solidarity vis-à-vis our group, or perhaps to tell us that the river system was owned by them and that we should move." One of the scientists predicted that the other wolves were also being warned away from the site of the trespassing. And this was true. Thomas writes:

> Uncanny as it seems, as long as we stayed there, the wolves never again visited the place where they first spotted us, the place that became our main camp, even though we certainly didn't threaten them but instead put out very odoriferous baits to lure them. They later tolerated and even visited me in my camp right by their den, and a wolverine came gladly enough to eat the baits, but . . . the wolves thereafter avoided our main camp, just as if the two who had seen us told the others where a surprising and untoward thing had occurred. In fact, they almost certainly had done just that.

None of us knew how they managed the communication, but then, wolf communication is merely one of many things about animals that people don't fully understand.

Although we don't tend to think about them in these terms, birds are also highly social creatures, and they are at their most intelligent in socialized settings. Irene Pepperberg emphasizes this point regarding Alex and other African gray parrots, who in the wild live in large flocks for many years. A lot of information about the environment and other birds requires processing by each of these birds. I've mentioned Pepperberg's model/rival, or M/R, learning environment, in which Alex's manifest capacity for jealousy is exploited for learning purposes. This M/R environment also exploits social interaction between the trainer and Alex and other parrots. Pepperberg knew what every teacher of young children knows, that actually handling an object helps the child to learn the name for this object. Labeling at a distance simply does not work well with children, and Pepperberg believed that the same bias would hold for parrots, and she was right. Like the child, the bird needs hands-on interaction.

OTHER MINDS

The brief discussion of highly evolved social intelligence and "social tools"—a discussion that could have been a book in itself—leads directly to the theoretical underlying question: Do some animals have a "theory of mind"? This is the official terminology, although the meaning of this phrase is more accurately conveyed as "theory of other minds." When Tepel pokes Mama, does Tepel actually have a sense that Mama is a being with independent intentions and beliefs, with a "mind of her own"? Or has Tepel simply learned from past episodes that poking Mama in this way results in a certain behavior?

When two lionesses intentionally make themselves known to the wildebeest while a third and fourth sneak into position for a blindside attack, does each have a sense of the intention of the others?

The question is important because an animal's knowledge of other minds implies a knowledge of its own mind. Or does it? The authors of *How Monkeys See the World* believe that vervet monkeys master some of the abstract-relationship tests because they encounter "dominance hierarchies" in their real world every bit as complex as those of the Montagues and Capulets, but Cheney and Seyfarth also note, "The fact that we can describe vervet monkey social behavior in terms of relationships and strategies does not, therefore, necessarily mean that knowledge of these principles is what guides the monkeys' actions. They might be following a few relatively simple rules of action: avoid some individuals, groom or copulate with others. At this point in our discussion we simply do not know."

Maybe the monkeys know only about other *behavior*, not about other *minds*. Or as philosopher Daniel Dennett puts the point in his typically clever way, it is theoretically possible to be an unthinking natural psychologist. Certainly a theory of other minds would come in handy for any primate, so it would have good reason to evolve, but this is not to say that it necessarily has. An animal does not necessarily need to consult any internal "model" of the mind in order to anticipate behavior, Dennett points out. The animal could just be equipped with a large list of if-then contingencies.

On the other hand, as I've noted, at some point a lengthy list would need to be replaced by some simple generalizations and ideas. But enough of these theoretical debates anyway! Let's look at some hard-and-fast research, beginning with the work of Premack and Woodruff. They asked if an intelligent animal such as a chimpanzee who knows what it's like to wear a blindfold understands what it's like for another chimp or a human trainer to wear a blindfold? To find out, they set up a situation in which a young chimpanzee required the assistance of a trainer in obtaining food. The chimp knew where the food was; the trainer had the key to the box. Four chimps participated in this study, and each had no trouble leading the trainer to the hidden food. Then one day the trainer arrived blindfolded and was unable to follow. In fact, the trainer had several "blindfolds": one across his eyes, others elsewhere across his face.

What would each of the chimps do now? The results are fascinating: Three of the four chimps took the trainer by the hand and physically led him to the box. Very logical, very productive, very smart: good common sense. The fourth chimp, however, took off the blindfold—the correct blindfold, leaving the other decoys in place. Does this prove that the fourth chimp understood about his own eyesight and about the trainer's eyesight—knew about his own consciousness and the trainer's as well? Perhaps, but one could also argue that the chimp simply didn't like the appearance of the blindfold; one could argue that the chimp wanted to be able to see the trainer's eyes, and by removing the blindfold thereby lucked into an intelligent-looking behavior. In this field, one can always argue.

In another Premack-Woodruff study, the chimpanzees dealt with two trainers, one of whom was established over time as friendly (he shared food) and the other as unfriendly (he did not share the food, plus he dressed like Darth Vader, which the chimps did not like). In time, the chimps learned to direct the friendly trainer to a container of food, and one of the chimps learned to deceive the unfriendly trainer. But again, the question arises whether the chimp truly had a sense of the mental state of the friendly versus the unfriendly trainer, or did he just learn the simple rule "unfriendly trainer equals no food"?

To my mind, a much better case for a concept of other minds is put forward by Sue Savage-Rumbaugh. In her laboratory in Atlanta, the chimpanzees Austin and Sherman learned to work with each other and their lexigrams to pass food and tools back and forth in carefully controlled situations. One of the two watched as a trainer put food into one of several containers, while the one who could not see the container controlled the tools needed to open them. What to do now? After several weeks, the chimps caught on and began asking the other, by way of the lexigram keyboard, to pass the tool, which was done. I discussed this work in the chapter on language, but it is even more significant as it relates to the question of other minds. As Savage-Rumbaugh writes in *Kanzi: The Ape at the Brink of the Human Mind:*

> Did Sherman know that Austin's mind or knowledge state was different from his own? It seemed so; otherwise, why would he bother to tell Austin which tool he needed or which food was hidden in a container? . . . It was the chimps who began to attend to each other, to coordinate their communications, and to correct each other's errors. For me, as I watched them, the question was reversed: How could they not know that they were communicating?

Another study I find compelling involves a chimp observing while a trainer loads one of four containers with a favorite food. That is, the chimp observes the baiting procedure but cannot see which of the four containers has the food. But she can see two trainers who are also observing the baiting. One of these trainers (the "knower") has a clear view, while the view of the other (the "guesser") is blocked by a screen. The challenge is to seek the help of one of the trainers in finding the food. Of four chimps tested, two chose the knower, indicating an understanding of the "seeing-knowing" relationship for another individual. One chimp chose this knowing trainer but then did not always follow her advice. The fourth chimp never caught on to the difference between knowing and guessing.

Other versions of this and similar tests have produced the same results: Some apes catch on, some don't. Similar tests with macaque monkeys failed to instill knowledge of the situation in any of them. None learned to trust the knower over the guesser. (By the way, children cross this comprehension threshold between the ages of three and four, but with a difference: The successful chimps required over a hundred trials before understanding the problem; when kids are finally ready to "get it," they do so fast, with just a dozen trials.)

In a similar experiment, the chimpanzee Sarah was shown a series of videotapes depicting one of her trainers experiencing some kind of problem, such as trying to operate a radio that was clearly unplugged. Then the videotape was stopped before the problem was solved, and Sarah was presented with a choice of pictures, one of which shows the correct solution to the problem. Sarah selected that correct answer at well above a chance rate. Interpretation: She understood that a problem was being confronted and inferred a sense of purpose to the individual. But the really fascinating point here is that Sarah would choose incorrect answers if the trainer depicted with the problem was not one of her favorites—intriguing behavior open to a range of interpretations, one of which is that Sarah was lying.

So Sarah does seem to have a concept of other minds, although this concept is limited, apparently. Other tests have suggested that she is not capable of understanding when the other mind holds a false belief. The setup of this study was simple. A cabinet contained good food on one side and horrible, disgusting stuff on the other side.

Sarah had no problem directing a trainer to the good food. Then a masked man entered the room and switched everything around. Sarah reacted with vehemence and threw things at this evil intruder. There's no question that she knew what had happened, but when the unknowing trainer—the trainer who held a now false belief—came back in, Sarah did not seem to understand that he might not know about the treachery. She didn't try to warn him, and she directed him to the side of the cabinet that now held the bad food.

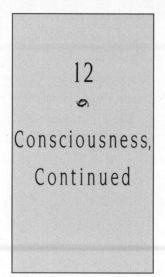

12

Consciousness, Continued

DECEPTION

We humans are not the only Machiavellians. Animals are good at politics and deception as well. R. W. Byrne and Andrew Whiten wrote an entire book on the subject, titled *Machiavellian Intelligence*, and every other book on animal behavior has a chapter or two on the subject. Including this one, because deceptive activity is not only fascinating in its own right, but also provocative as it relates to the question of consciousness. Deception seems to require a sense of the other mind as well as my own mind.

Let's begin this survey with the firefly, a common beetle whose overall communication skills are "fantastically complex," in the words of Donald Griffin—a reference, in part, to the biochemistry of the luminescent flashing. The male of the species *Photinus pyralis* seeks out females on a summer's eve by flying near likely bushes while flashing every six seconds for one half second. A responsive female in one of these bushes usually waits a couple of seconds before answering the male in the affirmative with her own half-second flash. The male then turns and flies in her direction, and increasingly excited flashes go back and forth between the pair. The "excitement" part of the narrative is a blatantly anthropomorphic assumption on my part, but nevertheless, mating usually follows in short order.

There is a catch, however. It happens that the female of a larger species of firefly, *Photuris pyralis*, mimics the reply of the *Photinus* female. If the hapless *Photinus* male responds to this deception and comes too close, this deceptive female will eat him on the spot and thus get a quick and easy, high-protein meal for her own eggs. However, only about 10 to 15 percent of the males that initially approach the deceptive *Photuris* female go all the way, so to speak, and put themselves in harm's way. Most somehow catch on to her ruse and fly away at warp speed!

Can the *Photuris* femme fatale actually have an intention to deceive the *Photinus* male? And does this male actually understand that he has been deceived when he takes evasive action? We're cautious in drawing this conclusion, and the same is true, I believe, when considering some species of scorpion fly, in which the male must present the female with a gift of food—an insect—before she will mate with him. Males either do their own hunting for this purpose or, sometimes, present themselves as females to other males who already have their insect. They then steal this bug and head for the real females themselves. Intentional behavior or sheer instinct? Deception among the insects is quite common. Perhaps they have to fool everyone because most of them are so small?

What about the behavior of the genus *Gonodactylus*? These creatures are predatory by nature and operate from caves. The battle for a good cave often requires ritualized posturing and gesturing and, to all appearances, bluffing. They recognize other individuals—by way of odor, it is believed—and avoid the caves of those who have defeated them. Members of *Gonodactylus* are also known among specialists as "stomatopods." Among the rest of us they are known as shrimp—mantis shrimps, to be exact.

The individual whose research brought to light the surprisingly complex behavior of this shrimp denies any consciousness for his subjects, as do most readers of this story, I suspect. They are shrimp, after all. But as Griffin points out—I was very surprised to learn this—mantis shrimp happen to have a well-organized central nervous system, one that is larger than a bee's. And we have seen what a bee can do. Therefore, Griffin concludes, "it is quite reasonable to speculate that mantis shrimps may experience very simple conscious feelings or thoughts about the fights by which they gain or lose the cavities that are so important to them and the antagonists whose odors they learn to recognize from previous encounters."

We already know that birds are quite intelligent in some respects, and that the brains of some birds are larger relative to body weight than the brains of the "lower" mammals. Donald Griffin reports the following case of avian deception on the part of a hummingbird who had detected a mist net strung across his territory. (The episode was observed by researcher A. C. Kamil.) Everyone studying hummingbirds knows that once a net has been discovered by a bird, it will never be effective against that bird, who understands to avoid it. This particular hummingbird even used this net as a perch! In fact, he happened to be perched on it when another male entered his territory. As we have learned, male hummingbirds are ferociously aggressive in defending their territories, usually charging directly at the intruder and driving him away. In this case, however, the net-knowl-edgeable defender of the territory flew *around* the perimeter of his acreage until the intruding bird was *between* him and the net. Then he attacked, successfully driving the unfortunate bird into the net.

Kamil does not relate this "anecdote" for purposes of attributing consciousness, but Griffin argues that it is suggestive of "intentional planning," if nothing else. Even more suggestive of conscious plan-ning and deception is the behavior of the shrike. I can only imagine the weeks and months of careful observation that must have been necessary to establish this behavior, now well known and reported in many sources, including *The Animal Mind*. Briefly put, certain shrikes who dwell in the treetops serve as sentinels for all the birds feeding below them in the lower reaches of the trees. The shrikes are watch-ing for dangerous hawks, which will take smaller, unsuspecting birds on the wing. This is not a deal with one-way benefit, however, be-cause the shrikes feed on insects stirred up by all the other birds below them.

As the shrikes move through the treetops, the other birds follow. When the shrike sees a hawk, it emits an alarm call, and the other birds dive for cover. And sometimes, when a shrike sees another bird about to capture a particularly juicy insect, the shrike will emit a false alarm. The other bird forgets the insect and flies for cover. The shrike then takes the meal. Should the other bird catch this insect despite the alarm call, the shrike may stifle the alarm midcall. This behavior seems pretty intentional to me, as though the shrike understands that he should not "waste" alarm calls or the other birds will catch on to the trick.

The shrike is not the only bird that has been observed emitting false alarms in order to get rid of predators temporarily. In fact, many birds are capable of all sorts of deception, none more intriguing than the "tonic immobility" of many ground-dwelling birds if they are captured by a predator. They play dead, in other words. (Why should it matter to the predator whether its prey is dead now or dead in a few minutes? The answer is unclear, but apparently it does matter, because sometimes the too-sudden lack of movement by the prey will induce the predator to drop the meal and move on. And as we know, the recommended procedure for surviving a bear attack is to curl up and lie as still as possible, despite the mauling.)

We assume that much of this feigning behavior by birds is instinctive, and surely it is, but there are also good reasons for seeing a measure of versatility. It turns out that death-feigning birds, such as bobwhite quail, are more likely to do so if they see two eyes in front of them, not just one. Why would this be, as clever, controlled experiments demonstrate? With very few exceptions, the predators of the world have a pair of eyes mounted fairly close together and looking forward. This allows for binocular vision, which in turn provides vastly superior information on distance, as we all know from trying to touch an object with one eye closed. On the other hand, prey animals, such as the wildebeest, have eyes mounted on either side of the head, which sacrifices "distance control" but provides a wider range of vision, which is more important for them. Presumably, the bird responds to two eyes rather than just one because two eyes mean "predator." If the feigning bird discovers just one eye staring down, it is more likely to take flight, instead of going to the trouble of playing dead.

Perhaps the most famous deceptive behavior in the animal kingdom is that of the female plover. This clever bird is world-famous—I read about it everywhere—thanks to the exhaustive research of Carolyn Ristau of Rockefeller University, whose essay for *Cognitive Ethology* on the piping plover is a jam-packed thirty-three pages. This bird has at least four quite distinct tricks she employs to lure a predator away from her nest of eggs, including the "broken wing" trick, in which she presents herself to the predator in just such a vulnerable state, executes a brief run away from the nest, feigns again, then takes off for another brief run away from the nest. Another deception is to run squeaking along the ground in the manner of a small rodent, which is also choice prey. A third is to sit in brood on a nest that is not there, always at some distance from the real nest. A fourth trick is to raise a general and highly visible ruckus, tempting the predator, then retreating, tempting, retreating, tempting, retreating—always away from the nest, of course.

These deceptions are not restricted to birds. The hognose snake is justifiably famous among biologists for its extravagant display of horrible death, beginning with violent writhing, concluding with inert, upside-down stillness and bleeding from the mouth. Meanwhile, it is quite alert all the while to the behavior of the predator. What to make of all these clever stratagems? The traditional explanation before Ristau's research was that most if not all such tricks are really just a classic case of "conflict behavior." This much-studied phenomenon among animals results from a conflict between the "fight" and "flight" instincts and yields confused and pointless behavior. (In tight situations, we humans are just as susceptible to conflict behavior as any other creature.) However, it is very difficult to reconcile this explanation with the plover's behavior, which gives no sense at all of being confused.

Sometimes the deceptive behavior seems incorrect in the way of instinct gone awry. For example, the deception may continue after it's too late: The eggs have already been eaten. This doesn't seem very intelligent, and it's the kind of point that doubters pick up on with a vengeance. One researcher wrote, "It is ludicrous to suppose that injury-simulation arose through birds deciding the trick was worth trying."

Ristau does not deny that there must be a strong instinctive component in the behavior, but she takes great care to point out the aspects of the behavior that seem more thoughtful. The birds keep an eye on the predator and adjust behavior accordingly, in many cases. The action almost always leads away from the nest, a calculation that is not necessarily easy, as the "engagement" shifts ground over time.

Also, the choice of deceptive tricks seems to vary with the nature of the intruder, with the full-blown behavior saved for the most dangerous. A mere cow is not a predator, so the plover doesn't bother with the broken-wing display with a cow. However, the lumbering bovine could unwittingly tread on the nest with tragic results, so the plover does park herself between the approaching cow and the nest and make a racket, thereby usually diverting the big creature. Most impressively, Ristau watched as the birds apparently discriminated between specific trespassers based on their previous experience with these trespassers. And they drew their inferences after just one encounter. In order to ensure control, Ristau chose humans as the only suitable "predator" for this phase of the experiment. Plovers dealt differently with the individual who sauntered near the nest but showed no interest as opposed to the individual who made what could be—and were—interpreted as threatening gestures toward the nest.

Ristau is a careful scientist. She concludes in *Cognitive Ethology*, "These experiments are only a beginning in the exploration whether . . . plovers are intentional creatures. The results so far suggest that they are."

If deception might be a marker that an animal has a concept of other minds and its own mind, we would expect to find choice examples among the predatory mammals and the primates. And we do. Following is a story told by Donald Griffin in *Animal Minds*. The narrative is based on Griffin's own experience at Amboseli National Park in Kenya while traveling with Robert Seyfarth and Dorothy Cheney, whose book about vervet monkeys I have cited quite a few times. Now, however, we are dealing with lions, not monkeys. One day Griffin and the Seyfarths were driving along a dirt road (there is no other kind in Amboseli) and paused to watch a herd of wildebeest, some on one side of the road, some on the other. While the trio watched, at least four, maybe five lionesses approached with a "businesslike gait." (There is nothing more "businesslike" than the gait of a hungry and confident contingent of lionesses.) All the wildebeest stopped feeding to observe them, and without pausing, two of the lionesses forthrightly climbed a small knoll and sat there in clear view of all the wildebeest. They were not trying to hide; just the opposite, in fact, or so it seemed. Shortly thereafter, a third lioness slinked along the road in a ditch, belly to the ground, and moved into position between the two groups of wildebeest. This animal was trying to hide, obviously, and had succeeded.

All was quiet for a couple of minutes. Suddenly a fourth lioness charged toward the wildebeest from a copse of trees on one side of the road. The wildebeest on that side rushed to join the others on the other side of the road, but in order to get there they had to get past the lioness slinking down the ditch. She now leaped into action and took down one of the wildebeests. Soon the charging lioness, who had presumably been part of the group to begin with, and the two lionesses who had positioned themselves so conspicuously sauntered over to the scene and commenced dining. The other wildebeests stopped to watch from a hundred meters away.

The lions' behavior in this story demonstrates mapping of the terrain, cooperative hunting, shrewd deception—a veritable galaxy of ingenious behaviors. So far as we know, lions are not capable of solving the reasoning problems in the laboratory that chimps can solve, but scenes like the one Griffin describes demonstrate again that we see animals at their most intelligent and most "conscious" while they are engaged in the most pressing activities of life in the wild. You could observe captive lions for a lifetime and never see such intelligent behavior.

Let's think for a moment about hiding. It seems to require a sense of self—otherwise, why hide?—but the range of animals that hide is enormous indeed. Snakes do it. Invertebrates. Birds. Mammals, of course. Many reports have come in regarding grizzly bears—always grizzlies, it seems—who take up positions of vantage from which they can see but not be seen, and Donald Griffin reports one story about the grizzly who hid its own tracks. Now, this, if confirmed, would say a great deal to be sure! Or is such behavior qualitatively different from the cat's instinctive efforts to cover its tracks, so to speak, after it has finished its business in the litter box? Anyway, practically everybody out there hides, and if we stop to consider the phenomenon, it can often be explained as a simple process of learning that the last time I got in this dark place I walked away alive, while my friend who stayed outside got eaten. So hiding may be a clever form of deception, but it is not evidence that an animal understands "I am hiding."

Among the primates, however, apparently purposive deception is everywhere. You could almost say that it's a way of life. One common and well-substantiated trick is for one male to "ignore" an object—food, very likely—while in the presence of an alpha male or any higher-ranking animal, in the hope of having unchallenged access to this object at a later time. A widely reported example of this evasive behavior is that of a male mangabey, a close relative of the notoriously fractious baboon, who was provided a sneak preview of food before his entire group was released into an enclosure. The first time this happened, this male went straight for the food but then had it taken away by a dominant male. In the second trial, the male stayed away from the food and was followed by the dominant animal, and both lost out to an enterprising third party. In the third trial, the subject male headed away from the food, bided his time, then rushed for, and gained, the prize. In all following trials, he followed this same procedure with good success.

Frans de Waal observed one ape wait several hours until the coast was clear, an impressive demonstration of deferred gratification. (It is quite difficult even for a chimpanzee, and almost impossible for other animals, to voluntarily squelch the desire for the immediate gratification of food.)

Marc Hauser reports that the macaques he observes on the Puerto Rican island of Cayo de Santiago, also called "Monkey Island," routinely assess the social situation before calling out about a new food source. Who's around? Friend or foe? Kin or non-kin? These are critical concerns, because if the monkey lies, in effect, by not reporting the food with foes and non-kin around, they will rough him up. What's most fascinating to Hauser is the behavior of the "peripheral male" who isn't a member of any group. This male almost never makes a food announcement and, even when caught, is never beaten up. This suggests that the rules of engagement, so to speak, are specific to the one social group.

Writing in *Bonobo: The Forgotten Ape*, de Waal tells us about the infant chimp Laura, who when instructed to clean her plate, did so amazingly quickly. Her caretakers were unable to figure out how she had accomplished this until they discovered the food in her diaper.

Several times de Waal observed one of his primate friends making overtures of reconciliation as a ploy to lure the enemy within reach, then attacking.

One final story from his book:

> A juvenile male tentatively reached for an apple that had rolled away from his mom's food pile. He stopped, seeming to realize that picking up the fruit would get him into trouble. Instead, he approached his younger sister, with an exaggerated play face. She was sitting near her mother in the direction of the apple but had not noticed it. While wrestling with his sister, the male got closer and closer to the apple. Then, with a sudden movement, he grabbed it. His interest in the play vanished . . .

In Wolfgang Kohler's famous dangling-banana experiments in the Canary Islands, so important in the study of tool use among the apes, dominant males often allowed their inferiors to build the tower of boxes that would reach the banana, then took over at the last moment—or tried to take over, because the inferiors often managed to destroy the tower in the process of vacating the scene. Accidental or intentional destruction?

An episode of deception that "made the rounds"—and therefore the literature—among ethologists was the behavior of the female baboon who sneaked away from the alpha male in her troop and mated with a young male behind a rock, unseen by the alpha. Moreover, she peeked out from behind the rock, apparently to make certain that the main male remained oblivious to her infidelity. Similar behavior has been observed (and filmed by the *Nature* crew) among the macaques on Cayo de Santiago. There have also been many reports of primates engaging in "acoustic hiding," as it's called—repressing the usual sounds of sexual behavior if this behavior might run afoul of the established order.

Jane Goodall tells us about the male chimpanzee Humphrey, who had the nasty habit of attacking females quite brutally when greeting them. One day Fifi sees Humphrey coming, and he's obviously in one of his bad moods. She looks around nervously, then suddenly stops and stares into the nearby bushes and gives a little hoot. Humphrey, "all bristling and swaggering," as Goodall describes him, strides to the bushes to investigate and conquer. But there's nothing there, and by the time he returns to Fifi, he has calmed down and grooms her instead of attacking. And Goodall also tells the incredible story of how chimpanzees are able to maintain almost total silence while out on patrol. They avoid dry leaves and rustling bushes. One time they maintained vocal silence for three hours: acoustic deception of a very high and calculated order.

IMITATION

At the Camp Leakey research center in Borneo, an adult orangutan decides to follow suit as one of the local staff washes clothes and takes a sponge bath on a pier over the lake. When the young man washes, the orangutan washes; when the man squeezes his clothes, the great ape squeezes the towel it has brought along; when the man pours water over his head, his shadow pours water over his head; tit for tat, as we see in a remarkable film sequence from *Nature*'s animal-minds series. There is no question that the orangutan is intrigued by the human's behavior and is copying it gesture for gesture. It's a charming scene and also an important one, because cognitive ethologists consider the ability to imitate another's behavior to be a sophisticated cognitive and social skill.

Imitation is the basis of cultural learning, which is one of the most powerful kinds of learning. Moreover, imitation, when broken down into its components, strongly suggests that the animal is able to keep an image or action from its environment "in mind" and then transfer this image or action to its own body. It suggests a sense of self—one that infants pick up quite early, around one year, according to Piaget. (In some experiments, babies less than a month old mimicked facial expressions such as sticking out the tongue—or is this just "deferred motor response," as Jacques Vauclair asks, rather than the "mental reconstruction of an entire motor sequence"? The question remains open, I believe.)

One of the first cases of imitation written about in the literature is from the notes of Charles Darwin, who jotted down his observation that a bumblebee would bore a hole through the underside of the flower of a kidney-bean plant, thereby obtaining nectar more easily than through the mouth of the flower, which is the normal means. Shortly after this observation, Darwin observed honeybees— not bumblebees—feeding through the underside of the kidney-bean flower. Darwin dismissed the possibility that the honeybees had been tipped to the new technique by the scent of the nectar escaping through the underside. He preferred to believe that the honeybees saw and then imitated the bumblebees.

This is anecdotal evidence, of course, and I haven't read where anyone has attempted to confirm Darwin's observation and conclusion. But rigorous tests have confirmed imitative talent by a large range of animals. Lab rats, to name one. The setup involves one group of rats learning a certain behavior to avoid a mild shock, while a second group observes. This second group does not know about the shocks; all these rats know is the behavior they see. When introduced to the experimental setup, however, this second group behaves as if it had been learning right alongside the first rats. In another experiment, one group of rats watches a joystick moving automatically while another group watches a fellow rat learn to move the joystick on his own in return for a reward. When their time comes, the group who have watched the rat perform much better than the group who have watched the joystick working automatically. Conclusion in both cases: They are imitating and learning from what they must have deemed successful behavior.

According to some studies, birds seem to be better imitators than monkeys, who are not all that successful as imitators in laboratory experiments, in spite of the famous "Monkey see, monkey do" quip. But I wonder about these experiments, because monkeys are clever little creatures when they need to be. Certainly their close relatives, the great apes who work with sign language, know a thing or two about imitation. Anyway, we know that parrots and the other psittacines are good imitators, and not just while mimicking spoken language. Pigeons can observe a fellow pigeon learning nearly any task and then almost immediately mimic the successful behavior.

Imitation is an incredibly powerful and quick form of learning. Instead of having to learn everything through your own mistakes, you can learn by watching others' successes. Jane Goodall and Christopher Boesch have each observed chimpanzees learning to "fish" for ants, one in Gombe, East Africa, and the other in the Tai forest in West Africa. In both cases young chimps study their mothers' actions intently before stealing or picking their own sticks, to try it for themselves. But when Goodall and Boesch compared notes, they realized that the two groups of chimps were using their fishing tools in very different ways. East African chimps use a long wand to gather as many termites as possible, sweeping them off with their hands and gobbling them down. Whereas chimps from West Africa use a much shorter stick, which collects far fewer termites, picked off with their lips. These methods are passed down from mother to offspring across generations, resulting in two different "tool cultures."

The most famous case of "imitation" among animals might be the potato-washing habit of a troop of macaques living on the Japanese island of Koshima. Or was it imitation? In the early 1950s, observers noticed that one female, Imo, carried her sweet potato to the surf and washed it. (This island was a preserve and home of "Mozu the Snow Monkey.") The sweet potatoes and wheat were periodically dumped on the beach. Eventually the washing habit spread through most of the troop, although the time required for this dissemination makes one wonder if imitation or independent discovery was the means involved. Three years after Imo's breakthrough, just ten other macaques were washing their tubers—ten out of sixty animals. After six years, seventeen macaques were food-washers. It was almost a decade before a majority of the troop was following suit. Clearly, this had become a cultural tradition handed down from one generation to another. Some years after Imo began washing her sweet potatoes, she began washing her wheat. The sand sank, leaving the grains floating in the surf, where she scooped them up. Clever, but again her fellow macaques picked up the habit only slowly, one by one.

Dolphins are superb imitators. Almost any movement the trainer can do that the dolphin's body allows it to do, the dolphin does. Trainer Lou Herman reports that dolphins have imitated a wide variety of behavior by human divers, seals, turtles, penguins, and skates. They can mimic one another, and they can mimic themselves by repeating an action if given the "do it again" signal. If given the "any" signal, they will do something else. This advanced talent was discovered by Karen Pryor, who writes about it in her book *Lads Before the Wind*. Pryor, a co-founder of Hawaii's Sea Life Park, trained the rough-toothed dolphin Hou to perform tricks for audiences. One day Pryor hit on the idea of withholding a reward until Hou did something new. Naturally, a couple of weeks went by as Hou had trouble comprehending this bizarre new goal, but then he caught on and henceforth came up with a new wrinkle in his act every day. How can dolphins follow these instructions without having a sense of what they just did, and how would they have this sense without having the sense of the "I" who just did something?

Lou Herman has worked with his two beloved dolphins, Ake'kamai and Phoenix, for nearly twenty years. He decided to devise a test to find out if they could copy an action the first time they were shown it (so there would be no time for trial-and-error learning.)

The setup is this. Lou asks Ake'kamai to do a back-flip. Phoenix can't see the instruction, but she can see Ake'kamai leaping up into the air, twirling around, and splashing back down to the water. Herman then asks Phoenix to imitate what she's just seen, and she copies perfectly, rising up above the water with a flip of her strong tail. The next time Ake'kamai is asked to do a balletic underwater somersault, Phoenix sees only the behavior before being asked to imitate, which she does perfectly the first time.

Not only do they seem to have an understanding of another's actions, they are able to remember and repeat their *own* actions. Once Phoenix has done a backflip, you can ask her to repeat what she's just done and she will. Such tests might seem basic, but there is beauty in simplicity, and Herman's work tells us a lot about the dolphin mind.

THE QUESTION OF CEPHALOPODS

Perhaps no creature poses more provocative questions about imitation and self-awareness than the coleoid cephalopods—squid, cuttlefish, and octopuses. Jacques Vauclair reports on his experiments with octopuses in which one observer octopus watches as another learns the rule in a red-ball/white-ball game. The rule is simple—attack the red ball, ignore the white ball—and the first subject learns it quickly. Given his chance, the observer octopus performs almost flawlessly almost immediately. (Unfortunately, this experiment has not been repeated.)

Writing in *Anthropomorphism, Anecdotes, and Animals*, Martin Moynihan provides a report on the amazing mimicry among *Sepioteuthis sepioidea*—the Caribbean reef squid, the most studied of these creatures: "Two young [squids] were discovered in very shallow water over white sand at midday. . . . Since they could not easily escape from the observer, they first shot out blobs of ink and then turned dark and floated with twisted arms, in obvious imitation of the blobs which were slowly disintegrating. The animals were, in fact, mimicking their own decoys." This display is just for starters.

These squid can change colors to an almost infinite degree, thanks to special pigment cells in their very thin skin. Each of these cells, with its supply of special chemicals, is individually hooked into the animal's central nervous system and can be manipulated independently of all the others. Changes are essentially instantaneous, and the results are a light show that virtually defies belief. Reef squid create mesmerizing waves and patterns of color in mating rituals and equally amazing but dissimilar patterns when faced with a dangerous predator. They camouflage themselves—and not just by turning black when in front of a black object or white with a white object. They can camouflage themselves when positioned against a half-white, half-black object, and the line between the two colors in the squid is clean and sharp. Moynihan writes, "The arrangement is never random. It is precisely the parts of the body that are near white that go white. The same for black. The parts may be left, right, front, rear, top, and/or bottom. All combinations are possible. One part may be black during one performance, white during the next, depending upon circumstances. More complex backgrounds may encourage more complex patterns of color."

When a group of Caribbean squid is confronted by a mildly threatening predator such as yellow jacks, most of the group will immediately project the same pattern, usually either "bars" or "streaks." But often the last squid to change will go exactly the opposite of all the others, and thus intentionally stand out in the eyes of the predator. What could be the point? Moynihan does not know, but it may well be a willful act. The truth is, we have no idea what communication is transpiring in the complicated exchanges observed among these squid. They are, as Moynihan writes, "kaleidoscopic and baffling. . . . There must be a switchboard linked to something like a cognitive map."

Moynihan was a senior scientist at the Smithsonian Tropical Research Institute in Panama who wrote about primates as well as these cephalopods. He was convinced that "awareness" should be our "default" assumption when it comes to complex behavior of animals. He says in conclusion to his fascinating discussion:

The flexibility and opportunism of coleoid behavior is suggestive. These animals have considerable abilities to solve different social problems in different circumstances. Choices are overt and decisive. I cannot believe that they are not deliberate and, in some sense, conscious. Alternative explanations would seem to be even more complicated, with even more loops and feedbacks. . . .

Other experts disagree with Moynihan and believe that the squid's behavior is purely instinctive. They point to the work of John Forsythe, who raised cuttlefish in a featureless environment and then released them into the Mediterranean Sea. With no prior experience whatsoever, they showed all the rich mimicry and patterning of wild cuttlefish.

THE MIRROR ON THE WALL

The line between consciousness and self-consciousness may be a fine one indeed—it might be the proverbial distinction without a difference—but self-consciousness (awareness of myself) is generally considered the highest order of consciousness that we *Homo sapiens* know anything about. Until now I have addressed this question of self-consciousness obliquely and by inference, and of course all explanations have been challenged. Understanding the limitations of inference, psychologists have devised tests to seek out self-consciousness directly.

The tool employed is the mirror. Sounds good: We humans look into mirrors explicitly to see ourselves, and we understand that the image we see is ourselves. Do animals? With some primates, this would certainly seem possible, because observers have reported for many decades that chimps stare at their reflected image in still water, and even reach out to touch that reflection. Wolfgang Kohler in the Canary Islands was the first serious researcher to report that primates could recognize themselves in the mirror, and the systematic investigation of this behavior was started by Gordon Gallup, a psychologist at the State University of New York at Albany. Today, mirror self-recognition, or MSR, tests are a staple of comparative psychology, and they require our close attention.

In the classic test, the subject animal—a chimpanzee, say—is introduced to a mirror over a period of time. (Chimps have no problem understanding the basic idea of a mirror.) When the animal is thoroughly familiar with the concept, she is then anesthetized, and a small mark of some kind is put on her forehead. What will be the chimp's reaction when she later sees this mark in the mirror? Will she recognize that it is a mark on herself? In most of the early studies, the chimp almost immediately uses the mirror to investigate the mark on her forehead. She goes straight to it with a finger. She knows that the image in the mirror is herself. Thereafter, the chimp is usually even more interested in mirrors than she has been before.

Children pass the MSR test at about the age of two, when they also begin to show the self-conscious emotions, shame and embarrassment. For many years, the test was considered proof positive of self-consciousness on the part of chimpanzees. Who could doubt the result? How could it be interpreted otherwise?

Well, Celia Heyes can interpret the test otherwise. We know Heyes by now as one who takes a very conservative stand on issues of animal thinking and consciousness, and she does not disappoint us in this case either. She believes that the mirror test can be explained as an advanced level of using visual feedback, but not as indicating a true sense of self. An animal does not have to have a sense of its own uniqueness in order to pass the test, she argues. Just as the chimpanzee could look through a telescope at the stars and not see the stars as we see them, so she can look into the mirror and not see a unique creature there. In short, self-recognition is not necessarily self-consciousness, just as cognition is not necessarily thinking. Or take the stag who knows how wide its antlers are and doesn't attempt to walk through too small an opening, or the fact that many mammals know that their shadows are related to their bodies. Does either instance require true consciousness on the part of the animal? Not really, even according to Donald Griffin, who thinks of this as "a sort of self-awareness." The stag might have learned about narrow passages between trees from harsh experience, and the horse, say, has become habituated "to the dark area on the ground that accompanies it on sunny days."

Heyes is not alone in her negative assessment of the MSR test. Nicholas Humphrey, who popularized the idea that certain animals—the chimps among them—are natural psychologists, did not believe that primates are self-conscious. In the 1980s, one group of careful and not unsympathetic scientists ran some MSR tests and found much less "mark-directed behavior" than they had expected. In one of their studies involving eleven chimps, a majority showed interest in the mirror and three showed other "self-directed" behavior following dozens of hours of exposure, but only one officially passed the MSR test. (This chimp understood almost immediately.) These results were very puzzling, and in fact the authors had trouble getting their work published because it ran so contrary to the presumption in primatology about the "robustness" of MSR among chimpanzees.

The deeper the investigation of animals and mirrors, the more puzzling the results. No elephant has ever passed the MSR test. Dogs do not pass the mark test, but dogs do engage mirrors in interesting ways, as any dog owner can prove to his or her own satisfaction with a great deal of patience. One trial seemed to demonstrate that pigeons can pass the MSR test, but these results have been noisily challenged, as we might imagine. And yet the use of mirrors as visual feedback is surprisingly widespread among animals who occasionally are studied in the laboratory.

Sue Savage-Rumbaugh's bonobo Kanzi enjoyed watching himself blow bubbles in the mirror, and the chimpanzee Austin enjoyed watching himself demonstrate the astonishingly adroit lips of all chimps by rolling a dime on edge from one side of his mouth to the other, and then back. Chimps can use television images to guide them in their manipulation of objects, and they can use the image to guide their arm while reaching for a banana—"a decidedly nontrivial bit of self-recognition," in the view of Daniel Dennett, who's no easy pushover on this question. There is a debate whether gorillas pass the test. They definitely have trouble with the standard setup, but Penny Patterson's famous Koko uses a mirror to groom, and recent studies do show "self-directed" and "mark-directed" behavior.

It turns out that the whole issue of mirror self-recognition is a classic case not of anthropomorphism but of anthropocentrism. We are looking for proof of our kind of self-awareness because this is the only kind we can understand. Any others are off the charts, literally. Monkeys are an excellent case in point. Confronted with a mirror image, monkeys see another monkey, judged by their vocalizations and, sometimes, threatening gestures. Allowed to handle a mirror, most baboons and monkeys will try to find the animal behind it, or try to kiss or lick the image. They do not seem to recognize the image for what it is: themselves. Or is this the behavior of young monkeys? In some cases, older monkeys do not try to find out what's behind the mirror and sit staring at it, although without interaction. And they may look behind them when they see someone in a mirror. So they know what a mirror is all about. Furthermore, when toys are attached to their necks, monkeys will use the mirror to touch the toys.

These results would seem to indicate that the monkeys understand just about everything regarding mirrors except the image in front of them. This is possible, or it is also possible, as Sue Savage-Rumbaugh concludes after her own analysis of the MSR test, that monkeys are just not interested in the dot on their heads. That's why they don't react when they see it in the mirror. This is a fascinating hypothesis, and it gains some credence when we learn from Savage-Rumbaugh that chimps and baboons will clean themselves of any "sticky-gooey fruit," while monkeys will not bother. She writes, "Perhaps monkeys are more dependent on other monkeys for self-tidiness than apes, or perhaps their self-concept does not deal as much with appearance as does the self-concept of apes." Other commentators have pointed out that monkeys and gorillas might not do well on MSR tests because of cultural constraints against looking other animals in the eye, which is taken by them as an act of bold aggression. On film we see the bonobo Panbanisha "pass" the MSR test with nonchalance, casually removing the dot that had been surreptitiously placed on her forehead. Apparently she did not know she was taking an internationally televised test!

Dolphins offer another excellent illustration of the problem. Ken Martin, director of Earthtrust at Hawaii's Sea Life Park, who has tested dolphins with the mirror, tells us:

> You see them kind of play with their image, which is called contingency checking. They move their pectoral fin, or their head, or they open their mouth and watch the contingency of that in the mirror. It's like my seeing myself on television and waving my hand. That's one of the ways you recognize it's yourself. Work has been done with killer whales who take

that to an extreme. They do rhythmic bubble blowing, and open their mouths, and stick out their tongues.

.Since dolphins and whales can't touch a mark on the forehead, the classic MSR test is not possible with them. One way Martin has come up with to get around the practical problem is to carefully compare mirror behavior with regular social behavior. And it turns out that dolphins are always very calm looking in the mirror, while they're much more active—hyperactive, even, from our perspective—when dealing with each other. Like everyone who works with intelligent social creatures, Martin believes that the cetaceans need self-awareness and other-awareness in order to deal with the complex society they live in, although this is a very different kind of society from our own. Acoustic identification is much more important to dolphins than visual identification. (I should note that the large cerebral cortex of the dolphins and other cetaceans is somewhat differently organized from the cortex of primates, and not as structurally complex. Or is this just in the eye of the beholder, who happens to be a primate?)

Dolphin society is closer to the matriarchal society of elephants than to that of the primates, including us. In fact, Martin thinks of primates as rugged individualists, dolphins as very smart sheep, and he says:

When you look at dolphins in the wild they are always with others, they do everything together, they do everything in synchrony. Being a dolphin is very much a team-player concept. Some form of group awareness might be very important for dolphins. They have common ancestors with the hoofed mammals, and it could well be that group awareness might be at least as important to them as self-awareness. In fact, self-awareness might be a strange concept to dolphins. You never see one alone in the ocean. Never.

So what if these cetaceans can't pass our MSR test? On these grounds alone, we're going to say that they can't have self-consciousness? This is absurd. It may very well be that primates and cetaceans and other animals are self-conscious on their own terms, which are, after all, the only ones that count to them.

13

The Heart
of the
Matter

THEY CAN SUFFER

To this point I have avoided, for the most part, the issue of suffering in animals, but now is the time. Daniel Dennett believes that the capacity for suffering may be an important benchmark for consciousness. As he writes in *Consciousness Explained*, "The capacity to suffer is a function of the capacity to have articulated wide-ranging, highly discriminative desires, expectations, and other sophisticated mental states." I agree with Dennett, but I agree with Jeremy Bentham more. Outraged by the arguments of the Cartesians who used our human rationality as the one and only threshold for consciousness, this eighteenth-century English utilitarian wrote, "a full-grown horse or dog is beyond comparison a more rational, as we all are a more conversable animal, than an infant of a day or a week or even a month, old. But suppose they were otherwise, what would it avail? The question is not, Can they reason? Or, Can they talk? But, Can they suffer?''

Yes. All the issues about animal minds and consciousness we have examined in this book are fascinating in and of themselves—we humans are curious creatures; we want to know things—but they influence far-reaching questions of politics and ethics. This is a short chapter, but it may be the most important.

Do we feel guilt—maybe just a little, furtive twinge of conscience—about our treatment of animals? Many of us, yes, on issues ranging from eating meat to torturing animals for purposes of experimentation. In his book *In the Company of Animals*, James Serpell suggests that this moral conflict stems from our reflexive, innate anthropomorphism. Otherwise, why would we care? Otherwise, why have we designated pets as a protected category of animals whom we treat exactly the opposite of those animals we eat or put into cages? In Western society, tens of millions of dogs and cats and other relatively small creatures eat and live better in all respects than do millions of people in the less developed countries. But a paradox within a paradox stares us in the face: While most of us treat our own pets with TLC and fuss about the quality of their diets—many eat a more balanced diet than we do—in the United States and the United Kingdom we put millions of other dogs and cats to death every year because nobody wants them.

In order to address this double paradox, we have a choice, Serpell argues: We can either deal with the ethics of our coldhearted treatment of pigs, which are intelligent creatures, or we can laugh at and disparage our tenderheartedness toward dogs, who are no smarter than pigs. In Western society, at least, we choose the latter alternative. Our attitude has been, quoting Serpell, "Humans have a right to eat meat; farmers have a duty to supply this demand as cheaply as possible and animals inevitably suffer as a consequence. Why complicate the issue with imponderable questions about the morality of it all?"

It is correct that in "the old days" life used to be much more difficult and contingent than it is today, at least in the developed world. Hunting and husbandry and domestication were economically necessary in the new scheme of things introduced in the Neolithic Age. Animals were wealth, plain and simple. (The word "pecuniary," formerly much more common than it is today, stems from the Latin *pecus*, cattle. Even today, in some societies, such as the Masai of East Africa, wealth depends upon the number of one's cattle.)

In our new information age, far removed as it is in many ways from that earlier one, husbandry and domestication are still economically necessary. Animals are still wealth of one form or another, although cultural norms play a large role in how the details work out, culture to culture. The usual exhibit in this regard is the cow: sacred in India, eaten with gusto here. Dogs in the Western world are practically sacred in a "secular" sense (Darwin emphasized dogs as evidence of evolutionary continuity throughout *Descent of Man* for the good reason that he knew his primary audience: the English, inordinate dog lovers one and all), but dogs are just "dogs" in much of the rest of the world, the house specialty of certain restaurants in Vietnam and Korea (including South Korea, whose busy ministers of trade undoubtedly hope that this quaint gustatory practice remains little known on our side of the planet). Roger Caras, president of the American Society for the Prevention of Cruelty to Animals, suggests that dogs became pets on this side of the Pacific and on the other side of the Atlantic because they're not a good meal in terms of meat on the bone. Dogs are skinny compared with, say . . . pigs. So one is pampered and the other tenderized.

Peter Singer blows right past the cultural distinctions and makes a very convincing case that the exploitation of any animal is morally equal to the exploitation of any human. When it comes to the question of which animals suffer, he doesn't believe in drawing lines. To my knowledge, it was Singer's book *Animal Liberation*, first published in 1975, that first brought the issue before a large audience in this generation. (*Animal Machines: The New Factory Farming Industry*, by Ruth Harrison, was published a decade earlier, but I don't think it had the same impact. All apologies if I'm wrong.)

Singer essentially draws a direct analogy between the reasons for inferring animal consciousness that we have looked at in this book and the reasons for inferring animal pain and suffering: equivalent nervous systems, observable behavior, and the evolutionary usefulness of pain and suffering. Then he takes up the argument of Bentham and the other utilitarians that the principle of equality among humans is not a description but a prescription. Equality cannot be a description, obviously, because humans are not equal in any "performance category" you care to consider. But equality can and must be a prescription, because, otherwise, someone has the power to draw the line. Otherwise, you find yourself defending the morality of experimentation on babies as preferable to experimentation on adults on the grounds that babies are our intellectual inferiors. Or as Thomas Jefferson stated, "Because Sir Isaac Newton was superior to others in understanding, he was not therefore lord of the property or persons of others." (And yet Jefferson was a slaveholder, of course, albeit one with a very guilty conscience who feared the day when God would wreak his vengeance on this culture.)

In conclusion Singer asks, "If possessing a higher degree of intelligence does not entitle one human to use another for his or her own ends, how can it entitle humans to exploit non-humans for the same ends?" The only option, Singer argues, is speciesism, an ungainly word for which he apologizes but doesn't find a suitable substitute. It is strictly analogous to sexism and racism.

So on what ethical grounds do we support marine theme parks, whose large-brained performing cetaceans are, in the final analysis, enslaved? How do we condone, or at least rationalize, experimentation during which animals undoubtedly suffer? The capacity for suffering—alone, by itself—is necessary reason for us to take into account the well-being of these animals. The fact that so many species breed only with extreme difficulty in captivity—with such difficulty that I should perhaps use the passive voice "can be bred"—seems to me and others a clear indication that such captivity is emotionally traumatic to the animals.

I would be remiss, however, if I did not take note of the vast improvements that have been made in many zoos, animal parks, and marine-life facilities during the past twenty-five years or so. In today's best zoos, huge sums of money go into the design and construction of "natural" habitats for the animals. Some, such as the San Diego Zoo, have (in addition to the splendid downtown zoo) a huge area of wide-open spaces where the larger animals can roam about. New York's Wildlife Conservation Society (formerly the Bronx Zoo) has been a world leader in habitat design and has a new gorilla facility that may be the finest in the world. Many defenders of zoos argue that some endangered species would soon become extinct were it not for zoos' captive-breeding programs, and sadly, this is undoubtedly true. Nevertheless, conditions in some small commercial zoos in the United States remain deplorable, and most of them should be shut down.

And there is the question of animal experimentation, such as the famous ones conducted by psychologist Harry F. Harlow. He was studying maternal deprivation in monkeys. Unsurprising result: The baby monkeys suffer and become depressed. It was Jeffrey Masson's book *Dogs Never Lie About Love* that introduced me to the English philosopher Mary Midgley's devastating critique of these experiments, from an ethical perspective. Her point could not be more simple: If monkeys and humans are comparable emotionally, then the cruelty of the work is self-evident; if monkeys and humans are not emotionally comparable, then what is the point? Other writers have made a slightly different, equally devastating argument: If we use the results of animal experimentation to draw conclusions about human physiology (most obviously regarding its reaction to new medications), we are logically obligated to infer in the opposite direction, so to speak, that conditions painful in humans must also be painful in animals.

Years ago, Jane Goodall was dismissed as "a *National Geographic* cover girl who didn't know anything." (That's her phrase, by the way, and I believe we can safely read a little sarcasm into it.) Goodall's descriptions of the emotional capacities of the chimpanzees at her research center in Tanzania were dismissed as—what else?—anthropomorphic and anecdotal. Today Goodall is the most famous primate researcher in the world. In her characteristically blunt fashion, Goodall says:

Certainly anyone who's had anything to do with primates or pigs really does know that they're intelligent. You can't spend time with animals and not realize this unless you're completely stupid yourself. . . . And I think also if you deny animals intelligence, even when it's obviously there, it makes it very much easier to do some of the extraordinarily unpleasant things that so many people do to animals. It's more comfortable to think that if you're cutting a piece out of a dog for some kind of animal experimentation, well, he's not intelligent, therefore he can't feel like we do.

For years, Jane had heard stories about animal labs but had avoided going inside one because she knew that the experience would be utterly depressing and that there would be nothing she could do to help. Then, in 1987, she was home from Africa on holiday with her family in Bournemouth, England. As she relates in the essay she wrote in *Intimate Nature: The Bond Between Women and Animals*, the whole family watched a videotape of scenes from inside a biomedical research lab in which "monkeys paced round and round, back and forth, within incredibly small cages stacked one on top of the other, and young chimpanzees, in similar tiny prisons, rocked back and forth or from side to side, far gone in misery and despair."

That footage changed her attitude. Now Jane felt she had to see these places for herself, and do what she could do. The lab had no choice but to open its doors to her. She was, after all, Jane Goodall. The scene she encountered was a "nightmare," worse even than she expected. On a subsequent visit to a different lab owned by the same company, she met JoJo, a chimp born in Africa and shipped to the United States ten years earlier, now living in a cage with an old rubber tire and nothing else. Goodall writes, "Very gently JoJo reached one great finger through the steel bars and touched one of the tears that slipped out above my mask, then went on grooming the back of my wrist. So gently. Ignoring the rattling of cages, the clank of steel on steel, the violent swaying of imprisoned bodies beating against the bars as the other male chimps greeted the veterinarian."

She now introduces into her narrative Jim Mahoney, who had been doing what he could to improve conditions in this lab, which was studying hepatitis, AIDS, and other viral diseases, but his means were limited. "His round over, Jim returned to where I still crouched before JoJo. The tears were falling faster now. 'Jane, please don't,' Jim said, squatting beside me and putting his arm around me. 'Please don't. I have to face this every morning of my life.' "

Jane asks whether chimps should be used in these experiments at all, no matter how valuable the resulting knowledge. Do we have the right? No, she believes. Some defenders of the industry have called her a rabid antivivisectionist, and she has been tempted to call them in turn sadistic vivisectionists. But she realizes that no purpose is accomplished by a lot of name-calling. The key to closing these labs, she believes, is education regarding the mental and emotional attributes of the primates. She told me, "Humans are a species capable of compassion, and we should develop a heightened moral responsibility for beings who are so like ourselves."

When she saw JoJo, she thought of David Greybeard, one of the chimps in Gombe who opened the door for her into that "magic world." In her essay, she continues:

I had been following David one day, struggling through dense undergrowth near a stream. I was thankful when he stopped to rest, and I sat near him. Close by I noticed the fallen red fruit of an oil nut palm, a favorite food of chimpanzees. I picked it up and held it out to David on the palm of my hand. For a moment I thought he would ignore my gesture. But then he took the nut, let it fall to the ground and, with the same movement, very gently closed his fingers around my hand. He glanced at my face, let go of my hand, then turned away. I understood his message: "I don't want the nut, but it was nice of you to offer it."

For JoJo and thousands of other primates in their cages, "nature's sounds are gone, the sounds of running water, of wind in the branches, of chimpanzee calls that ring out so clear and rise up through the treetops and drift away in the hills. The comforts are gone, the soft leafy floor of the forest, the springy branches from which sleeping nests can be made. All are gone."

Can there be any question that our biblically ordained as well as self-proclaimed hegemony over animals comes with—or should come with—great responsibilities? The first national recognition of this fact was a bill introduced in the House of Commons in 1821 and promptly laughed out of consideration. Just two years later, however, the Society for the Prevention of Cruelty to Animals was founded, and then received Royal Charter in 1840.

Today, certain countries, notably England, Sweden, and Switzerland, have meaningfully tough, though not perfect, antivivisection laws. Many more nations have no laws whatsoever. None in the United States. The Animal Welfare Act of 1970, last amended in 1985, is woefully insufficient. Fully 90 percent of all laboratory animals—rats, mice, and birds—are completely exempt from all provisions, including those concerning housing and transportation. But the biggest loophole states that nothing in the law shall interfere with the "experimental design" of a testing program. In other words, if an integral part of the experimental design requires starving the subject animals, starvation is fine. Medical experimentation on brain-dead humans is illegal, while any equivalent experimentation on fully conscious chimpanzees might be completely legal. Furthermore, the review boards established to oversee experimental designs are staffed by the institutions conducting the research. As is so often true in the United States and other countries, the fox is guarding the chicken coop.

Cruelty to animals by individuals is covered by the states, but only twenty-two of the fifty states have felony laws on the books. In New York, where I live, for example, it may be a felony to set my neighbor's house on fire, but is not a felony to douse his dog with gasoline and toss the match. The section of the New York statute addressing experimentation is also weak and full of loopholes. For example, one section reads, "Pain and discomfort shall be minimized by proper use of tranquilizers, analgesics, and anesthetics. *Exceptions may be made when provisions . . . would defeat the purpose of the experiment.*" (My emphasis.)

On the other hand, some ethicists as well as laypeople are afraid that this question cuts both ways. As I said in my Preface, they are afraid that if we do not maintain a hard-and-fast distinction between ourselves and all other animals, we might find ourselves at the precipice of a slippery slope that could lead to all manner of abuses of humans—the same abuses we now put upon other creatures on the grounds that they are fundamentally different from us. If they are not fundamentally different from us, we are not fundamentally different from them. What's good for the goose . . .

Donald Griffin replies in *Animal Minds*, "Morals and ethics should surely be based on accurate understanding of the relevant facts, and since they have survived the Copernican and Darwinian revolutions, strengthened rather than weakened by correction of factual errors, there is no reason to fear a different outcome once evolutionary continuity of mentality is recognized."

Questions about animal minds are not merely fascinating. The answers matter for our treatment of them and, perhaps, of ourselves as well. For this reason alone, as Donald Griffin writes, "Cognitive ethology presents us with one of the supreme scientific challenges of our times, and it calls for our best efforts of critical and imaginative investigation."

CAUTIONARY NOTE

While working on this book, I was forced to think about the relationship between ontology—what we know about the world—and epistemology—how we know what we know. It is this "how" that creates a lot of problems in the cognitive sciences. For one obvious point: We are trying to understand our own thinking and consciousness by means of our own thinking and consciousness—a circularity guaranteed to confuse. And we are trying to understand animal minds by means of our own minds—an inherently anthropocentric enterprise, as we saw with the MSR test.

Moreover, our wonderful language is a very real problem, as made clear by Daniel Dennett, one of the most creative and provocative of all the thinkers in the cognitive sciences. Dennett's book *Consciousness Explained* is powerful, if perhaps just a bit extravagantly titled. But his shorter volume, *Kinds of Minds*, is a more focused consideration of animal consciousness. Dennett argues that although language is the "royal road" to our knowledge of other human minds—with language we defeat philosophical solipsism; with language we know that other men and women have minds more or less like our own—but it is a flawed tool for the job of understanding animal minds. We ask questions of the natural world in the only way we can—with our language—and in effect we expect animals to answer with this same language!

In a truly brilliant metaphor, Dennett writes that our language has too much "resolving power" for this job. It is like studying poetry through a microscope. When we think and talk and write about animals and their minds, it *is* like studying poetry through a microscope. The answers will never be totally fulfilling; they may well be misleading, and inevitably, something vital will be lost.

Acknowledgments

This book would not exist in its present form without the extraordinary editorial contribution of Mike Bryan. Mike, the author or co-author of a dozen books on such widely disparate subjects as golf, baseball, Wall Street, entrepreneurial enterprise, and religious faith, was infinitely patient with this neophyte as I struggled with my first book. He is also a terrific teacher. I might have finished this book eventually without Mike's help, but I certainly could not have met some of the publisher's deadlines without him. Thank you, Mike, for everything.

My friend and colleague Bill Moyers must also take "blame" for the existence of this book. Bill, who has many books to his credit, strongly encouraged me to write this one, and he kindly introduced me to my new colleagues at Doubleday in New York, including assistant publisher Marly Russoff and senior editor Roger Scholl. Bill was a great inspiration, as were my other public-television colleagues, friends and prolific authors Robert Kotlowitz, Alex Kotlowitz, Robert MacNeil, and Jim Lehrer.

Doug Young, my editor at Headline Books in London, and Heather Holden Brown, head of nonfiction, were especially helpful, as were Kelly Davis and Julianna Lessa.

I must thank my employer, 13/WNET, New York's public-television station, for management's essential support. So many were helpful, but I must single out Bill Baker, our president; Michael Bessie, board member; Tammy Robinson, head of programming; Carmen Di Rienzo, Esq.; Bill Grant, who succeeded me as head of science, natural-history, and features programs; Fred Kaufman, executive producer of *Nature*; Janet Hess, science editor; Susane Lee, producer, whose editorial assistance was invaluable; and the entire *Nature* staff, especially Eileen Fraher, the brilliant manager of us all on the *Nature* series.

The generous cooperation of the production team of our television series on animal behavior at Green Umbrella, Ltd., in Bristol, England, was also essential. To Paul Reddish, executive producer; producers Sanjida O'Connell, Lizzie Greene, and Andrew Murray; Rachel Kelly, production manager; and most especially producer Zoe Heron, who spent three years as the principal researcher on this project before a frame of film was shot or a word written, I am deeply grateful. The scope and accuracy of Zoe's research were nothing short of prodigious. And, of course, my warm thanks to Peter Jones, the founder and CEO of Green Umbrella and one of the most talented producers of natural-history films in the world.

To my attorney, Robert N. Gold, and my agent, Joe Spieler, who deftly handled the business side of this book, I am most grateful, as I am to Anu Krishnam, who did the photo research.

For their cooperation and support I thank Donald Griffin; Cynthia Moss; Jane Goodall; Professor Nicholas Dodman, DVM, Tufts University; Professors Peter Platt, Barnard College, and Joan Ferrante, Columbia University; John Walsh of the World Society for the Prevention of Cruelty to Animals; Elena Araya of the American Society for the Prevention of Cruelty to Animals; Dean Smith of the American Antivivisection Society; Patty Bryan; Dr. Nick Bryan; and many others who are quoted in this book and for whom its subject is their life's work.

Despite all the fine help I had, I have most probably made some errors anyway. The mistakes in the book are mine alone.

And, of course, I am deeply grateful to my friend, Dr. Dennis De Stefano, to whom this book is dedicated, for his patience, encouragement, keen editorial eye and for his ability to put my plight into humorous perspective when I went around asking with great angst, "How did I get myself into this book mess?" Thank you, Dennis.

Bibliography

Allen, Colin, and Marc A. Bekoff. *Species of Mind: The Philosophy and Biology of Cognitive Ethology.* Cambridge: MIT Press, 1997.

Bleibtreu, John. *The Parable of the Beast.* New York: Collier Books, 1968.

Budiansky, Stephen. *If a Lion Could Talk: Animal Intelligence and the Evolution of Consciousness.* New York: The Free Press, 1998.

———. *The Nature of Horses: Exploring Equine Evolution, Intelligence, and Behavior.* New York: The Free Press, 1997.

Camhi, Jeffrey M. *Neuroethology: Nerve Cells and the Natural Behavior of Animals.* Sunderland, Mass.: Sinauer Associates, 1984.

Caras, Roger A. *A Perfect Harmony: The Intertwining Lives of Animals and Humans Throughout History.* New York: Simon & Schuster, 1996.

Cheney, Dorothy L., and Robert M. Seyfarth. *How Monkeys See the World: Inside the Mind of Another Species.* Chicago: University of Chicago Press, 1990.

Conniff, Richard. *Spineless Wonders: Strange Tales from the Invertebrate World.* New York: Henry Holt and Co., 1996.

Coren, Stanley. *The Intelligence of Dogs: Canine Consciousness and Capabilities.* New York: The Free Press, , 1994.

Darwin, Charles. *Descent of Man* (Great Minds Series). Prometheus Books, 1997.

Dawkins, Marian Stamp. *Through Our Eyes Only? The Search for Animal Consciousness.* Oxford: Oxford University Press, 1998.

Dennett, Daniel. *Consciousness Explained.* Boston: Little, Brown, 1991.

———. *Kinds of Minds: Toward an Understanding of Consciousness.* New York: Basic Books, 1996.

de Waal, F. M., and Frans Lanting. *Bonobo: The Forgotten Ape*. Berkeley: University of California Press, 1997.

Dodman, Nicholas. *The Dog Who Loved Too Much: Tales, Treatments, and the Psychology of Dogs*. New York: Bantam Books, 1996.

———. *The Cat Who Cried for Help: Attitudes, Emotions, and the Psychology of Cats*. New York: Bantam Books, 1997.

Dukas, Reuven, editor. *Cognitive Ecology: The Evolutionary Ecology of Information Processing and Decision Making*. Chicago: The University of Chicago Press, 1998.

Fortey, Richard. *Life: A Natural History of the First Four Billion Years of Life on Earth*. New York: Alfred A. Knopf, 1998.

Fouts, Roger, with Stephen Tukel Mills. *Next of Kin: What Chimpanzees Have Taught Me About Who We Are*. New York: William Morrow and Co., 1997.

Gazzaniga, Michael. *Mind Matters: How Mind and Brain Interact to Create Our Conscious Lives*. Boston: Houghton Mifflin Co., 1988.

Gould, James L., and Carol Grant Gould. *The Animal Mind*. New York: Scientific American Library, 1994.

Griffin, Donald R. *Animal Thinking*. Cambridge, Mass.: Harvard University Press, 1984.

———. *Animal Minds*. Chicago: University of Chicago Press, 1992.

Hogan, Linda, Deena Metzger, and Brenda Peterson, editors. *Intimate Nature: The Bond Between Women and Animals*. New York: Fawcett Columbine, 1998.

Knapp, Caroline. *Pack of Two: The Intricate Bond Between People and Dogs*. New York: The Dial Press, 1998.

Masson, Jeffrey Moussaieff. *Dogs Never Lie About Love: Reflections on the Emotional World of Dogs*. New York: Crown Publishers, 1997.

Masson, Jeffrey M., and Susan McCarthy. *When Elephants Weep: The Emotional Lives of Animals*. New York: Delacorte Press, 1995.

McFarland, David, editor. *The Oxford Companion to Animal Behaviour*. Oxford: Oxford University Press, 1981.

Mitchell, Robert W., Nicholas S. Thompson, and H. Lyn Miles, editors. *Anthropomorphism, Anecdotes, and Animals*. Albany, N.Y.: SUNY Press, 1997.

Moss, Cynthia. *Elephant Memories: Thirteen Years in the Life of an Elephant Family*. New York: William Morrow and Co., 1988.

O'Connell, Sanjida. *Mindreading: An Investigation into How We Learn to Love and Lie.* New York: Doubleday, 1997.

Pinker, Steven. *How the Mind Works.* New York: W. W. Norton, 1997.

Premack, David, and Ann James Premack. *The Mind of an Ape.* New York: W. W. Norton, 1984.

Pryor, Karen, and Konrad Lorenz. *Lads Before the Wind: Diary of a Dolphin Trainer.* Sunshine Books, 1997.

Restak, Richard M. *The Mind.* New York: Bantam Books, 1988.

Ristau, Carolyn A., editor. *Cognitive Ethology: The Minds of Other Animals.* Hillsdale, N.J.: Erlbaum Associates, 1991.

Ryden, Hope. *Lily Pond: Four Years with a Family of Beavers.* New York: Lyons Press, 1997.

Savage-Rumbaugh, Sue, and Roger Lewin. *Kanzi: The Ape at the Brink of the Human Mind.* New York: John Wiley & Sons, 1994.

————, Stuart G. Shanker, and Talbot J. Taylor. *Apes, Language, and the Human Mind.* Oxford: Oxford University Press, 1998.

Serpell, James. *In the Company of Animals: A Study of Human-Animal Relationships.* Oxford: Basil Blackwell, 1986.

Sheldrake, Rupert. *The Rebirth of Nature: The Greening of Science and God.* Rochester, Vt.: Part Street Press, 1994.

Shepard, Paul. *The Others: How Animals Made Us Human.* Washington D.C.: Island Press/Shearwater Books, 1996.

Singer, Peter. *Animal Liberation.* New York: Avon Books, 1990.

Skinner, B. F. *About Behaviorism.* New York: Vintage Books, 1974.

Slater, P. J. B. *An Introduction to Ethology.* Cambridge: Cambridge University Press, 1986.

Sorabji, Richard. *Animal Minds and Human Morals: The Origins of the Western Debate.* Ithaca, N.Y.: Cornell University Press, 1993.

Sparks, John. *The Discovery of Animal Behavior.* Boston: Little, Brown, 1982.

Stevens, Christine. *Animals and Their Legal Rights.* Washington, D.C.: Animal Welfare Institute, 1987.

Thomas, Elizabeth Marshall. *The Hidden Life of Dogs.* New York: Pocket Books, 1993.

Thorpe, W. H. *The Origins and Rise of Ethology.* Westport, Conn.: Heinemann Education Books, 1979.

Vauclair, Jacques. *Animal Cognition: An Introduction to Modern Comparative Psychology*. Cambridge, Mass.: Harvard University Press, 1996.

Wilson, Edward O. *Consilience: The Unity of Knowledge*. New York: Alfred A. Knopf, 1998.

———. *Sociobiology: The Abridged Edition*. Cambridge, Mass.: Harvard University Press, 1980.

Index